Ginn Elementary English

6

BY DOROTHY MILLER

John C. Maxwell, Series Adviser

GINN AND COMPANY
A XEROX COMPANY

Acknowledgments

Grateful acknowledgment is made to the following authors and publishers for permission to use copyrighted materials:

Coward-McCann, Inc. for "Fragment from Nothing." Reprinted by permission of Coward-McCann from *The Creaking Stair* by ELIZABETH COATSWORTH. Copyright 1923, 1929, 1949 by Coward-McCann, Inc.

E. P. Dutton & Co., Inc. for an excerpt from the book *Ring of Bright Water* by GAVIN MAXWELL. Copyright, ©, 1960 by Gavin Maxwell. Reprinted by permission of E. P. Dutton & Co., Inc.

Essex Music Limited for "The Cowboy's Life." Attributed to James Barton Adams. Collected, adapted and arranged by JOHN A. LOMAX and ALAN LOMAX. © Copyright Ludlow Music Inc., New York, N.Y. All publication rights controlled by Essex Music Ltd., London, for the British Empire and Commonwealth of Nations (excluding Canada, Australia and New Zealand). Used by permission.

Harcourt, Brace & World, Inc. for "Primer Lesson" from *Slabs of the Sunburnt West* by CARL SANDBURG, copyright, 1922, by Harcourt, Brace & World, Inc.; renewed, 1950, by Carl Sandburg. Reprinted by permission of the publishers; "Splinter" from *Good Morning, America*, copyright, 1928, 1956 by CARL SANDBURG. Reprinted by permission of Harcourt, Brace & World, Inc.; paragraph from *North to the Orient* by ANNE MORROW LINDBERGH. Reprinted by permission of Harcourt, Brace & World, Inc., publishers.

Holt, Rinehart and Winston, Inc. for "Mending Wall" from *Complete Poems of Robert Frost.* Copyright 1930, 1939 by Holt, Rinehart and Winston, Inc. Copyright © 1958 by Robert Frost. Copyright © 1967 by Lesley Frost Ballantine; "Theme in Yellow" and "Under a Telephone Pole" from *Chicago Poems* by CARL SANDBURG. Copyright 1916 by Holt, Rinehart and Winston, Inc. Copyright 1944 by Carl Sandburg. All reprinted by permission of Holt, Rinehart and Winston, Inc.

Little, Brown and Company for selections from *The Incredible Journey* by SHEILA BURNFORD, by permission of Atlantic/Little, Brown and Co. Copyright © 1960, 1961 by Sheila Burnford; for an excerpt from *Drums Along the Mohawk* by Walter D. Edmonds, published by Little, Brown and Company; for "Phaëthon" from *Mythology* by EDITH HAMILTON, by permission of Little, Brown and Co. Copyright 1942, by Edith Hamilton.

The Macmillan Company for "Skating," reprinted with permission of The Macmillan Company from *Pillicock Hill* by HERBERT ASQUITH. Printed in Great Britain in 1926; "Skyscrapers," reprinted with permission of The Macmillan Company from *The Pointed People* by RACHEL FIELD. Copyright The Macmillan Company 1924, 1930; "The Moon's the North Wind's Cooky" and "An Indian Summer Day on the Prairie," reprinted with permission of The Macmillan Company from *The Congo and Other Poems* by VACHEL LINDSAY. Copyright The Macmillan Company 1914, renewed 1942 by Elizabeth C. Lindsay; "Night Was Creeping" ("Check"), reprinted with permission of the Macmillan Company from *Rocky Road to Dublin* by JAMES STEPHENS. Copyright The Macmillan Company 1915, renewed 1943 by James Stephens.

McGraw-Hill Book Company for excerpts from *Endurance; Shackleton's Incredible Voyage* by ALFRED LANSING. Copyright 1959 by Alfred Lansing. Used by permission of McGraw-Hill Book Company.

The Viking Press, Inc. for "Crossing" from *Letter from a Distant Land* by PHILIP BOOTH. Copyright © 1953 by Philip Booth. Reprinted by permission of The Viking Press, Inc.; "The Sky" from *Under the Tree* by ELIZABETH MADOX ROBERTS. Copyright 1922 by B. W. Huebsch, Inc., 1950 by Ivor S. Roberts. Reprinted by permission of The Viking Press, Inc.; three short excerpts from *The Good Master* by KATE SEREDY. Copyright 1935, 1953 by Kate Seredy. Reprinted by permission of The Viking Press, Inc.; and for an excerpt from the short story "Flight" from *The Long Valley* by JOHN STEINBECK. Copyright 1938, © 1966 by John Steinbeck. Reprinted by permission of The Viking Press, Inc. and McIntosh and Otis, Inc.

2

3

Illustrations for this book are by the following artists: Robert Borja, Seymour Chwast, Beatrice Darwin, George Guzzi, Harvey Kidder, Don Leake, Jerry Pinkney, and Tommy Shoemaker. Script cuts are by Contis Studios.

Contents

CHAPTER ONE

Your Language

1 Man Makes Language

"Ouch!" yelped Caveman as he burned his tongue on the broth.

"Yum, yum," exclaimed Mrs. Caveman as she bit into the juicy mammoth steak.

"Bow-wow," cooed Baby Caveman as the dog made off with a choice bone.

So began language, some people think. How do *you* think language began? Do you think people learned to speak words by making noises that showed pain, pleasure, and excitement? Did these sounds eventually come to stand for feelings and ideas as others—family and friends—saw, heard, experienced the same things, and then uttered the same sounds? Perhaps. No one really knows.

You too may say *ouch* and *yum, yum,* but *you* have 599,998 other words to express your ideas and feelings, because you have inherited a language that has borrowed from other languages and has grown over the centuries to at least 600,000 words.

What are words? Some language scientists define words as meaningful noises. Some say they are noises which symbolize or stand for something, as, for example, the word *dog* stands for a certain kind of four-legged animal. Others say words are units of sounds or letters which communicate ideas. However we define what a word is or what a word does, it is important to recognize that the word is a useful tool because it has a meaning generally agreed upon by those using it. If the listener or reader

11

does not understand what the word stands for, no communication can occur.

- In what ways are words to *you* like notes to a musician or paint to an artist?
- How are words important to a statesman, a doctor, a lawyer, a clergyman, a teacher, a nurse, a stewardess, a pilot, a secretary, a salesman, a TV broadcaster, and an actress? How are they important to *you*?
- How do words allow us to communicate ideas or feelings that gestures or facial expressions alone could not communicate?

WORKING TOGETHER

A. Discover how much we need words by playing this charade game. Think of a sentence and try to communicate it to your classmates without using words.

12

How does communicating by gestures compare with communicating by words? Which method is easier? Which is more exact?

B. Can you tell about an occasion when you could not use words, and how you "spoke" without them? Were you in a foreign country? Were you in a place where talking and writing were not permitted? Was your voice temporarily "out of order"?

WORKING BY YOURSELF

A. On a piece of paper, list feelings you might have, such as anger, joy, or sadness, and write the best sentences you can think of to communicate these feelings to another person.

B. How could man keep written records of himself and his surroundings without words? In what ways would another system be satisfactory? Unsatisfactory? Write your answers in your notebook and be ready to discuss them with your classmates.

symbol

The word *symbol* comes from the Greek word *symbolon,* which means "token or sign." A symbol is something that stands for or suggests something else. It may be a visible sign of something invisible.

The handshake is a symbol of friendship.

symbolic   symbolism   symbolize

13

2   The Development of English

We are not quite sure how or when the first words came into being ages and ages ago. Nor are we quite sure how separate language systems developed in various parts of the world. We really do not know, for example, why the English came to use the word *house* and the Spanish the word *casa* to mean the same thing. But we do know quite a bit about how American English has developed over the last three hundred years.

For example, many of the words we Americans use came from other languages; as you know, we have built many out of Latin and Greek roots. When you study French, German, or Spanish, you will discover that many of our English words are also built out of words or parts of words from these languages. Our word *dandelion*, for instance, came from the French *dent de lion* (tooth of lion)—a good picture name for the flower with sharply indented leaves. Our word *canyon*, meaning "a narrow valley with steep sides, usually with a stream at the bottom," came from the Spanish word *cañon*, related to the Spanish word meaning "street."

- What other English words do you know that have been borrowed from foreign languages?

14

A. Take turns reading the familiar words below. You may be surprised at the languages from which English borrows them.

Indian	*French*	*Spanish*	*Italian*
chipmunk	bureau	cafeteria	piano
hickory	chaperone	patio	piccolo
moccasin	depot	rodeo	solo
squash	theater	stampede	soprano

Scandinavian	*Dutch*	*German*	*Chinese*
egg	caboose	frankfurter	tea
lift	cookie	kindergarten	chow
schooner	skipper	pretzel	kowtow
ski	waffle	waltz	sampan

15

B. How many of the following words have you used, heard, or seen in print recently? These are not words absorbed from other languages, but they are relatively new English words. Read the words aloud. What do they show about another way in which English can grow?

1. ack-ack	11. jalopy
2. blackout	12. jeep
3. bridgehead	13. penicillin
4. bulldozer	14. plastic
5. carport	15. radar
6. cinerama	16. supersonic
7. commando	17. technicolor
8. dogfight	18. video
9. drive-in	19. walkie-talkie
10. flak	20. winterize

C. What words have the fields of music and art given us? Be prepared to explain the meaning of each word you discover.

D. List and explain the meanings of as many new words as you can that have grown out of recent developments in the following fields.

1. architecture   2. space exploration   3. transportation

Many English words have developed from proper names of people and places; the words below are just a few. Find each in your dictionary, and when you have discovered its source, note it on a piece of paper and use the word in a sentence. Follow the example below:

1. *atlas*   Source: in Greek mythology, Atlas was a giant forced to carry the heavens on his shoulders.

To find the location of Marrakesh, Lois consulted an *atlas*.

1. atlas	4. canary	7. marathon	10. tantalize
2. sandwich	5. cardigan	8. muslin	11. titanic
3. calico	6. magnolia	9. saxophone	12. watt

3   How Your Word Store Can Grow

READING AND THINKING

Little Wilbur, pointing to the candy case, says, "Me want that."

Twelve-year-old Martha says, "I would like one of the fudge and nut bars in the back row, please."

Little Sandy looks up at a plane in the sky and says, "Zoom!"

Twelve-year-old Chuck says, "Look at that Navy Skyhawk! It's a supersonic jet."

When you were Wilbur's or Sandy's age, you were learning to make sounds that *imitated* sounds you heard. You imitated sounds, for example, that planes, horns, and thunder made. You imitated sounds that people made when they talked. In time you came to understand that sounds stood for certain things—mother, father, candy, home, bed, dog, go, come, and eat. And so you began to learn *words* almost as naturally as you learned to eat and walk.

- What were probably some of the first words you learned?

In ten years your vocabulary has grown from "zoom" and "me want" to hundreds and hundreds of words. What has made it grow? New experiences, new interests, new friends, new school subjects, new books—all have added to your storehouse of words, often without your realizing it.

- In what other ways can you build yourself an even bigger storehouse of word power?

DISCUSSING

A. Read aloud these sentences that Carol found in a book she had borrowed from the library:

The boat plunged through pounding, *turbulent*, stormy seas, its hull battered by *mountainous* waves. A mighty blast sent its *spinnaker boom* crashing to the deck.

18

How do you think Carol learned the meaning of the italicized words? If the word *turbulent* is new to you, as it was to Carol, can you find clues to its probable meaning by looking at words around it, such as *stormy* and *pounding?*

Clues to the meaning of a word which come from a word or from a surrounding group of words in the same or a nearby sentence are called *context clues.*

B. How do you think Carol learned what *mountainous* means? Can you see a familiar *root* or *main* word in *mountainous?*

C. Why would it be difficult to determine the meaning of *spinnaker boom* by using context clues or root clues? How would you find its exact meaning?

D. Below are sentences which contain some words which are probably unfamiliar to you. These unfamiliar words are italicized. How many word meanings can you unlock by finding word roots? How many by finding other clues?

1. A *tumultuous* cheer rose from the crowd.

2. A stenographer quickly *transcribed* her shorthand.

3. The disease is caused by a *microscopic* insect so tiny it was discovered only recently.

4. They dangled *precariously* from the pole. The slightest movement would cause them to fall.

5. His reply was *inaudible.*

6. The boy gave a *raucous* laugh. He was very rude.

7. The waves beat *relentlessly* against the hull. At last it *disintegrated* and sank from sight.

8. It was an *awesome* sight. We were almost overcome by the wonder of it.

9. The liner presented a *majestic* sight as it steamed proudly to sea. No queen was ever more *regal.*

10. It was a *ferocious* creature, snarling and baring its fangs at the slightest sound.

A. Latin and Greek are two valuable sources for many great languages, one of which is English. List words you know which are built on the Latin and Greek words in the list below and be ready to compare your list with those of your classmates. You may get some ideas from the pictures which appear above the two columns of root words and their meanings.

On your paper number from one to twenty-six and list one English word for each root.

1. *aqua-* water
2. *audi-* hear
3. *centum-* hundred
4. *cyclus-* wheel
5. *demos-* people
6. *dict-* speak
7. *duc(t)-* lead
8. *form-* shape
9. *manus-* hand
10. *metr-* measure
11. *mis(t)-* send
12. *pars(t)-* portion
13. *pend-* hang

14. *phon-* sound
15. *physi-* nature
16. *port-* carry
17. *rupt-* break
18. *scope-* view
19. *techn-* skill
20. *temp-* time
21. *terra-* land
22. *therm-* heat
23. *vers(t)-* turn
24. *vid(s)-* see
25. *vive-* live
26. *voc-* call

20

B. Find the root common to each word in the lists below. Be ready to tell the meaning of the root and of each word. Use each word in a sentence.

1.	2.	3.	4.
spectacle	picture	describe	contain
spectator	pictorial	prescribe	sustain
spectacular	picturesque	inscribe	contents
inspect	depict	scribbler	abstain

C. The make-believe words in the following sentences cannot be found in a dictionary because they are not real words, but the Greek and Latin roots which were combined to form them can be found in a dictionary. Decode each italicized word by finding the meanings of the roots it contains. For example:

> Mother says I have *lavaphobia*. (*phobia:* fear of + *lava*, from *lavare:* to wash; *lavaphobia:* fear of washing)

1. If I didn't have *laboraphobia*, I would do my *scholopus*.
2. I want to be a *cineaster*.
3. The pitcher has a good *celeriglobe*.
4. Walter and I are having a *fratribellum*.
5. My sister says I *dormadict*.

MORE FOR YOU

Your teacher will have you choose which of the following selections to work on.

A. Read the selection from the book *The Incredible Journey*, in which the author Sheila Burnford describes one member—the English bull terrier—in a party of three animals on their journey through the Canadian wilderness. On a sheet of paper, list the unfamiliar words and explain how you would find their meaning.

When the old dog woke shivering with cold he was alone. The cat was some distance away, belly to ground and tail twitching excitedly, stalking his breakfast. Stealing through the morning air came a familiar smell of smoke and something cooking—beckoning irresistibly.

The mists were rolling back from the valley, and a pale sun was lighting the sky when the old dog came through the windbreak of tall Norway pines and down outside the farmhouse door. His memory was short; already human beings were back on their rightful pedestals, cornucopias of dog food in their hands. He whined plaintively. At a second, louder whine, several cats appeared from the barn nearby and glared at him with tiger-eyed resentment. At any other time, he would have put them to instant flight; now he had more pressing business and chose to ignore them. The door swung open, a wondrous smell of bacon and eggs surged out, and the terrier drew up all the heavy artillery of his charm: with an ingratiating wag of his tail he glued his ears back, and wrinkled his nose in preparation for his disastrous winning leer. There was an astonished silence, broken by the deep, amused voice of a man. "Well!" said the owner of the voice, surveying his odd visitor, whose eyes were now rolled so far back that they had almost disappeared into his head. He called into the house, and was answered by the pleasant, warm voice of a woman. There was a sound of footsteps. The tail increased its tempo.

The woman stood for a moment in the doorway, looking down in silent astonishment at the white gargoyle on the step, and when he saw her face break into a smile that past master in the art of scrounging proffered a civil paw. She bent down and shook it, laughing helplessly, then invited him to follow her into the house.

Dignified, the old dog walked in, and gazed at the stove with bland confidence.

22

B. In his book *Zoo Doctor*, William Bridges, Doctor of Veterinary Medicine at New York's Bronx Zoo, described one of his patients. Read his description below and on a sheet of paper list the unfamiliar words, noting how you would find their meanings.

Sudana certainly did look sick. Something was wrong inside those four tons of flesh and bone. The big African elephant was leaning, actually leaning—a thing she never did when she was her usual sturdy self—against the steel bars at the front of her compartment in the Elephant House. Her enormous ears were folded back against her neck and shoulders, and not once did she flap them in greeting to her friend the doctor. Most ominous of all, her normally restless tail hung straight down, never once twitching the curved brush of hairs at the tip.

"What's the matter, old girl? This isn't like you, Sudana. You've never given me a bit of trouble in twenty years!" The doctor talked steadily and soothingly while he slowly, deliberately, without any sudden motions, climbed over the guardrail and reached through the bars to lay a hand on the elephant's trunk. He felt it in several places and then slipped his hand under her ear and down the length of her rough foreleg and back along her body. It was like rubbing coarsely finished cement—warm cement. Sudana had a fever, and a high one.

After carefully estimating Sudana's weight, the doctor decides that her eight thousand pounds of bulk will require about four cupfuls of medicine. Dr. Bridges knows Sudana won't like the taste of the medicine, but he also knows she must have it to get well. He tells the keeper not to give Sudana any water, hoping she'll get thirsty enough to take the medicine in her drinking water. The paragraphs on page 24 describe what happened when Sudana was given the medicated water.

Sudana smelled the water. She squeezed through the door even before it was fully opened and headed straight for her water trough, trunk outstretched. Dipping its tip deeply, she drew up a couple of gallons, and curled her trunk to eject the cool fluid into her parched mouth.

What was this?

Water dribbled from her mouth. Her trunk continued to squirt the liquid onto her tongue, but something was wrong. *Very* wrong! Somebody was playing a mean trick!

Violently Sudana's trunk jerked out of her mouth, and medicated water gushed from her lower lip. She aimed her trunk at the doctor and her perfidious keeper. They ducked, but it was too late. They got the full effects of a gallon of cold sulfadiazine-and-water straight in their faces.

24

4 How English Grows

From day to day, from second to second, you are not precisely the same person, either physically or mentally, that you were a second ago. This constant change is common to all living things. On a larger time scale, it is also present in your language. English—or any *living* language—must change and grow to fit the changing needs of its users.

- From the examples below, can you see one way in which English has grown in order to serve us better?

agree	*dis*agree
angle	*tri*angle
behave	*mis*behave

The letters which you have seen attached to the beginning of a word to change or modify its meaning (really to make another word) are called *prefixes*. Like the word roots we have examined, most of them are inherited from Latin and Greek. The meanings of prefixes can be found in a dictionary, where each prefix is entered followed by a dash, for example, *dis-, tri-, mis-*.

Another way English grows is represented by the words below:

attend	attend*ance*
confide	confid*ence*
encourage	encourage*ment*

Sometimes letters are attached to the end of a word to form another word; these letters are called *suffixes*. Suffixes, like prefixes, can be found in your dictionary, listed with a dash before them, for example, *-ance, -ence, -ment*. By learning the meanings of common prefixes and suffixes, you can more than double your storehouse of words.

25

A. Look at the two columns of words below. Explain the meaning of each word in Column I. How do the prefixes added to the words change their meanings? Define the underlined parts of the words in Column II, consulting your dictionary when necessary.

I	II
continental	transcontinental
cycle	bicycle
day	midday
fortunate	unfortunate
historic	prehistoric
man	superman
operate	cooperate
press	express
view	review
way	subway

B. Try your skill at analyzing the following words, just as you did the above list of words and their prefixes.

I	II
help	helpful
instruct	instruction
kind	kindness
manage	manager
rest	restless
ring	ringing
trouble	troublesome
vigor	vigorous
work	workable
danger	dangerous

C. Are you a good word detective? Can you tell from the following words what the underlined word parts mean?

biochemistry   geography   telegraph
biography   geology   telephone
biology   geometry   television

The underlined word parts, which combine with another word root to form an English word, differ from prefixes in that they are nouns in the language from which we borrow them, while prefixes are usually prepositions.

Consult a dictionary to see if you were right about the meanings of the above word parts. How many additional words can you build using the combining forms *bio-*, *geo-*, and *tele-?*

WORKING BY YOURSELF

A. There are a number of English words, as well as the Latin and Greek ones we have observed, that are used as prefixes. Some are: *after*, *fore*, *over*, *under*, and *up*. In your notebook, write two words built from each of these; then use your words in sentences.

B. Add prefixes or suffixes to complete the numbered words in this paragraph. Number your paper 1 through 17 and write after each number the prefix or suffix used. Then wait for your teacher to have you read the paragraph aloud.

The camp_1_ soon realized that it was use_2_ to try to _3_place the ropes within a reason_4_ length of time. It seemed hope_5_ to try to _6_lay the _7_rooted floor planks or _8_tangle the twisted canvas until the winds _9_creased. _10_construct_11_ would have to be _12_layed until the end of the relent_13_, howl_14_ gale. Meanwhile, _15_comfort_16_ as they were, the campers _17_mained calm.

Compile your own reference chart of *word roots*, *prefixes*, *suffixes*, and *combining forms* and keep it in a convenient place in your notebook. Look at it to refresh your memory when necessary, and add to it whenever you can. Share any new finds with your classmates.

5   Learning New Words: The Dictionary

READING AND THINKING

As they cultivate their language, even the best word detectives sometimes need more than context, root, prefix, and suffix clues to arrive at the meaning of a word. You may remember that Carol, good word detective that she was, did not have enough evidence to give her the exact meaning of *spinnaker boom*.

- What was your decision about how she should learn exactly what the words meant?

A dictionary is a most valuable book if you know how to use it well. Bill, for example, read that ". . . the chest opened and out poured florins." Jewels? Money? Fish? Insects? When he looked in the dictionary, he found out exactly what a *florin* is. He also learned something about its history. However, Bill floundered for some time before obtaining his information. Why might he have had trouble?

28

WORKING TOGETHER

A. How quickly can you arrange in alphabetical order the words that confused Bill? One person may write the words at the chalkboard as you and your classmates alphabetize them.

floor	flop	flourish	Florida
flour	florid	florist	florin
floral	flower	flavor	flood

B. Look carefully at the dictionary page printed on page 30. Can you notice one aid which the dictionary provides for finding words? Where on the page do you find the same word that appears at the very top of the page in bold print above the left-hand column? Where do you find the same word that appears at the top of the page above the right-hand column?

The words printed at the top of a dictionary page are called *guide words,* since they help guide you to the word you wish to find.

C. On one page of a dictionary *arose* is at the top of the left-hand column and *art* is at the top of the right-hand column. Which of the following words appear on the page?

arrange	arrive	ash
arson	arrow	arouse
army	artist	ascend
article	ask	arrest

D. As you examine the sample dictionary page which follows in your book, discuss all the information that it provides for any single word. Then answer the following questions:

1. What might a girl both do and wear?
2. Could a *flounder flounder?*
3. Would you cross the sea in a *flotilla* or on *flotsam?*
4. Can *flounder* mean the same or nearly the same as *flub?*

Flor en tine (flôr′ən tēn), 1. of Florence. 2. a native or inhabitant of Florence. *adj.*, *n.*

flor id (flôr′id), 1. ruddy; highly colored: *a florid complexion.* 2. flowery; much ornamented; showy: *florid language, florid architecture. adj.*

Flor i da (flôr′ə də), a State at the southeast corner of the United States. *n.*

flor in (flôr′ən), 1. a gold or silver coin of varying value current at various times in different countries of Europe. 2. an English silver coin worth 2 shillings. 3. an old English gold coin worth about 6 shillings. *n.*

flo rist (flō′rist), person who raises or sells flowers. *n.*

floss (flôs), 1. silky fiber like that in milkweed pods. 2. shiny, untwisted silk thread for embroidery. Waxed floss is used for cleaning between the teeth. *n.*

flo til la (flō til′ə), 1. small fleet. 2. fleet of small ships. *n.*

flot sam (flot′səm), parts of a wreck found floating on the water. *n.*

flounce[1] (flouns), 1. fling the body angrily or proudly. 2. a sudden angry or proud fling of the body. *v.*, **flounced, flounc ing,** *n.*

flounce[2] (flouns), 1. wide strip of cloth, gathered along the top edge and sewed to a dress, skirt, etc., for trimming; wide ruffle. 2. trim with a flounce or flounces. *n.*, *v.*, **flounced, flounc ing.**

Girl wearing a dress with flounces

floun der[1] (floun′dər), 1. plunge about; struggle without making much progress: *Men and horses were floundering in the deep snow beside the road.* 2. be clumsy and make mistakes: *The girl was frightened by the audience and floundered through her song.* 3. a floundering movement or action. *v.*, *n.*

Flounder (1 ft. long)

floun der[2] (floun′dər), flatfish that has a large mouth. *n.*, *pl.* **floun ders** or **floun der.**

flour (flour), 1. the fine meal made by grinding grain, especially wheat. 2. cover with flour. *n.*, *v.*

flour ish (flèr′ish), 1. grow in vigor; thrive; be prosperous: *His newspaper business grew and flourished.* 2. wave in the air: *John flourished the letter when he saw us.* 3. waving about: *The donkey gave a flourish of his heels.* 4. a display or show: *The agent showed us about the house with much flourish.* 5. a showy trill or passage in music. 6. an extra ornament or curve in handwriting. *v.*, *n.*

R. E. Avery

Flourishes in handwriting

flour y (flour′i), 1. of or like flour. 2. covered or white with flour. *adj.*

flout (flout), 1. mock; scoff at; treat with disdain or contempt: *The foolish boy flouted his mother's advice.* 2. a mockery; sneer; insult. *v.*, *n.*

flow (flō), 1. run like water: *A stream flows past the house.* 2. current; stream: *There is a constant flow of water from the spring.* 3. glide; move easily: *a flowing movement in a dance, flowing verse.* 4. hang loosely: *flowing robes, a flowing tie.* 5. any smooth, steady movement: *a flow of words.* 6. pouring out: *a flow of blood.* 7. the rise of the tide. 8. rate of flowing. *v.*, *n.*

flow er (flou′ər), 1. blossom. The flower is the part of a plant or tree which produces the seed. Flowers are often beautifully colored or shaped. 2. a plant grown for its blossoms. 3. produce flowers; bloom; cover with flowers. 4. the finest part of a thing: *The flower of the land would be killed by a war.* 5. the time when a thing is at its best. 6. be at its best. *n.*, *v.*

flow ered (flou′ərd), 1. having flowers. 2. covered or decorated with flowers. *adj.*

flow er et (flou′ər et), small flower. *n.*

flow er ing (flou′ər ing), having flowers. *adj.*

flow er pot (flou′ər pot′), pot to hold dirt for a plant to grow in. *n.*

flow er y (flou′ər i), 1. having many flowers. 2. full of fine words and fanciful expressions. *adj.*, **flow er i er, flow er i est.**

flown (flōn), See **fly**[2]. *The bird has flown. The flag is flown on all national holidays. pp.* of **fly**[2].

flu (flü), influenza. *n.* [Used in common *talk*]

flub (flub), do (something) very clumsily; make a mess of. *v.*, **flubbed, flub bing.** [Used in common *talk*]

fluc tu ate (fluk′chü āt), rise and fall; change continually; waver: *Prices fluctuate. The temperature fluctuates. v.*, **fluc tu at ed, fluc tu at ing.**

fluc tu a tion (fluk′chü ā′shən), continual change; going up and down; wavering. *n.*

flue (flü), a passage for smoke or hot air, such as there is in a chimney. *n.*

flu en cy (flü′ən si), 1. smooth, easy flow: *The orator had great fluency of speech.* 2. easy, rapid speaking or writing. *n.*

flu ent (flü′ənt), 1. flowing smoothly or easily: *a reply in fluent French.* 2. speaking or writing easily and rapidly: *a fluent speaker. adj.*

fluff (fluf), 1. soft, light, downy particles, such as come from cotton or from new blankets. 2. a soft, light, downy mass of fur or feathers. 3. make into fluff; shake or puff out (hair, feathers, etc.) into a fluffy mass. *n.*, *v.*

fluff i ness (fluf′i nis), softness and lightness. *n.*

fluff y (fluf′i), 1. soft and light like fluff: *Mother's whipped cream is fluffy.* 2. covered with fluff: *fluffy baby chicks. adj.*, **fluff i er, fluff i est.**

flu id (flü′id), 1. any liquid or gas; something that will flow. Water, mercury, air, and oxygen are fluids. 2. like a liquid or a gas; flowing: *She poured the fluid mass of hot candy into a dish to harden. n.*, *adj.*

fluke[1] (flük), 1. the flat, three-cornered piece at the end

FLUKE

FLUKE

Anchor showing flukes

hat, āge, cãre, fär; let, ēqual, tèrm; it, īce; hot, ōpen, ôrder; oil, out; cup, pút, rüle, ūse; ch, child; ng, long; th, thin; ᴛʜ, then; zh, measure; ə represents *a* in about, *e* in taken, *i* in pencil, *o* in lemon, *u* in circus.

E. Use your dictionary to find the unusual plural form of each of the following words. Is more than one plural form given? Note too the meanings of each word.

    crisis   hippopotamus   memorandum   opus

F. Explain what the following sentences illustrate about the word *pass*. Then define the word *pass* as it is used in each sentence.

    1. I have a *pass* for the movies tonight.
    2. The quarterback faded to throw a *pass*.
    3. I hope I can *pass* this test.
    4. *Pass* me the sugar, please.
    5. The soldiers will *pass* in review.
    6. The explorers found a mountain *pass*.

WORKING BY YOURSELF

A. Each of the words below has more than one meaning. On a sheet of paper, write at least two sentences for each word, showing two possible meanings of the word.

1. change	8. spring
2. flat	9. stand
3. foot	10. string
4. order	11. taste
5. scale	12. tie
6. screen	13. time
7. sense	14. track

If necessary, consult your dictionary to make sure you have used each word correctly. How many other meanings for each word can you find? Which word has the most meanings?

B. Using dictionary information, draw the following figures:

    parallelogram   quadrant   lintel   keystone

Since your desk dictionary, an abridged one, contains the pronunciation, origin, and meaning of between 80,000 and 130,000 words, it usually will serve you well. But you should also become acquainted with an *unabridged* dictionary. This huge dictionary, which can be found in most libraries, contains as many as 600,000 words, often meanings for each word which are not found in desk dictionaries, and some sections which desk dictionaries do not have.

A. An unabridged dictionary gives about 200 meanings for the word *set*. Consult an unabridged dictionary and list five meanings for *set* that your desk dictionary does not contain.

B. Use an unabridged dictionary to discover what a scissor-tailed flycatcher and a Percheron look like. Write a few sentences describing each.

C. Make a list of the sections you find in an unabridged dictionary that are not in your desk dictionary.

abridged

Abridged comes from two Latin words meaning "to make brief."

In English, an *abridged* book is one which has omitted some words or p... s, without losing the meaning of the original book.

Now that I have read the abridged book, I should like to compare it to the unabridged version.

abridgement   abridge

6 Pronouncing New Words

When Bill finally spied the word *florin* in his dictionary, he was pleased to see that one of the first things he could discover about it was its pronunciation.

> **flor in** (flôr′ən), **1.** a gold or silver coin of varying value current at various times in different countries of Europe. **2.** an English silver coin worth 2 shillings. **3.** an old English gold coin worth about 6 shillings. *n.*

- Why is pronunciation such an important part of our spoken language?

Through a system of notations called *diacritical marks,* a dictionary indicates just how to sound the letters of a word. A complete key to these diacritical (dī′a·krĭt′i·käl) marks is in the front of a dictionary; a shorter one is at the bottom of each page. The keys show what each mark means by giving a familiar word that contains that sound. For example, the straight line over a vowel (ā, ē, ī, ō, ū) informs us that the vowel is given its *name* sound or *long* sound.

- Look at the key on your dictionary page. How would each vowel be pronounced in its long sound?

A curved line over a vowel (ĕ) or a vowel with no mark over it represents a *short* sound.

- Which method is used to represent the short vowel sound on the dictionary page in your book?
- Consult the dictionary key again to find the pronunciation of each short vowel.

• What words besides those in the dictionary key can you think of to illustrate long and short vowel sounds?

When you use any dictionary, you should follow its own pronunciation key, for its key may differ from that of another dictionary. One dictionary, for example, may not mark long vowel sounds at all. Another dictionary may not mark short vowels. You would have to know the system before you could pronounce words you looked up in any dictionary.

As further aids to the pronunciation of the word *florin*, the dictionary supplied Bill with a respelling of the word and with a division of the word into syllables, marking the accented syllable. The sound of the *i* in the unaccented syllable of *florin* is represented by ə, the symbol for a vowel sound heard only in unaccented syllables. This symbol is called a *schwa*. In the dictionary key on page 30 the schwa represents the *a* in *about*, the *e* in *taken*, the *i* in *April*, the *o* in *lemon*, and the *u* in *circus*.

Many words have more than one accented syllable. In the word *undecided*, for example, there is a primary accent on the third syllable and a secondary accent on the first syllable. See if you can hear the accents in *undecided* (un′di sīd′id), *blueberry* (blü′ber′ē), and *guarantee* (gar′ən tē′).

WORKING TOGETHER

A. Copy these words from the sample pronunciation key reprinted at the bottom of page 30: *hat, age, care, far, let, be, term, it, ice, hot, go, order, oil, out, cup, put, rule, use.* Pronounce each word. Now write beside each at least one other word that contains the same sound as the marked vowel. Read your list aloud to see if your classmates agree with your choices.

B. Using the longer pronunciation chart at the front of a dictionary, mark the vowels in these words: *man, far, palm, vacation, error, angel, pity, order, undo.* Pronounce each word.

C. Looking at the dictionary page reprinted on page 30 of your book, decide how to pronounce the words *florid, flotsam, flourish, fluctuate,* and *fluent.* Then be ready to use each word in a sentence.

D. These words are sometimes mispronounced because the wrong sound is given a vowel. List each word, consult a dictionary, and mark each vowel. Pronounce each word.

alias	Italian
bade	mischievous
err	suite
genuine	theater

E. Write the following words on a sheet of paper, dividing them into syllables. Place an accent mark before or after the syllable that receives the main accent. Write a sentence using each word; then be ready to read your four sentences to your classmates.

admirable	precedent
comparable	preferable

F. Using what you know about word parts, write your own definition of the word *dictionary.*

G. Each word below has two meanings, depending upon the syllable accented. Using your dictionary, (1) divide each word into its syllables, (2) show the accents, and be ready to (3) pronounce each word, and (4) use each word in a sentence.

rebel	desert	contest
convert	present	refuse
object	progress	permit
increase	insult	transfer
record	conduct	contrast
produce	suspect	convict

7 Varieties of English Usage

"Hi, Queenie. Say, you're a real knockout in that groovy gown!"

English words and expressions are often divided into *Standard English*, *Colloquialisms*, and *Slang*. These three groups are not meant to separate correct from incorrect English, but rather to show that there are appropriate times and places for words, just as there are for actions.

- What words could the boy in the picture above have used more appropriately?

36

- Read the definitions below. Then decide what kind of English you think the boy in the picture was speaking.

Standard (American) English: words or expressions that have become acceptable in most communities throughout the United States

Colloquialism: an expression used mainly in informal conversation; usually phrases, not words

Slang: informal language accepted by a small group of people; usually words, rather than phrases

- In what speaking or writing situations would you use each of the following words or expressions?

Standard English	Colloquial English	Slang
He's a talkative person.	He's a bag of wind.	He's a gasser!
What a bothersome, obnoxious girl she is!	She gives me a pain in the neck!	What a creep!

Some dictionaries note whether words are colloquialisms or slang. The sample below uses still another label.

stuck-up (stuk′up′), too proud; conceited; haughty. *adj.* [*Used in common talk*]

sock[2] (sok), 1. strike or hit hard. 2. hard blow. 3. squarely; right. *v., n., adv.* [*Slang*]

Reprinted by permission from the *Thorndike-Barnhart Junior Dictionary*, Sixth Edition. Copyright © 1965 by Scott, Foresman and Company.

The levels of usage in English show us two other examples of how our language changes. First, we see that words and expressions can pass from one kind of English to another as they become more widely used in speaking and in writing. For example, *hot dog* was originally a slang expression, but is now probably standard English, since it has replaced its acceptable synonym, "sausage sandwich."

A second way that English changes is clear from the fact that slang words usually go out of use very quickly. For example, though the word *gasser* in sentence 3 on page 37 was once in frequent use, it is seldom heard now. Your parents can probably give you more examples of slang you would consider old-fashioned.

DISCUSSING

A. What are some words or expressions you use in informal conversation with your friends that you would not use in writing a composition?

B. How do the words and expressions you mentioned in *A* differ from those your parents might use in speaking to their friends?

C. What words and expressions did you and your friends use last year or a few years ago that you no longer use?

D. Look for some advertisements in newspapers and magazines. Bring them to class and be prepared to read them aloud and discuss the kind of English they represent.

E. Discuss the kinds of English used by fictional characters or real persons on several TV programs. What does each character's or person's use of English show about him?

F. Consider two or three TV commercials. How does the company selling a product use language to attempt to influence a viewer to buy its product?

WORKING BY YOURSELF

A. Write a conversation of about ten to fifteen lines in which two friends discuss one of the following topics.

1. A movie they both saw recently
2. A person they both know
3. Something they plan to do in the future

Be ready to choose a classmate to read the conversation with you.

B. Using the same topic you chose for *A*, write a short summary for publication in a class or school newspaper. Think about the different kinds of English you have used in each assignment, and be ready to discuss the differences with your classmates.

C. On a sheet of paper number from 1 to 10 and write a definition for each underlined word or expression in the sentences below. Use a dictionary if necessary. Perhaps your parents or grandparents can help you with some of your definitions.

1. The music is <u>cool</u>.
2. That new show is the <u>cat's pajamas</u>.
3. The customer handed the waiter a <u>fin</u>.
4. Several workers stared angrily at the <u>fink</u>.
5. Jeff is a good <u>egg</u>.
6. The class thought the program was <u>corny</u>.
7. That's a <u>classy</u> jacket you're wearing.
8. The umpire made a real <u>boner</u>.
9. He really <u>goofed</u> on that play.
10. He's an <u>oddball</u>.

MORE FOR YOU

Compile a list of currently popular words or expressions used by you and your friends. See how your language fashions have changed by consulting your list in a few months or a year.

8 A Review

A. In your dictionary find the origin of the following words. Use the table of abbreviations so that you can be sure you know the language from which we borrowed each word.

1. adobe	5. cargo	9. jockey	13. stanza
2. ballet	6. coffee	10. orange	14. tobacco
3. camel	7. corral	11. poodle	15. veneer
4. candy	8. cotton	12. potato	16. zebra

B. Write the definitions of these words. Use each in a sentence.

1. adlib	3. countdown	5. snorkel
2. cloverleaf	4. hedgehop	6. starlet

C. Many dictionaries contain sections listing names of important places and people; others provide such information within the body of the dictionary. Find whether or not your dictionary has separate sections for names of important places and people. What are such sections called?

1. Use your dictionary to find out why the name *Clemens* is of interest to boys and girls.

2. Find out why *Oak Ridge* is important to Americans.

3. Find a city, a river, and a lake in your state and be ready to tell what the dictionary says about each.

4. Discover the meanings of the following proper names:

     Deborah   *George*   *Irene*   *Michael*

D. If you have available a dictionary which lists proper nouns, write the dictionary respelling for each of the following proper nouns, and be ready to read the nouns aloud.

1. Carlisle	5. Dumas	9. San Jose
2. Cheyenne	6. Gloucester	10. San Juan
3. Chihuahua	7. Oahu	11. Thames
4. Chopin	8. San Joaquin	12. Worcester

E. Write the plural form of each of these words:

1. crisis
2. oasis
3. basis
4. monkey
5. handful
6. deer
7. tomato
8. echo
9. index
10. loaf
11. parenthesis
12. self

F. The words below are often mispronounced because people accent the wrong syllable. List each word, use a dictionary to help you divide it into syllables, place the accent at the right place, and pronounce the word.

1. admirable
2. defense
3. detail
4. entire
5. infamous
6. mischievous
7. municipal
8. preparatory
9. research

G. Sometimes at the end of a written line, writers divide words at the wrong places or try to divide words that cannot be divided. List only those words that can be divided into syllables and show at what point each word can be broken at the end of a line.

1. auditorium
2. beginning
3. bicycle
4. coming
5. depend
6. enjoy
7. happen
8. holiday
9. receive
10. running
11. search
12. straight
13. sudden
14. summer
15. thought
16. through
17. vacation
18. wrote

H. Unscramble the following word roots and suffixes, forming correct words. Use your dictionary if you need help.

1. govern _____ (-*ize*)
2. summar _____ (-*ic*)
3. subtract _____ (-*ment*)
4. glori _____ (-*ness*)
5. pur _____ (-*ary*)
6. hope _____ (-*ion*)
7. prim _____ (-*ous*)
8. hero _____ (-*less*)
9. wilder _____ (-*ful*)
10. speech _____ (-*ify*)
11. secret _____ (-*ity*)
12. grav _____ (-*ive*)

41

CHAPTER TWO

Your Spoken Language

1 Carving Your Words

> Speak clearly, if you speak at all;
> Carve every word before you let it fall.
> —Oliver Wendell Holmes

The advice given by Oliver Wendell Holmes in the quotation above is probably the result of his own experience. A great success in two fields—medicine and writing—Oliver Wendell Holmes stood many times before large audiences and earned the reputation of a gifted public speaker. Whether he was lecturing in his spare time about English poets, or, as Professor of Anatomy at Harvard College, lecturing about the human body, his own advice would have served him well. Oliver Wendell Holmes's suggestion can also be useful to you.

You know how important the dictionary is in helping you to speak and write correctly. However, it would be possible to pronounce a word as the dictionary indicates, to use it correctly in a sentence, and still *not* communicate your meaning to others.

- To what important part of spoken English was Oliver Wendell Holmes referring in the quotation at the beginning of this lesson?

- In what ways do you think you might follow Oliver Wendell Holmes's advice?

Each description that follows refers to a basic part of oral communication which any speaker must consider. As you read the descriptions, try to decide what the basics are.

1. When Myra explained several of her original paintings to the class, children at the back of the room looked puzzled and became restless before Myra had finished.

volume

The English word *volume* can be traced back to a Latin word that meant "a roll, usually of parchment or papyrus containing writing." In the Middle Ages, *volume* came to mean "a collection of written or printed sheets bound together to form a book." Still later, *volume* was used to mean "one of a number of books forming a related set or series."

The way words and their meanings change in a living language is shown further by the fact that in the 1600's and 1700's the same word, *volume*, signified the particular bulk, size, or dimensions of a thing. Not until about 1800 did the word *volume* take on the meaning it has in this lesson—that is, "the strength or power of sound."

In which volume of the encyclopedia did you find your information?
The TV volume is turned up too high.

voluble   voluminous

Have you decided why some members of Myra's audience were not interested in her talk? Now consider Juan's problem; like Myra's, it cuts off some of his listeners.

2. As Juan announced the Boy Scouts' fund-raising drive, many of his classmates winced, and a few even covered their ears.

pitch

The *pitch* of a voice, as of a musical note, is its highness or lowness. Voice pitch is determined by the number of vibrations set into motion along the vocal cords in a given unit of time, and by the length of the vocal cords themselves.

If you were strumming a rubber band, how would you lower the sound produced? How would you raise the sound?

When Mrs. McIntosh is excited, her voice becomes high-pitched.

3. While Naomi read her short story to the class, many listeners slumped down in their seats, yawning occasionally.

tone

The Greek word *tonos,* "the act of stretching," gives us our English word *tone.* The way we change our voice pitch in speaking affects our *tone,* which is the total mood or emotion the voice conveys. See if you can read aloud this short dialogue in the *tones* you think the speakers used.

Mother: Matt, your room is very messy.
Matt: Too bad!
Mother: *Don't use that tone with me, young man!*

tonal   monotone   monotonous

- How do the descriptions of Myra, Juan, and Naomi show each speaker's failure to consider *volume, pitch,* or *tone* in oral communications?
- Why are enunciation—giving each vowel and consonant the sound it should have—and pace of speaking also important in oral communication?

Read and think about these other famous remarks on the subject of speaking:

"The manner of speaking is full as important as the matter, as more people have ears to be tickled than understandings to judge."—*Lord Chesterfield*

"Let your speech be always with grace; seasoned with salt."—*New Testament:* II Corinthians, xi, 6

"Let thy speech be better than silence, or be silent."
—*Dionysius the Elder*

SPEAKING AND LISTENING

A. Tell your class something about yourself—a trip you have taken, a hobby you enjoy, your family, a favorite school activity— in a short two- or three-minute talk. As each boy and girl speaks, your teacher may ask the other members of the class to rate him on a chart like this one by placing a check next to the word which best describes the speaker's enunciation, pace, volume, pitch, and tone. Each speaker may also rate himself.

SPEAKING CHART			
ENUNCIATION		**PITCH**	
careless		pleasing	
distinct		shrill	
fuzzy		too deep	
lazy		too high	
PACE		**TONE**	
hesitant		harsh	
just right		pleasing	
too fast		rasping	
too slow		twangy	
VOLUME		What suggestions for improvement can you make to the speaker?	
just right			
too loud			
too soft			
too uneven			

B. Try to show pleasure, disappointment, and disgust by changing your tone as you read each of these sentences:
1. I'll watch the baby while you play ball.
2. I am going shopping with Mother after school.
3. My cousin is coming to visit us.
4. The weatherman says it will snow tomorrow.
5. They are waxing the gym floor.
6. I can only go if we're home before dark.
7. It was a false alarm.

C. If you use your voice well, you can change your tone from time to time to give the same words and the same sentences different meanings. Try it with the following sentences.

1. Bill? (*questioningly*)
   Bill! (*with amazement*)
   Bill! (*with anger*)
2. Laddie, come here. (*excitedly*)
   Laddie, come here. (*sternly*)
   Laddie, come here. (*coaxingly*)
3. Where were you? (*eagerly*)
   Where were you? (*accusingly*)
   Where were you? (*impatiently*)

WORKING BY YOURSELF

A. On a sheet of paper make a list of at least six rules which *you* consider important for good speaking. Compare your list with the one in the Handbook. On what points does your list agree with the one in the book?

B. How often do listeners have to ask you to repeat what you have said? Try to keep a written record for a week, noting also the sounds you seem to have most trouble communicating. Then begin your own campaign to speak distinctly.

2 Oral Reading: Poetry

SPEAKING AND LISTENING

The distinctness of your speech in every conversation or discussion you take part in and in every announcement you make is important to you and your listeners. It is even more important, perhaps, when you read aloud a special kind of literature—poetry.

- Why are sounds and a clear, accurate pronunciation of them especially important in poetry?
- From the poems you have read, how would you say poetry creates and re-creates many sounds?

As you read the following poems and excerpts from poems to yourself, try to note words that sound like what they describe. Then be ready to read the poems aloud to your classmates. As you read, speak as clearly and distinctly as you can, without emphasizing any sounds unnaturally.

PAUL REVERE'S RIDE

A hurry of hoofs in a village street,
A shape in the moonlight, a bulk in the dark,
And beneath, from the pebbles, in passing, a spark
Struck out by a steed flying fearless and fleet—
That was all! And yet, through the gloom and the light,
The fate of a nation was riding that night;
And the spark struck out by that steed in his flight
Kindled the land into flame with its heat.

Henry Wadsworth Longfellow

Think about each poem you are reading.

- What words and lines communicate the mood to the reader?
- What is the main idea of the poem?
- What words help to re-create sounds?

49

THE COWBOY'S LIFE

The bawl of a steer,
To a cowboy's ear,
Is music of sweetest strain;
And the yelping notes
Of the gay coyotes
To him are a glad refrain.

The rapid beat
Of his broncho's feet
On the sod as he speeds along,
Keeps living time
To the ringing rhyme
Of his rollicking cowboy song.

James Barton Adams

THE BLITZEN OASIS AFTER RAIN

Every leaf glistens; the whole world glitters;
Lombardy poplars, rustling with a silken rustle,
Drip from pointed leaves gold-flashing sundrops.
Each sudden gust shakes down a sparkling shower,
A bright rehearsal of the thunderstorm.
Small birds, silenced, now begin to twitter,
Swallows dart again, tracking the crooked mazes of the air,
Shuttles of the air, skimming the pool,
And on the steaming door of the blacksmith shop
A yellowhammer beats his sharp, reverberant tattoo.
The wind runs along the willows,
Footing them to paths of silver.
From drenched alfalfa fields, a honey smell:
Aromatic odors, blown from all the brave
And bitter weeds that dare the desert—
Greasewood, sagebrush, rabbit-brush, deathweed, wormwood,
Bitter and fragrant.

Against the black horizon lightning darts;
Thunder grumbles sullenly afar,
A mad old bull, cast out, defeated.
Beyond the irrigation ditch,
Beyond the line of cottonwoods,
Beyond the barbed-wire fence,
Out in the still unslaked, defiant waste,
A sagebrush thrasher bubbles up his joy.

Charles Erskine Scott Wood

51

THE SOUNDS IN THE MORNING

The sounds in the morning
Go all down the street:
The tapping of sticks
And the patter of feet,
The wind in the plane-trees
That whisper and rustle,
The pigeons all sleepy,
The newsboys all hustle,
The *clippety-clop*
And the *clip-clop* again
Of soldiers and horses,
More horses than men,
The clatter of milk-cans,
The chatter of maids,
The slop of their buckets,
The sort without spades,
And sometimes the mooing
Of slow-moving cows
Brings the smell of the lowlands
To me as I drowse,
And sometimes the bleating
And scuffle of sheep
Draws down the high hill-tops
To me half-asleep,
Dogs barking, bells chiming,
The twitter of sparrows—
Till the sun through the slats
Of my blind shoots his arrows,
And the world of my ears
Seems to dwindle in size
As I jump out of bed
To the world of my eyes.

Eleanor Farjeon

3 Explaining by Announcing

"He'll have a lot of explaining to do," growled Father as he looked at the cracked windowpane.

"Why hasn't this errand been done?" demanded Mother.

Fortunately, few of our explanations have to do with broken windows and neglected chores. But we *do* spend much of our lives both in and out of school *explaining*—using our voices to tell someone how to make something, how to do something, where something is, the reasons for certain actions and events, and why we think as we do about various issues and problems.

- How many times yesterday in school and at home were you asked to make an explanation of some kind?

Explaining *who*, *what*, *when*, *where*, and *why* can take various forms; one of the most frequent forms is an announcement.

53

"Now be sure to explain to your class about our bake sale," said Mrs. White as the Girls' Club meeting broke up.

When Sue, Nancy, and Joan announced the bake sale in their homerooms, this is what they said:

Sue: "We're having a bake sale Tuesday—uh, I mean Wednesday. You're all expected to come. It's going to be at the playground entrance, I think. See you then."

Nancy: "Our club is having a bake sale next Wednesday at four o'clock by the playground gate. Everybody is invited."

Joan: "Do you love cookies? The Sixth Grade Girls' Club is having a bake sale next Wednesday at four o'clock to raise money for our Children's Hospital fund. Our booth will be set up at the main playground entrance. If you love cookies, fudge, and all kinds of pies and cakes, be sure to be there before we're sold out. Bring your mothers. They won't want to miss this either."

- Which girl probably interested the most people in the bake sale?
- How did she make the bake sale something you might want to attend?
- What did she tell you that you would need to know?
- How did she catch your attention and interest?
- What guides can you establish for making an effective announcement?

DISCUSSING

A. Decide what facts would be needed in order for you to make clear and interesting announcements on each of these topics:

1. A play	3. A lost dog
2. A picnic	4. A found book

54

B. Real communication is a two-way process. For every speaker there is a listener. A good listener listens not only because it is the courteous thing to do, but because he knows he will learn much of interest and value, whether it be directions for landing his aircraft or the announcement that Susie has a new puppy.

You will spend more of your life hearing and listening than doing anything else, except breathing. How would you explain the difference between just hearing and *listening*?

WORKING BY YOURSELF

A. Add any important details you need in order to prepare an announcement based on each of the situations below. Sort out the five W's—*who, what, when, where, why*—and then arrange them in a clear and interesting announcement. Make notes to be sure that you include all the necessary information, but do not memorize the announcement. Be ready to present it to the class.

1. A volleyball game between the fifth and sixth grades after school in the gym on Friday
2. A meeting of the Science Club on Saturday at Barry Wilson's home
3. A collection of books and magazines for the Veterans' Hospital
4. Tryouts for the school orchestra after school today
5. Postponement of the Boys' (or Girls') Club trip to the pool scheduled for Saturday
6. Special Art Club show next week on the auditorium stage
7. A display of new books acquired by the library
8. The publication of the first edition of the school newspaper

B. Test your ability to listen by taking notes on a piece of paper as your classmates make their announcements. What information should you be able to offer someone who has not heard the announcement at first hand? Your notes may be simply five words which get down *who, what, when, where,* and *why* in an abbreviated way.

> *Sixth-grade class picnic*
> *City Park*
>
> *June 20*
> *end of school*

4 Explaining How

READING AND THINKING

Have you ever thought about what a busy word *how* is? If you are like most people, you spend a great deal of time explaining how. You explain to others how hockey is played or how paper is produced, how to reach your school or how to find mushrooms. You may even explain how to do something in which you are especially interested, or which you do especially well. Tom, for example, enjoys making puppets and hopes to have his own troupe someday. Knowing this, his teacher asked him to tell the class about his hobby and to explain how he makes puppets. Here is Tom's explanation:

If you've never made puppets, I'll tell you an easy way to get started. Take the cardboard tube from a roll of paper towels or wax paper. Cut the tube so you have a little tube six inches long to work with. In one end cut five slits, evenly spaced, each three fourths of an inch in length. Fold these flaps you have made toward each other and paste them down to make the top of the head. Down from the top one inch make two slits for ears and one for a nose. Make these slits one-half inch long. Then out of cardboard cut shapes for the ears, nose, and arms. You can make these as funny-shaped as you want to. Use tempera or show-card colors to paint the face and mouth as well as the cut-out ears, nose, and arms. After the paint dries, use any colored yarn for hair. Then you're ready to dress the puppet. You can take . . .

Tom went on to explain several ways of clothing the puppet and of using his hand to make the puppet perform. On the chalkboard, he drew some shapes of ears and noses from which to choose, and he sketched several costumes.

- Did Tom make his explanation clear enough so that you could follow him without chalkboard diagrams?
- How did you know what Tom was going to explain?
- Did he understand what he was explaining? Give reasons for your answer.
- How did he divide his explanation?
- How much information did he give?
- What kinds of details did he provide?
- What words did he use to supply these details?
- At what points does Tom's explanation need to be made clearer?

Below are the notes Tom used for his talk. Read them aloud, and then discuss the type of information and detail which he included.

Statement of what is to be explained : The making of puppets

1. *Basic materials needed*
   a. *cardboard tube*
   b. *scissors*
   c. *cardboard*
   d. *paint*
2. *Steps in making puppet*
   a. *Cut 5 slits each 3/4" long.*
   b. *Fold flaps toward each other and paste down.*
   c. *One inch from top of tube cut slits each 1/2" long.*
   d. *Cut cardboard ears and nose and insert in slits.*
   e. *Use paint to color face.*
   f. *Use yarn to make hair.*
   g. *Dress puppet.*
3. *How to make puppet perform*

After you study Tom's notes, prepare notes for your own explanation of one of the following subjects, and be ready to present your explanation orally to the class.

1. How to make something of wood, cloth, or cooking materials
2. How to play a game
3. How to operate a machine, an instrument, or some other piece of equipment
4. How to tell a joke
5. How to spin a yarn
6. How to save money
7. How to lose friends
8. How to train a dog

5 Explaining Why

READING AND THINKING

Explanations that tell *why* are likely to be of the "I believe" or the "I know" kind. The reasons which support them are based either on OPINION, what we *feel* about something, or on FACT, what we *know* about something. But unless we have REASONS to back up what we feel or think we know, our explanations will mean little.

For example, Sam may say that he thinks football is a more exciting game than baseball. He can't really prove that football is more exciting, but he can give good reasons why he thinks it is. He may say that since he likes action, football, in his opinion, is a better game because there is almost constant action and more action, and many kinds of action. Then he would go on to give specific examples for each of his reasons. His outline would look like this:

Statement – I think football is a better sport to watch than baseball because it is more exciting.

    Reason 1 – There is constant action – no long waits between innings or pitches

    Reason 2 – There is more action – every man is doing something during every play

    Reason 3 – There are all kinds of actions – punts, passes, tackles, blocks, runs, pile-ups

Restatement – The constancy, amount, and variety of action in football makes it more exciting to watch than baseball.

- Why is Sam's explanation a good one, even though you may not agree with him?

Be ready to read Martha's and Ted's explanations aloud. How often do your own explanations sound like these?

1. "Did you enjoy these books, Martha?" asked the librarian as Martha returned her books to the library.

"I like this one all right, but I didn't think much of that one," answered Martha.

"Oh, why not?" asked Miss Wright.

"Oh, I don't know," said Martha. "It just wasn't so good. I didn't think much of it."

"Ted, can you tell us why Brazilians still speak Portuguese?" asked Mr. Lawson.

"It has something to do with Brazil's being a colony," responded Ted.

"Is Brazil a colony now?" Mr. Lawson asked.

"Well—I don't think so," Ted finished.

WORKING TOGETHER

We have seen how reasons give powerful support to *why* explanations, whether these explanations deal with historical or scientific facts, or our opinions on current subjects. Pool ideas to fill in the reasons or proofs in each outline below:

I

Statement: The Yankees were pennant winners more often than any other team because

Reason 1. . . . .
Reason 2. . . . .
Reason 3. . . . .

Restatement: Therefore, the Yankees were always the "team to beat."

II

Statement: Amelia Earhart made a great contribution to America's early achievements in aviation because

Reason 1. . . . .
Reason 2. . . . .
Reason 3. . . . .

Restatement: For these reasons she is remembered as the Lady Lindbergh.

WORKING BY YOURSELF

Following the patterns above, plan a *why* explanation for one of these topics.

1. Why a T-quarterback does not need to be as big as a tackle
2. Why jets can fly faster than sound
3. Why we speak English in the United States

4. Why America needs a good conservation program
5. Why people first settled our town or city
6. Why our state is called the _____ state
7. Why styles change
8. A *why* topic of your own

When you are satisfied with your explanation, (1) check the first sentence to be sure you have stated clearly what you are about to explain; (2) check next the order of your reasons; (3) to make your reasons move smoothly and sensibly from one to the next, link them together with such words as *next, then, too, in addition, also,* and *finally;* (4) be sure your last sentence sums up what you have proved; (5) review your Speaking Chart for helpful reminders. Then give your explanation to the class.

MORE FOR YOU

Find out how well you can distinguish fact *why's* from opinion *why's* by examining a local newspaper. Compare a news story with an editorial. You may also be interested in comparing the treatment two different newspapers give to the same news event.

6 A Review

A. Here are some additional *how* topics. Choose one of these and be prepared to give your explanation to the class.

1. Explain school regulations concerning the use of the lunchroom or playground.

2. Explain to a parent where he can find the principal's office.

3. Explain to your parents the report-card system your school uses.

4. Explain to a stranger how to get from your school to the nearest restaurant.

5. Explain how to get from your home to a town fifteen or twenty miles away.

6. Explain how to plant a flower bed, raise hamsters (or some other pet), or teach a dog tricks.

7. Explain how to find the meaning of a word in the dictionary and what other kind of information may also be found there.

8. Explain how to find and borrow a book from the library.

B. Ask your parents to use the Speaking Chart on page 47 to rate your voice at the dinner table and in the living room tonight.

C. In your notebook begin a list of suggestions that will help you make your voice pleasant and clear. Here are three to start with:

1. Hold yourself erect and look at your listeners.

2. Open your mouth so that words can come out clearly.

3. Move your tongue. Don't let it be lazy.

Add some rules of your own concerning volume, pitch, pace, and tone as you discuss them in class or discover them for yourself. If possible, test your suggestions and analyze your own speaking problems by working with the school tape recorder.

D. Use your voice to express each emotion specified in parentheses as you read the two sentences below.

1. There must be someone at the door. (*with interest*)
   There must be someone at the door. (*with concern*)
   There must be someone at the door. (*with annoyance*)
   There must be someone at the door. (*with fear*)
   There must be someone at the door. (*with surprise*)

2. You have a good book. (*we don't*)
   You have a good book. (*why complain?*)
   You have a good book. (*some aren't*)
   You have a good book. (*not a good magazine*)

E. There is an old French proverb which says "The spoken word belongs half to him who speaks, and half to him who hears." Write a paragraph explaining what this has to do with *listening*.

F. Study the following reasons for mispronunciations, and then practice the correct pronunciation of each sample word with your class.

1. Some words are mispronounced because a speaker omits a letter or syllable. For example, he says *goverment* instead of *government*, *pome* instead of *poem*, or *accidently* instead of *accidentally*.

2. Sometimes a speaker adds a letter to a word. He says *acrosst* instead of *across*, *filum* instead of *film*, or *drownded* instead of *drowned*.

3. Sometimes a speaker sounds letters which should not be sounded in a word. He says cor*p*s, of*t*en, or depo*t*.

G. Listed below are words that are often mispronounced. Point out the reason or reasons from exercise **F** which seem likely to cause the mispronunciation. Then practice pronouncing each word correctly with your classmates.

athletics, escape, favorite, height, heir, library, probably, salmon

The System of Language:
Nouns and Verbs

1 Words Follow an Order

READING AND THINKING

Have you ever really looked at a tree? From its finger-like roots, up the bark of its sturdy trunk, out to its branches and tiny limbs, and to the very tips of its leaves, the tree is arranged according to a definite plan or order. The representation of this natural order is one of the striking qualities about the picture you see at the opening of Chapter Three. Though the tree in the painting is not exactly like a real tree, any more than two real trees are exactly like each other, you recognize it as a tree because its parts are in a certain familiar *tree* order.

You can see order in yourself as well as in things around you. Your body follows a certain plan which makes you a person, and not a bird or an earthworm. Birds and earthworms, in turn, possess a distinct order of their own.

Considering the pattern and order which surround man, it seems natural that he should have the sort of mind that would lead him to develop his *words* according to a pattern. In the design of the trees, of himself and of the creatures around him, in the order of the seasons and of day and night, are the repetition, regularity, and order that man, either consciously or by instinct, built into his language. Every language, from most to least widely spoken and written, has the order which makes it a system.

- What languages do you think are most widely used today?
- How would you define a *system*? Check your ideas on the following page.

system

The Greek word which gives us *system* in English is *synistanai,* or "to combine" or "cause to stand."

A *system* is a combination of things organized to serve a common purpose. For example, the human digestive *system* is composed of many organs working together toward the common purpose of breaking down food we eat so that it is usable in our bodies.

Our language is also a *system*. It consists of many parts organized to serve the common purpose of communication.

From these two examples of *systems,* you will see how important the *organization* of the parts of a system would be. Each part of the system has its own job to do; unless each part carries out its function, the entire system will not stand.

What is the name of the system which allows us to find books in the library?

Do you know any of the working parts of a radar system?

systematic   systematize   systemic

- How can you explain the fire drill system in your school?
- Think about your use of systems in daily life. What is your system of attacking chores at home? What is your system of studying for a test? What is your system of saving money?
- What kinds of system or order can you see in the words you use? What is the common purpose of your language system?

DISCUSSING

A. Mention other examples of the order in nature. Try to imagine life on earth without this natural order.

B. Why is it necessary for language to have some system or order?

C. How does a language become ordered? Who determines what the order will be?

D. Larry decided that English needed the word *blooky* to symbolize the kind of tiredness he feels after having studied long and hard for a test. How can he use the word and be understood by a classmate? By a pupil in another room?

WORKING BY YOURSELF

Two kinds of language order have been ignored in the following sentences. Rewrite the sentences on a sheet of paper and try to restore word law and order. Then be ready to explain what language order was ignored in each sentence.

1. Whipped winds wild willows the through.
2. Lazily on pads lily lounged ladies lovely little.
3. We birded watch for fives hour before spottings a tanagered.
4. Cried neighbor, his "Look out car that for!"
5. Boy which is the one guilty?

2 The Four Major Word Groups

Almost ninety percent of the words in English fall into four major groups: nouns, verbs, adjectives, and adverbs. These are the four major working parts of our language. All other words are like bolts, screws, and lubricating oil which help the major parts fit together and work well.

One way of talking about the groups of words is to *define* them. For example, a *nail* is usually defined as a pointed, headed piece of metal that is used to fasten wood together. But doesn't that sound like a *screw*, too? Yet a nail and a screw look quite different and don't really function the same way. The example illustrates how difficult it is to make a definition—any definition—describe an object fully and accurately.

We meet the same problem when we try to define parts of language. The definitions can't always be complete and accurate; therefore we will be ready to apply certain tests to determine the groups that words belong to. See again how incomplete definitions can be in the following examples.

---

motion an act, process, or instance
of changing place

70

Does the dictionary definition explain how motion affects your vision or hearing? Does it describe the feeling in the pit of your stomach that some motion produces?

cat a carnivorous animal long domesticated and kept by man as a pet or for catching rats and mice

Does the definition tell you how soft and furry a cat is? Does it tell you the kind of sounds it makes in its various moods?

Just as man learned about the order of the sun and the tides by observing them often enough to discover their pattern, we can learn about the order of words through observation. To understand the system of words in English, we will observe their positions and functions in relation to other words in the sentence, and their forms or spellings.

WORKING TOGETHER

A. See how alert you are by choosing an object in the classroom, then closing your eyes and describing it to your classmates. Have you *observed* it carefully?

B. Select a classmate to go to the chalkboard and draw an object as another classmate describes it to him. How clear has the description been? Has it provided enough information for the pupil at the chalkboard to draw the object so that you would recognize it?

C. Discuss what information you would add to make the definitions of *motion* and *cat* more complete.

WORKING BY YOURSELF

A. Write your own definitions for five words of your choice. Be ready to read the definitions to your classmates and have them guess what you have defined. You might then compare your definitions to those in the dictionary. To what extent do both your definitions and the ones in the dictionary succeed in describing the object?

B. Some misunderstandings or disagreements are caused by the fact that no two persons have exactly the same definition for a given word. Since a person's definition of a word partly determines the feelings or emotions the word arouses in him, you can see how misunderstandings might occur. Read the following comments and discuss why you think they might have caused a disagreement between the persons involved.

    1. My mother says you're a bookworm.
    2. You can't trust him—he's a politician.
    3. Your uncle isn't much of a success.
    4. That book you recommended was dull.

72

3 Nouns in Context: Positions and Functions

READING AND THINKING

"...the movie was superb..."

"...she steals..."

"...he's a good quarterback..."

- How would you interpret these snatches of conversations?

The three periods before and after each quotation above mean that the quotations are *out of context,* or removed from the total group of words which surrounded them when they were originally spoken. Just to see how important the *context* of a word or group of words can be, look at the complete statement from which each of the above quotations was removed:

"I certainly wouldn't say that <u>the movie was superb.</u>"

"Sometimes <u>she steals</u> a glance at him."

"Nobody thinks that <u>he's a good quarterback.</u>"

- How does the meaning of each quotation change when it is placed in the context of the entire original statement?

Perhaps the examples on page 73 will show you why, as one way of classifying words, we will always consider them in the *context* of a sentence. This is the way we now want to examine the first word group, NOUNS, by seeing their positions and functions in relation to the other words in a sentence. Typical positions and functions of nouns in sentences are shown in the five sentences below.

       N **V**
1. The <u>dog</u> ate.

       N **V**   **N**
2. The <u>dog</u> ate our <u>steak</u>.

       N **LV**   **N**
3. The <u>dog</u> was a <u>thief</u>.

       N **LV** **Adj**
4. The <u>dog</u> was swift.

       N **V**   **N**   **N**
5. The <u>dog</u> gave his <u>owner</u> a <u>chase</u>.

- How would you describe the position and function, or job, of each underlined word in the five sentences above?
- In terms of the functions of the underlined words, what would be the difference between "The <u>dog</u> bit a <u>thief</u>," and sentence 3 above?

In addition to having certain positions and functions, a word that acts as a noun will usually fit this test frame:

(The) _____ is good.

(The) _____ are good.

- Try to determine which of the following words can act as nouns by fitting them into the test frame:

 tin, courage, rapidly, summer, elms, playground

In the sentences on page 74, notice four words which signal that nouns are coming: *the, our, a,* and *his.* These words are called *determiners,* or *noun markers.* Sometimes the noun immediately follows the determiner; sometimes other words come between the determiner and the noun: *The big black dog ate.*

Determiners fall into two main types: (1) those which are *always* determiners, and (2) those which are *often* determiners. Examples of the first type are:

a, an	our	their
my	the	your

Some words of the second type are:

all	few	no
another	her	one
any	his	other
both	its	several
each	many	some
enough	more	this, these
every	most	two . . . ninety-nine

WORKING TOGETHER

A. Apply the three noun tests below to the underlined words in the sentences which follow them.

> Test 1—positions and functions
> Test 2—noun test frame
> Test 3—presence of determiners

1. Few cars lacked safety belts.
2. Ralph was chairman yesterday.
3. The books were overdue.
4. Your sister broke her toy.
5. Many activities were planned at the meeting.

B. Decide whether or not the following words can act as nouns by substituting them in the test frame on page 74.

run	beautiful	boy
chicken	loudly	postman

C. Notice again how important word order is in our language. What happens when nouns used as subject and direct object are out of position?

The <u>dog</u> ate our <u>steak</u>.
The <u>steak</u> ate our <u>dog</u>.

The <u>dog</u> ate our <u>steak</u> from the <u>platter</u>.
The <u>platter</u> ate our <u>dog</u> from the <u>steak</u>.

Why does sentence 3 on page 74 not change its meaning when we interchange the positions of the two nouns?

D. To determine which of the following words can be nouns, try to place *a* or *an* and *the* before each.

ocean	beautiful	rapidly	porch
run	agreement	doorway	puppy
yard	handsome	pleased	happy

WORKING BY YOURSELF

A. Using the noun test frame given in this lesson, determine whether or not the words in the following list can be used as nouns. Number your paper from 1 to 10 and write **N** if the word can be used as a noun, and *no* if it cannot.

1. act
2. friendly
3. hope
4. pines
5. play

6. records
7. salmon
8. typist
9. warmth
10. wasted

B. On a sheet of paper write ten sentences using ten different determiners. Draw a circle around each noun and underline each determiner.

4 Pronouns: A Subclass of Nouns

READING AND THINKING

Personal pronouns, one subclass of nouns, fill the same positions and perform the same functions as nouns. As you see from the list below, personal pronouns are words we use all the time:

I, me	we, us
you	you
he, him	they, them
she, her	
it	

Another test for finding out if a word is a noun is to substitute an appropriate pronoun for it. For example:

Mike saw the man.

He saw him.

The sun dropped behind the hills.

It dropped behind them.

- What happens to the determiner when a pronoun is substituted for a noun?
- What pronouns can be substituted for nouns in the sentences on page 78, which are repeated from Lesson 3?

N V
1. The <u>dog</u> ate.

N V N
2. The <u>dog</u> ate our <u>steak</u>.

N LV N
3. The <u>dog</u> was a <u>thief</u>.

N LV Adj
4. The <u>dog</u> was swift.

N V N N
5. The <u>dog</u> gave his <u>owner</u> a <u>chase</u>.

Other pronouns, sometimes called *indefinite pronouns*, can also fill noun positions and perform noun functions. You will recognize that some of them can also be used as determiners.

anybody	everybody	many	nobody
anyone	everyone	mine	no one
both	few	more	some
each	hers	most	theirs
enough	his	neither	yours

- Look at the pairs of sentences below. How can you decide whether the underlined words are determiners, or indefinite pronouns?

<u>Many</u> were lost.   <u>Many</u> report cards were lost.
<u>Both</u> were sent.   <u>Both</u> astronauts were sent.

78

An important rule to follow as you use pronouns to substitute for nouns in your speaking and writing is that pronouns must refer to nouns already specified. Pronouns must also be the same number (singular or plural) and the same gender (masculine, feminine, or neuter) as the nouns they replace. For example:

1.

a. Jerry knew what book he wanted to borrow.

b. He asked the librarian if it was available, and she told him it was.

2.

a. The players lined up to be photographed.

b. Several were not in uniform, and the coach was angry.

c. He had reminded them the day before that they would not be photographed in street clothes.

In the sentences above, each underlined pronoun refers to a noun already mentioned. This noun is called the *antecedent* of the pronoun—the word which goes before it and is replaced by it.

• Which words are antecedents in the sentences above?

When a speaker or writer uses pronouns carelessly, his meaning can become vague. Avoid vagueness by checking to see that when you use pronouns, they always refer to specific nouns.

WORKING TOGETHER

A. Use each of the indefinite pronouns on page 78 in a sentence, remembering that *anybody, anyone, everyone, nobody,* and *no one* are singular words and will be followed by determiners and personal pronouns which are also singular. For example:

Everyone left his coat in the closet.
Nobody had his on.

B. A noun test frame is given below. Use it to test the underlined words in the five sentences following it. You may find that not all the underlined words can be nouns. For those words which *can* act as nouns, go on to substitute appropriate pronouns, and then fit each of the pronouns into the test frame.

```
(The) _____ is good.
(The) _____ are good.
```

1. The precious <u>metal</u> sparkled in the <u>dust</u> as the <u>prospector</u> <u>gasped</u> for breath.
2. Shimmering <u>moonlight</u> dazzled the <u>water</u> while the <u>boat</u> creaked <u>solemnly</u>.
3. The gleaming <u>kayak</u> knifed through the <u>waters</u> noiselessly.
4. The <u>runner</u> collapsed <u>after</u> he had burst through the <u>line</u>.
5. The sheepdog's <u>eyes</u> were concealed by shaggy <u>hair</u>.
C. Substitute nouns for pronouns in the sentences below.

1. It growled ferociously from behind them.
2. He returned it to her.
3. We went to him with them.

WORKING BY YOURSELF

On a sheet of paper write two sentences for each word below, using the word first as a determiner, then as an indefinite pronoun. Draw an arrow from the determiner to the noun it marks and underline the indefinite pronoun.

1. both	5. his
2. each	6. some
3. few	7. enough
4. more	8. several

5   Nouns: Form Traits

READING AND THINKING

If you were asked to describe your father to someone who had never seen him, you might mention his wavy brown hair streaked with silver, his brown eyes edged with laugh crinkles, and the cleft in his chin. The things you would have described are some of his physical *traits*, qualities of his appearance that distinguish him from anyone else's father. A longer description might go on to summarize his personality traits.

In discussing words, we also consider *traits* which distinguish one group from another.

- What traits of *form*, or spelling, can you see among the following words? What do the words have in common?

I		II		III	
book	books	church	churches	child	children
boy	boys	dish	dishes	deer	deer
dog	dogs	fox	foxes	foot	feet
film	films	grass	grasses	man	men
plane	planes	quiz	quizzes	ox	oxen

- What does the change in spelling of each word in Groups I, II, and III represent?

The plural form of most nouns is made by simply adding -*s*, as in Group I above. Some nouns, however, are made plural by adding -*es*, as in Group II. Nouns ending in -*s*, -*ss*, -*sh*, soft -*ch*, -*x*, -*z*, and -*zz* require the -*es* ending to make their plural forms pronounceable. Some nouns, such as those in Group III, follow no rule in forming the plural. The dictionary will guide you in forming these irregular plurals.

Several other spelling changes which some nouns undergo in the plural form are represented below.

Nouns ending in the letter *y* following a consonant are made plural by changing the *y* to *i* and adding the suffix *-es:*

baby — babies   lady — ladies
caddy — caddies   ally — allies

Some nouns ending in the letters *f* or *fe* are made plural by adding *-s*. Others, however, change the *f* or *fe* to *v* and add the suffix *-es:*

half — halves   loaf — loaves
calf — calves   wife — wives

The plurals of most nouns ending in *-o* following a consonant are formed by adding *-es*. Musical terms ending in *-o* and nouns ending in *-o* following a vowel, however, form plurals by adding *-s*.

tomato — tomatoes   echo — echoes   piano — pianos
hero   — heroes   alto — altos   studio — studios

Though quite rare, there are some nouns that have only plural forms:

scissors   trousers
pliers   slacks

- Do you know other nouns which change in any of the above ways?
- Can you think of any nouns that have the same form in both singular and plural?

Aside from a few exceptions, then, another good test to determine if a word is a noun is to attempt to form a plural of the word in one of the ways illustrated in this lesson.

WORKING TOGETHER

A. Tell what words you can think of that form plurals in the following five ways described in this lesson.

-s	-es	irregular plurals	-ies	-ves

B. Use a plural noun in the blank in each sentence below.

1. A flock of _____ flew overhead.
2. He drives _____ on the range.
3. I hooked six _____ in that stream.
4. It is time to shear the _____.
5. Three polar _____ attacked the party of explorers.

C. Another signal that a word is a noun may lie in the suffix you discover at the end of the word. What common noun suffix can you see in the words below?

development   equipment   investment
encouragement   establishment   management

Sometimes we can recognize a familiar root word to which a suffix has been added. What are the root words above? Are they nouns? If not, what are they?

D. Some other noun suffixes appear in the words below. What are they? Add five words to each group.

defender	arsonist	goodness
manager	plagiarist	kindness
performer	pianist	wilderness
density	convention	childhood
gravity	exhibition	brotherhood
oddity	nation	manhood

83

WORKING BY YOURSELF

A. On a sheet of paper write the plural forms of the following words. If you are unsure of any, use the dictionary. Note any that have *two* acceptable forms.

1. horse	6. shelf	11. sky
2. church	7. knife	12. dairy
3. hoof	8. tomato	13. box
4. beef	9. louse	14. wharf
5. wolf	10. family	15. porch

B. Rewrite the following sentences, using the plural form of the underlined word in each sentence. Make any other changes that are necessary. Be ready to explain any such changes.

1. That boy is in the sixth grade.
2. The man works for IBM.
3. This oak is the sturdiest tree we have.
4. A woman slipped and fell on the ice.
5. This library is open on Saturday.
6. The mouse scurried across the floor.
7. A leaf fluttered and blew across the pavement.
8. That box is a gift for Ellen.
9. The scarf flapped in the wind.
10. This freighter has a huge winch for loading cargo.
11. A fox ran across the field.
12. We rode the trolley.
13. That tomato is ripe.
14. The radio went dead.
15. An elf cast the spell.
16. The pants were gray.
17. This secretary knows shorthand.
18. There was a patch on his jacket.
19. Mother cooked a turkey.

6 Nouns: Possessive Forms

READING AND THINKING

"Sue's hair is braided today," remarked Russ.

"Sally's is in a ponytail," answered Sue.

Sally commented, "Russ's latest haircut is just like his older brother's."

"I think Mrs. Ruffle's dog has the most unusual hairdo of all," decided Sue. Russ and Sally had to agree.

The brief conversation on page 85 illustrates another important form change of nouns.

- Which nouns in the conversation have something added to their singular forms?

- How has each change affected the information given you by the noun?

Forming the possessive of a *singular* noun is usually easy. Simply add *'s* at the end of the noun, as *Sue's, Sally's, Russ's, brother's* and *Mrs. Ruffle's.* To form the *plural* possessive of nouns requires special care. However, if you have learned to form the plural correctly, you will have no trouble with the plural possessive.

Singular	Singular Possessive	Plural	Plural Possessive
boy	boy's	boys	boys'
cat	cat's	cats	cats'
dog	dog's	dogs	dogs'
painter	painter's	painters	painters'
player	player's	players	players'

- How has the plural possessive been formed for nouns whose plurals end in -*s?*
- Think about how you would form the possessives of the italicized nouns in the following sentences.

1. The *artists* shirt was splattered with paint.
2. A *pitchers* eye must be sharp and accurate.
3. Those *pilots* records are excellent.
4. The *speakers* voice trembled.
5. The *students* heads were bent over their papers.

The nouns below are examples of those which can confuse you if you are not careful to remember the special way to deal with them.

Singular	Singular Possessive	Plural	Plural Possessive
goose	goose's	geese	geese's
man	man's	men	men's
mouse	mouse's	mice	mice's
ox	ox's	oxen	oxen's
woman	woman's	women	women's

- How is the plural possessive formed when the plural of a noun does not end in -s?

Notice that the possessive is usually formed by nouns which symbolize *living* things. Thus, we would say:

The dog's leg is broken.

But we would seldom say:

The table's leg is broken.

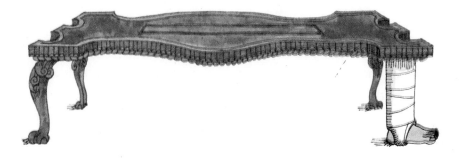

We would probably say:

The leg of the table is broken.

Personal pronouns also have possessive forms, but, although some of them end in -s, they never require apostrophes. Possessive forms of personal pronouns which cause trouble because of their -s endings are: *ours, yours, his, hers, its,* and *theirs.* Notice that there are no apostrophes in the possessive pronouns in the sentences below. Why is there an apostrophe in the first *It's* in sentence 2, but not in the second one?

1. That dog must be <u>yours</u>.
2. It's wagging <u>its</u> tail.
3. The book is <u>his</u>, not <u>hers</u>.
4. The horse broke <u>its</u> leg.
5. That building is taller than <u>ours</u>.
6. The bats are <u>yours</u>, but the mitts are <u>theirs</u>.

WORKING TOGETHER

A. To test yourself change the following word groups into plural possessives. For example:

The lockers of the children = The children's lockers

1. hats of the men
2. coats of the women
3. yoke of the oxen
4. books of the children
5. tails of the mice

B. Review what you have learned about form traits of nouns by supplying the missing information in the sentences below.

1. Words which are nouns indicate number by having _____ and _____ forms.

2. Nouns are able to show _____ by use of _____ and _____.

3. Nouns frequently end in certain _____, several of which are _____, _____, _____, __ ___, and _____.

A. On a sheet of paper number from 1 to 14. Write the following sentences, supplying apostrophes wherever they are needed to show possession.

1. We were surprised at the length of the elephants trunk.

2. Jimmy wore his firemans hat.

3. Peoples homes were flooded.

4. We kept the players scores.

5. My brother works on Saturdays in a mens store.

6. All the libraries have bought many new childrens books.

7. That store is having a sale of womens dresses.

8. You could hear the angry customers complaints for days.

9. The girls giggles were contagious.

10. The boys laughed at the womens hats.

11. The childrens feet were growing so fast they would soon need mens and ladies shoes.

12. You could see the deers prints in the soft earth.

13. Sheeps wool is warm.

14. The elevator will stop at the mens department, the womens department, and the childrens department.

B. Test whether or not the words below the example are nouns by writing the singular form, the plural form, the possessive singular, and the possessive plural. Then use each form in a sentence.

Example:	girl	girls	girl's	girls'
	animal	____	____	____
	bird	____	____	____
	camel	____	____	____
	dentist	____	____	____

7   Verbs: Function and Position Traits

READING AND THINKING

1. The dog _____.
2. The dog _____ our steak.
3. The dog _____ a thief.
4. The dog _____ swift.
5. The dog _____ his owner a chase.

By removing just one word from each of the sentences you examined on page 74, you can see how much meaning—how much communication—depends on the words which you have removed. You are left with questions such as, "The dog what?" "What did the dog do to the steak?" "What about the dog and a thief?"

● What words would fit in and complete each sentence?

The words that you have inserted belong to the second major class of words in our language, VERBS. To check your choices, and any other words you wish to examine as verbs, use the verb test frame below.

	(happily)
The children _____	(happy).
	(it)

● How would you state the function of the verbs in the five sentences above and of the verbs in the sentences which follow?

     N   **V**
1. Roosters <u>crow</u>.

    N   **V**
2. Dogs <u>bark</u>.

         N   **V**

3. Thunder crashed.

         N   **V**   **N**

4. The cat washed his paws.

      N   **V**   **N**

5. Dad drives his new car.

   N (pro) V   **N (pro)**

6. She finished them yesterday.

- How does the position of a word in a sentence help you to recognize it as a verb?
- What other words can you fit into the **V** position in the six sample sentences?

A *verb* usually follows a subject noun or pronoun, and comes before a noun or pronoun acting as an object.

- Which nouns are subjects in the sentences above?
- Which nouns are direct objects?

WORKING TOGETHER

A. Fit verbs into the following sentences.

1. Miss White _____ English.
2. The principal _____ the class.
3. Mary and I _____ the movie.
4. Chip _____ his car.
5. Bob _____ the windows.
6. My grandmother _____ teen-agers.
7. My sister _____ Latin.
8. My brother _____ college.
9. He _____ football.
10. I _____ many books.

B. Find out which words in the list below are verbs by trying to use them in the blanks in the following sentences.

sweetly	them	picture
mist	while	whisper
flipping	moved	sorry
hers	swallowed	shuffles

1. Don't even _____! We must have absolute silence.
2. He was _____ a coin to decide what he should do.
3. We used to live on Elm Street, but now we have _____ to Peach's Point.
4. I can _____ what that boy will look like in ten years.
5. When Tom was ill, he _____ painfully.
6. We know he is angry when he _____ off without a word.

Which of the words you have filled in can function as another word class without any spelling changes at all?

C. Use any form of the verbs below in a sentence with a personal pronoun subject. For example: *He went home.*

1. go	3. come	5. swim	7. fly
2. do	4. burst	6. throw	8. bring

WORKING BY YOURSELF

A. On a piece of paper number from one to ten and write the verbs in each of the following sentences. Be prepared to explain how you know each is a verb.

1. Jan goes to kindergarten.
2. Dad sometimes drives or flies to Boston on a business trip.
3. His partner drives home with him.
4. He left a week ago.
5. He once took me with him on a trip.

6. I liked that.
7. I traveled that far only once before.
8. My older brother travels there with Dad.
9. Dad sometimes becomes tired of traveling.
10. I sent you a postcard from Boston on my last trip.

8 Verbs: Form Traits

READING AND THINKING

Major form traits of verbs are the typical endings which you may be able to discover from the following sentences.

We trained our dog by rewarding his tricks with bits of food. Our neighbors probably wish he hadn't learned so well. When they hear a scratch on the door, they know it is Oscar on his morning rounds. He offers a paw, shakes hands, and waits for his treat. Then he moves on to the next house and repeats his performance. For Oscar, every day is Halloween.

93

If you recognized the verbs, you noticed -*s* added to the verbs to form the third person singular present tense (he *offers, shakes, waits, moves, repeats*) and -*ed* added to form the past tense of *train* (*trained*). There are other endings that sometimes identify verbs, but the most common are -*s*, -*ed*, -*d*, and -*t*, as used above to show present and past verb tense.

PRESENT

I wait	we wait
you wait	you wait
he, she, it waits	they wait

PAST

I waited	we waited
you waited	you waited
he, she, it waited	they waited

If you reconsider the last sentence on page 93, you will notice the verb *is*, which belongs to a special subgroup of verbs called LINKING VERBS. Their spellings may not fit the patterns we have just seen, yet they are in the verb class.

- How would you explain why words like *am, is, are, was,* and *were* are usually placed in the verb class?
- What two elements of a sentence do linking verbs connect?

Let the following sentences containing italicized linking verbs help you decide.

1. The salesman *was* angry.
2. Those boys *are* the winners.

Another form trait of verbs is that they are often accompanied by an auxiliary or helping word in order to indicate *time* or *tense*. These auxiliaries are sometimes called *verb markers*, since they signal that a verb is present. In sentences such as those which follow, the entire verb, consisting of both the auxiliary word and the main verb, is called a verb phrase.

N (pro)	(aux)	V	N
1. I	*am*	writing	a theme.
2. I	was	writing	a theme.
3. I	will	write	a theme.
4. I	have been	writing	a theme.
5. I	had been	writing	a theme.
6. I	have	written	a theme.
7. I	had	written	a theme.
8. I	can	write	a theme.
9. I	could	write	a theme.
10. I	may	write	a theme.
11. I	might	write	a theme.
12. I	ought to	write	a theme.
13. I	should	write	a theme.
14. I	did	write	a theme.
15. I	must	write	a theme.

- Which words are the auxiliaries in the sentences above?
- Which words are the main verbs?
- Which words are clues to the tense or time indicated in each sentence?

You will remember that some words like *am, is, was, are,* and *were* can also be verbs by themselves as well as *auxiliaries* or *verb markers.* For example:

> I *was* at the party.
> You *were* late yesterday morning.
> He *is* an amateur pilot.

Note carefully that *of* is never an auxiliary. We say *could have,* not *could of; would have, should have.*

> Jim *could have* played better.
> I *should have* tried harder.

auxiliary

Auxiliary comes from a Latin word meaning "help."

In English, an *auxiliary* is a person or thing that provides some kind of help.

Meg's father belongs to the auxiliary unit of the Fire Department.

He is an auxiliary in the Fire Department.

Can you find the auxiliary in this sentence?

WORKING TOGETHER

Read the following sentences aloud and test the verb tense endings (-*s*, -*ed*, -*d*, and -*t*) by supplying as many verbs as fit.

1. The sapling _____*t* in the strong wind.
2. Mary _____*s* books.
3. Dad _____*s* his car.
4. Mother _____*ed* the house.
5. Grandmother _____*ed* the turkey.

WORKING BY YOURSELF

Applying the tests for verb changes in form described in this lesson, determine whether or not the following words are verbs. Write a sentence for each word that can be used as a verb.

juggle	wren
appear	magnify
late	float
jiffy	deflate

96

9 Learning Irregular Verbs

Dear Michel,

Last week my family drove to the lake. Guess what—I finally swum across the lake. You should have saw my sister's face. I wish I had brung my camera so I could of had a picture of it.

One morning Dad took me fishing. As soon as I had threw in my line, I felt something tugging on it. I pulled as hard as I could to get my catch out of the water. What a disappointment when I brung up an old shoe!

Write soon and tell me what you seen and done since your last letter.

Your friend,
Larry

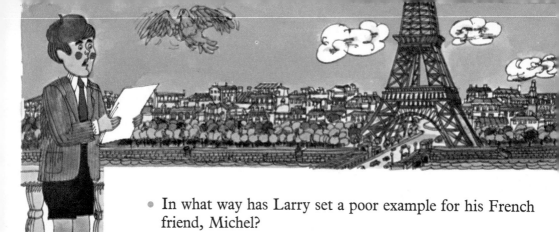

- In what way has Larry set a poor example for his French friend, Michel?

Many of Larry's errors could have been avoided if he had been acquainted with the five principal parts of verbs. These would have told him the patterns verbs regularly follow to form the different *tenses* which indicate the different *times* when actions occur. Observe the principal parts of familiar verbs in Chart I below.

Chart I

1) Simple form: *walk, wait, sing* (verb base before anything is added)

2) Third person singular: *walks, waits, sings* (-s form)

3) Present participle: *walking, waiting, singing* (-ing form, has an auxiliary when used as verb)

4) Past tense form: *walked, waited, sang* (adds -ed or changes form *within* the verb)

5) Past participle: *walked, waited, sung* (adds ed or -en or changes *within*, has an auxiliary when used as verb)

Since so many different verb tenses are formed using the principal parts of verbs, it is important to be familiar with those principal parts. Notice how many tenses of present, past, and future time you can form using auxiliaries with the five principal parts of a verb.

Chart II

Simple form: *speak*
Third Person Singular: *speaks*
Present Participle: *speaking*
Past Tense Form: *spoke*
Past Participle: *spoken*

Present: I, you, we, they *speak;* he, she, it *speaks*
I *am speaking;* he, she, it *is speaking;* we, you, they *are speaking*

Past: I, you, he, she, it, we, they *spoke*
I, he, she, it *was speaking;* we, you, they *were speaking*
I, you, we, they *have spoken;* he, she, it *has spoken*
I, you, he, she, it, we, they *had spoken*

Future: I, you *shall* (or *will*) *speak;* he, she, it, we, they *will speak*
I, you *shall* (or *will*) *have spoken;* he, she, it, we, they *will have spoken*

- Reconstruct Chart II mentally, substituting the verb *choose* for *speak.*
- Looking back at Larry's letter, which errors can you correct using Charts I and II?

Because there are about two hundred frequently used English verbs which are irregular, to avoid verb errors Larry would also have needed to study a chart like the one below.

Present	Present Participle	Past	Past Participle
begin	(aux) beginning	began	(aux) begun
break	breaking	broke	broken
bring	bringing	brought	brought
catch	catching	caught	caught
choose	choosing	chose	chosen
do	doing	did	done
draw	drawing	drew	drawn
drink	drinking	drank	drunk
drive	driving	drove	driven
freeze	freezing	froze	frozen
go	going	went	gone
ride	riding	rode	ridden
rise	rising	rose	risen
run	running	ran	run
see	seeing	saw	seen
speak	speaking	spoke	spoken
swim	swimming	swam	swum
take	taking	took	taken
throw	throwing	threw	thrown
write	writing	wrote	written

- Clearly the list above is incomplete. Can you add to it the irregular verbs *cut*, *hold*, *know*, and *wake*?

A. Since irregular verb forms must be memorized, practice will help you master them. Read the following sentences aloud, using caution in choosing the correct form of each verb. Consult the verb chart on page 100, if necessary.

1. Jack has (*go*) to the circus in Oakdale.
2. Mary (*do*) a good drawing in art class yesterday.
3. Sam (*see*) a play in New York last year.
4. The girls have (*bring*) pansies for their mothers.
5. The boys have (*break*) a window in the old garage.
6. The class (*choose*) Mary to be secretary yesterday.
7. We have (*drink*) the cool water from the drinking fountain.
8. The officer said that the man (*do*) it.
9. Tim has (*do*) the scenery for the play.
10. Martha (*draw*) all the posters last week.
11. Dad has (*drive*) a car for years.
12. The pond in the park has (*freeze*) enough for skating.
13. Everybody has (*go*) to the picnic.
14. Bill has (*ride*) Old Patch since the horse was a colt.
15. The sun has (*rise*) above the busy skyline.

16. The dog has (*run*) as far as he can.
17. We have (*see*) many Big League ball games.
18. Willie Mays has (*steal*) his second base of the game.
19. Dad has (*take*) me to the opening game every season.
20. Ted (*throw*) his coat on the chair.

B. Working with one of your classmates, prepare a short dialogue which uses *six* of the verbs on the list in any of their forms. Each person should speak three times. Present your dialogues before the rest of the class. Remember how important enunciation is—be sure to form each letter clearly.

WORKING BY YOURSELF

A. With the verb charts in this lesson as guides, rewrite Larry's letter, correcting each verb error.

B. Make a chart like Chart II using a pronoun and the necessary helpers, or auxiliary verbs, to form as many tenses as you can for the verb *see*.

10 Using the Verbs Lie and Lay

READING AND THINKING

If you are doubtful about which verb describes Father's action in each of the drawings opposite, you are not alone in your confusion. Probably more misused and confused than any other English verbs are the two in this lesson. To begin to understand the use of these verbs, we must be clear about the *meanings* of the two words.

102

lie: to recline; to be at rest; to be in a horizontal position on a support of some kind.

lay: to place or put; to apply; to set in order or position.

- Try to observe differences in patterns of sentences in which the two verbs occur in the following examples:
  1. I usually lie down after dinner.
  2. Don't lay that book on the stove.
  3. He lies on the grass when spring comes.
  4. If you lay the umbrella under your seat, you may forget it.
- What always follows the verb *lay?*

Many people use *lay* and *lie* incorrectly because they forget the principal parts of each. From the chart below you can see why they become confused:

	Present	Present Participle	Past	Past Participle
lie (recline)	lie	lying	lay	lain
lay (place)	lay	laying	laid	laid

Notice the pattern followed by the second letters of the principal parts of *lie* and *lay*. *Lie* forms an *i, y, a, a* pattern; *lay* forms an *a* pattern throughout all its principal parts.

See how we explain the two sketches of Father now, using each of the forms of *lie* and *lay*.

lie: Dad <u>lies</u> down. Dad <u>is lying</u> down. Dad <u>lay</u> down yesterday. Dad <u>has lain</u> down. Dad <u>had lain</u> down.

lay: Dad <u>lays</u> the book down. Dad <u>is laying</u> the book down. Dad <u>laid</u> the book down yesterday. Dad <u>has laid</u> the book down. Dad <u>had laid</u> the book down.

WORKING TOGETHER

A. Read the following sentences aloud, filling in the correct form of *lie* or *lay*.

1. Yesterday I _____ down for awhile after school.
2. Ruff is _____ in front of his kennel.
3. He has been _____ there all morning.
4. The kindergarten children are _____ down for a nap.
5. Magazines were _____ on the librarian's desk.
6. The baby _____ fast asleep in his crib.
7. Dad _____ his tools in a neat row on his workbench.
8. Every morning I find the tools _____ there in perfect order.
9. Many people _____ on the beach sunning themselves.
10. I have _____ there often myself.

B. Compose a telephone conversation between two friends in which each uses three tense forms of *lay* and *lie*. Choose a classmate with whom you read the conversation to your class.

C. Use each of the following forms of the verbs *lay* and *lie* in sentences of your own.

has lain	laid	was lying
has laid	lay	were laying

11 Verbs and Subject Nouns Cooperate

READING AND THINKING

The good writer or speaker fits his words together as carefully as the artist fitted the pieces of the mosaic above. Our language provides that the separate words or parts of the sentence must be working *together* toward the goal of communication.

If you recall the sentence patterns outlined in Lesson 3 when we discussed nouns (page 74), you remember that two necessary parts of an English sentence are the *subject noun* and the *verb*.

To succeed in communicating, the subject and verb should be in agreement.

- Can you see how noun and verb in the following sentences "disagree" or fail to work together?

  He ⸙ don't know my brother.

  You ⸙ was late today.

  When the teacher ⸙ come in, we get quiet.

  It ⸙ don't matter, really.

  A few boys ⸙ was playing football in the park.

The jagged line between each subject and verb shows the discord, or lack of agreement between them. To bring them into agreement, ask yourself these questions:

- Is the subject noun singular or plural?
- Is the verb singular or plural?
- What word shall I change so that *both* subject and verb will be either singular or plural?

Now try to correct the sentences on page 105 mentally.

WORKING TOGETHER

Even though you may frequently hear sentences like those you have just corrected, most speakers of English do not accept such sentences as sound in speaking or writing. In fact, such sentences probably give others the impression of language carelessness more rapidly than many other unaccepted forms in speaking or writing.

Sharpen your awareness of the need for agreement between subject and verb by composing sentences orally, using forms of the verbs listed below. Use each verb in both the singular and the plural, keeping subjects of the verbs in the same number. Then use the past participle of each verb in a sentence. Remember to use an auxiliary with each past participle. Follow this example:

Singular	1. She enjoys singing.
Plural	2. We enjoy movies.
Past Participle and auxiliary	3. They have enjoyed their new house.

come	know	see
do	like	try
have	say	want

WORKING BY YOURSELF

A. Number your paper from 1 to 5 and write the following sentences, inserting an appropriate subject noun or pronoun in each. Be ready to read your sentences aloud.

1. While _____ were studying, the phone rang.
2. _____ doesn't have any pets.
3. After _____ come home, dinner will be served.
4. _____ wants to go to the circus.
5. _____ don't know the new neighbor yet.

B. Following the directions for the previous exercise, this time insert an appropriate auxiliary in each sentence. Once again, be prepared to read your sentences aloud.

1. The tides _____ changed twice today.
2. _____ n't he own a bicycle?
3. Mike _____ have the same color eyes as his brother.
4. We _____ going to have a party.
5. Larry _____ n't like the city.

C. Copy the five sentences below on a sheet of paper, changing the singular subjects to plural, and the plural subjects to singular. Remember to make the necessary changes in the verbs and determiners.

1. Several children are presenting reports.
2. Who is your favorite author?
3. My sister is in the parade.
4. How many books do they have?
5. A tiger lily doesn't roar.

107

12　A Review

A. Substitute a pronoun for each noun in the sentences below. The sentences will be choppier and less clear with pronouns used in place of all nouns, but you *can* show that it is possible to make such a substitution as another means of recognizing nouns.

1. The children arrived early.
2. The soldiers marched proudly.
3. Martha gave the magazines to Mary.
4. Dad gave a jacket to Sam.
5. The principal spoke to Marge and me.

B. Use an acceptable verb in the following test frames.

1. Mother has _____ to the supermarket.
2. The potatoes were _____ on the bonfire.
3. We will _____ the books tomorrow.
4. Tom and I may _____ the stage scenery next week.
5. The boys have been _____ to come early.
6. The girls are _____ the costumes.
7. Jerry will _____ the lead in the class play.
8. The entire class has been _____ hard.
9. Our parents will be _____ to see the performance.
10. We have _____ a number of posters.

C. Most nouns form the plural by adding -*s* or -*es* to the singular. Test this characteristic of nouns by forming the plural of each of the following words. Then use each word in a sentence to show that it functions as a noun.

automobile	home	school
family	house	teacher
garage	potato	tomato

D. Use each of these words twice, once as a noun, and once as a verb: *run, watch, play, struggle,* and *win.* You may change the form of the words as necessary.

E. Use the noun test frame on page 74 to choose the words which can act as nouns from the list of words below. Which will fit the frame?

dancer	guitarists	players	slow
diving	happy	pleasant	steaks
game	live	program	swim
government	lonely	situation	weather

F. Use the verb test frame on page 90 to choose the words which can act as verbs from the list of words below. Which words fit the frame?

are jumping	handsome	playing
beautiful	happily	sang
coming	joy	singing
danced	painted	were laughing
had been swimming	performed	were skipping

G. Copy the following sentences. Place **N** above all nouns and **V** above all verbs. Be prepared to explain the clues you used to identify each noun and verb.

1. The mailman delivered the letters.
2. The clerk wrapped the packages.
3. Each boy cleaned his locker.
4. Mr. Ross rang the bell.
5. The officer directed traffic.
6. Our class has been reciting a poem.
7. I will be going to camp for several weeks.
8. Mother and Dad will visit me on weekends.
9. My sister has been a counselor.
10. We will live in tents on the edge of the lake.
11. A gabbist burds the brammer.
12. Tugments beamed a hipnation.
13. The soofer was drilling a plemmer.
14. Our mooster gammed six garbers.
15. An ambulist has been slooping the gimpments.

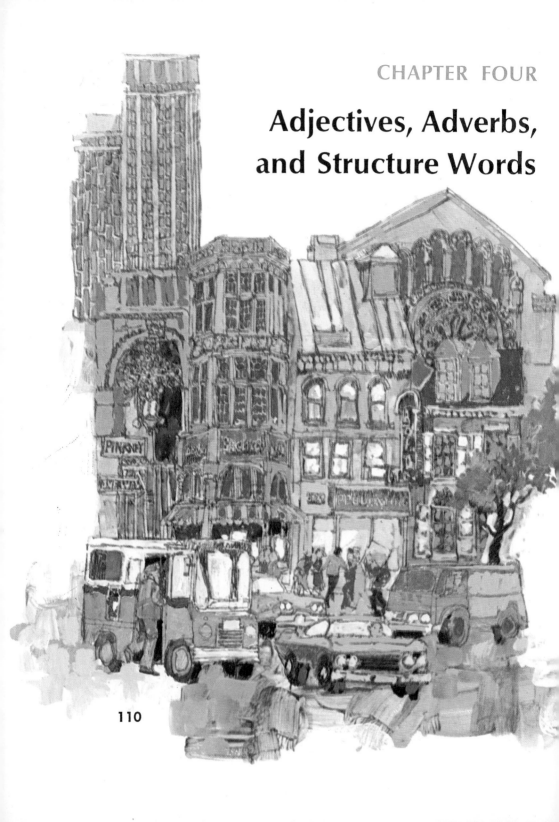

CHAPTER FOUR

Adjectives, Adverbs, and Structure Words

1 Adjectives: Form and Position Traits

READING AND THINKING

Just as position in a sentence is a clue to the identity of nouns and verbs, so, too, position in a sentence signals the third group of words we will discuss, ADJECTIVES. There are two positions in which adjectives appear most frequently: (1) before a noun (often between a determiner and a noun) and (2) following a linking verb, such as *is, are, was, were, seem, seems, seemed, appear, appears, appeared, become, becomes,* and *became.*

- Where do adjectives appear in the following sentences?

   Det   **N**
The furious man hobbled down the street. He waved his

       Det   **N**   **Det**
cane at the troublesome, frisky dogs. He wore a rumpled,

   N   **Det**   **N**
shabby hat. He had a forbidding appearance.

- Where do you find adjectives in the sentences below?

        LV   **LV**   **LV**
The snow is soundless. It seems cottony. It looks peaceful.

        LV   **LV**
The leader appeared capable. He was dependable.

- What adjectives would describe the scene on page 110? Try using them in both positions mentioned above.

Examine the endings of the adjectives above. Two other common adjective endings are *-er* and *-est,* although you must remember that not every word ending in *-er* or *-est* is an adjective.

- For what other group of words is -er a common ending?
- How can you determine the word group of the underlined words in the sentences below?

1. Susan is <u>older</u> than Mary.
2. Martha is the <u>oldest</u> one of the five sisters.
3. My pear is <u>riper</u> than yours.
4. This is the <u>ripest</u> pear in the bowl.

One way to be sure that -er, -est words are adjectives is to substitute them in a test frame.

Words which are adjectives usually fit into this test frame:

> The _____ boys seemed (very) _____.

The <u>older</u> boys seemed <u>older</u>.
The <u>ripest</u> bananas seemed <u>ripest</u>.

- What do the -er, -est endings on adjectives show?
- Must a word be able to add these two endings to classify as an adjective?
- How else can an adjective show comparison?

Several other endings sometimes indicate adjectives. For example, some adjectives such as *friendly*, *timely*, and *homely*, end in -*ly*, although -*ly* is also a common ending for the next class of words we will discuss. Most -*ly* adjectives are formed by adding -*ly* to a noun. A good way to test an -*ly* adjective is to place it before a noun: *friendly* boy, *timely* topic, *homely* man.

WORKING TOGETHER

A. Place as many other -*ly* adjectives as you can before these three nouns: *boy, topic, man.*

B. Place these -*ly* words before any nouns you wish: *lively, loudly, chilly, coolly.* Which -*ly* words are adjectives?

112

C. You discovered that *-ful, -less, -some, -ive, -ed, -ing, -y, -able,* and *-ious* are common adjective endings. What other adjectives can you think of with these endings? Test each before the two words below.

Adj
_____ child

Adj
_____ event

D. Decide which of the following words are adjectives by testing them in the frame given on page 112.

Turkish	inquisitive
rude	respectful
smooth	penniless
highway	rowdy
brave	wretched

E. How many *-er* and *-est* adjectives can you fit into the sentences below? Read the sentences aloud, adding appropriate adjectives.

1. Jack has a _____er dog than Tom.
2. Kitty owns the _____est bicycle in the school.
3. Laddie is _____er than Stubby.
4. Chico is the _____est cat on the street.
5. Our school is _____er than theirs.
6. Our school is the _____est in the county.
7. Their apartment is _____er than Brown's.
8. Terry's home is the _____est in the town.
9. This ribbon is _____er than that one.
10. Our costumes are the _____est in the entire parade.

F. Mention at least two adjectives having the same suffixes as those listed below.

spacious	laughable	meddlesome
furry	tired	hopeful
merciless	constructive	exciting

On a sheet of paper number from 1 to 10 and write the words you think are adjectives in the sentences below. Be prepared to explain how you have tested them. List any adjectives which can also act as nouns without changing form.

1. The shaggy dog slept outside his little kennel.
2. A green parakeet perched on the old bent twig.
3. The wind was very sharp and brisk.
4. The thick fog seemed chilly and damp.
5. A fuzzy little kitten opened his sleepy eyes and yawned.
6. An ancient castle tower stood in an overgrown thicket.
7. The sleek silver plane circled above the airport.
8. The gallant ship foundered in the heavy seas.
9. A careful driver is a good driver.
10. A careless driver is a menace.

2 Using Adjectives to Specify

READING AND THINKING

When adjectives are omitted from writing, as they have been from the paragraph on page 115 in *Working Together*, you realize how much more *specific* adjectives can make your communication, both written and oral. Instead of vague, hazy pictures, you can give clear, vivid ones by using well-chosen adjectives. The ability to make meaning specific is not limited to adjectives, as you can see if you examine the nouns in the following paragraphs. The nouns too are well-chosen, specific words. Adjectives simply modify the nouns, or make them still more specific.

- What specific nouns can you think of for the general words *house*, *street*, and *vehicle?*

- What specific adjectives can you think of for such vague, general ones as *nice*, *pretty*, or *good?*

WORKING TOGETHER

A. Mention at least three specific, picture-making adjectives to describe each of the following places.

your street   your classroom   your schoolyard

B. Try your skill at inserting adjectives in the blanks in the paragraph below. Use as many different adjectives as you can. For any nouns in the paragraph that you can make more specific, substitute nouns of your own.

The __(1)__ __(2)__ man looked __(3)__ standing there in the __(4)__ __(5)__ stream of people hurrying by. His __(6)__ eyes scanned the __(7)__ , __(8)__ faces of passersby, then rested on the __(9)__ __(10)__ shops that lined the street. Many __(11)__ , __(12)__ , and __(13)__ objects were proudly displayed in the windows; never had the __(14)__ fellow seen such __(15)__ things. Next his __(16)__ and __(17)__ glance discovered a flock of __(18)__ pigeons being fed by a __(19)__ __(20)__ lady dressed in __(21)__ __(22)__ clothes. Little did he realize that in his __(23)__ __(24)__ suit, __(25)__ hat, and __(26)__ __(27)__ shoes, he appeared almost as __(28)__ as she. He had arrived from his __(29)__ __(30)__ home only yesterday, and he had known at once that his __(31)'__ __(32)__ life had begun a __(33)__ chapter.

MORE FOR YOU

Write a paragraph describing very carefully an object or person that you see every day. Give special attention to your choice of nouns and the adjectives which modify them. Then be ready to write your paragraph at the chalkboard, omitting the adjectives so that your classmates can fill in the blanks. Compare your classmates' choices with yours.

3   Adverbs: Position Traits

READING AND THINKING

From what you already know about adverbs, what would you observe is a common adverb position in a sentence? See it again in the following sentences.

Ted quickly turned when he heard footsteps behind him.

The model plane plunged downward when its wing tip broke.

Mr. Rogers rapidly read the message.

Jerry bellowed loudly when the suitcase was dropped on his toe.

When it suddenly began to rain, we left hurriedly.

You will discover that some adverbs sound equally comfortable before or after a verb; others are less awkward *after* the verb, as "plunged downward"; sometimes adverbs may surround a verb, as in, "Ted *usually* pitches *better* in afternoon games."

Another position in which adverbs typically appear is illustrated in these sentences:

Mark closed the door quietly.

Sam thrust the pole upward.

Ted pitched the ball rapidly.

From the examples below, you can see that adverbs appear in various positions in sentences. Sometimes they can even be shifted from one position to another. Frequently you must use your ears to tell you where they fit most comfortably into the rhythm of the sentence.

We watch television seldom.

We seldom watch television

They often go to the lake.

They go often to the lake.

They go to the lake often.

The adverb *only*, however, should be placed as close as possible to the word it modifies because placement determines *meaning;* shifting its position shifts its meaning, as well as its part of speech.

Adj   *Only* Bob and I earned $10.   (Others did not.)
Adv   Bob and I *only* earned $10.   (We got the rest as a gift.)
Adj   Bob and I earned *only* $10.   (No more.)

You have observed that adverbs may occupy many positions in a sentence. If, however, you wish to determine whether or not a word acts as an adverb, try to place it at the *end* of the sentence, for if a word is an adverb, it usually makes sense in this final position.

Another test for adverbs is that they usually fit the following test frame:

> He worked _____.

Perhaps you have noticed something about the kind of information adverbs give.

- Looking back at those we have listed, or used in sentences, what questions would you say they answer? Consider also the adverbs *here, there, now, then, often, seldom, always, maybe,* and *never.*

WORKING TOGETHER

On the opposite page are lists of words commonly used as adverbs. Read aloud the ten sentences below the lists, placing appropriate adverbs in the positions you think best. Be ready to suggest several other positions in which the adverbs might appear in the sentences.

along	carefully	joyfully	sideward
aloud	happily	lazily	sometimes
apart	homeward	loudly	somewhere
backward	hopefully	sadly	swiftly

1. He walked to the store.
2. They sat in the park.
3. We whistled as we went.
4. The boat plowed through the waves.
5. I placed the books on the table.
6. I will put my sweater on.
7. He was putting the sign on the bulletin board.
8. She was humming as she passed.
9. The snake slithered through the sand.
10. She spoke to the audience.

B. Discuss adverbs you would use to describe each action you see happening in the picture below. Perhaps your teacher will select a pupil to list suggestions on the chalkboard.

A. On a sheet of paper, write ten sentences using adverbs ending in *-ly*, *-ward*, and adverbs showing *when, where,* and *how.*

B. Number from one to ten on a piece of paper, and write adverbs which suitably fill the blanks in the following paragraph. Be ready to read the completed paragraph aloud.

The ancient, bearded man shuffled __(1)__ across the park, squinting __(2)__ at the children when they ran __(3)__ by. He __(4)__ gave a glance at the mounted ·policeman who whistled __(5)__ as he rode __(6)__ . __(7)__ he reached a bench and measured its position __(8)__ before he __(9)__ lowered himself onto it. Now he could rest __(10)__ .

4 Adverbs: Form Traits

READING AND THINKING

When we discussed adjectives, we mentioned one form trait—one common word ending—which we would also find in the fourth group of words, ADVERBS.

- Do you remember what the ending was? You can observe it in these adverbs:

calmly	gloomily	quickly
carefully	happily	rarely
carelessly	noisily	regularly

- What happens if you remove the *-ly* ending from these adverbs?
- What spelling change must you make to form some of the adverbs?

Another common adverb ending is evident in the following words. Can you see what it is?

backward	eastward	upward
downward	forward	westward

Since both adverb suffixes that you have observed can also be adjective suffixes, you may wonder how to distinguish between the two word classes. The position and function of such words in context will be your guides. For example:

The kite sank on a <u>downward</u> stream of air.
The kite sank <u>downward</u>.
Though Sam was not rude, he was a <u>forward</u> boy.
Sam ran <u>forward</u> to the finish line.
The children were <u>lovely</u> as they slept.
The magazine gave a <u>timely</u> report of the problem.
The children shouted <u>noisily</u> in the playground.
Mark strode away <u>energetically</u>.

- In what positions did you find the adjectives and the adverbs?
- What are the functions of the adjectives and the adverbs?

Another group of adverbs can be recognized by the combination of such words as *time, way,* and *where* with *any, every, no,* and *some.*

- What combinations of this kind can you think of?

WORKING TOGETHER

A. The prefix *a-* forms at least sixty adverbs. The words *aloud* and *alone* are two examples. How many can you form with *a-*? Some of the words you form may also function as prepositions or adjectives. Place a verb before or after them to make your words function as *adverbs.*

B. Read aloud the following list of adverbs. Try to see how they are formed by pointing out the word from another class to which an adverb signal has been added.

1. wearily	6. grudgingly
2. energetically	7. lawfully
3. dully	8. criminally
4. enthusiastically	9. gaily
5. willingly	10. seriously

C. Use each of the ten adverbs above in a sentence. Then remove the adverb suffix from each word and use the remaining adjective forms in sentences.

WORKING BY YOURSELF

Number your paper from 1 to 12 and list the adverbs in each of the following sentences. Have good evidence for your decisions, and be ready to explain your choices to the class.

1. I am always willing to go anywhere you suggest.
2. Close the door quietly and step over here immediately.
3. Suddenly Dad started to laugh, and Christopher and I realized he wasn't really angry.
4. We never use this room.
5. We often stop to see Aunt Jennie when we go there.
6. Peter is always late, seldom remembers his books, and never hands his work in on time.
7. We headed homeward, singing noisily as we trudged along.
8. Traffic moved forward steadily but slowly.
9. Nancy stepped backwards, tried frantically to recover her balance, and then fell into the pool.
10. Only an old man and his four dogs live there now.
11. I have been here only once before.
12. The sun was beating down intensely.

Write a paragraph describing very carefully a baseball pitcher, a quarterback or another athlete in action, your mother cleaning the living room, or your father washing the car. The picture below may give you an idea for a description. Give special attention to verbs and the adverbs that modify them. Then be ready to write your paragraph on the chalkboard, omitting the adverbs so that your classmates can fill in the blanks. Compare your classmates' choices with yours.

5 Structure Words: Determiners and Auxiliaries

READING AND THINKING

> *Huge dinosaur lumbered heavily prickly bushes*
> *would be food.*

Having studied the four major classes of words in your language, you can recognize the group to which each word in the above sentence belongs. Yet something is missing; you are really not quite certain about the meaning of this "sentence." Watch what happens when we add the missing quantity:

The huge dinosaur lumbered heavily toward the
prickly bushes which would be its food.

The four groups of words you have examined so far are the most important in the system of English. However, other kinds of words, such as those you have seen added to the sample sentence above, are also necessary to the system.

- Why has the meaning of the sentence become clear?

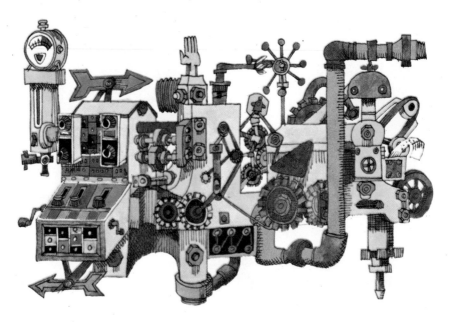

All words which are not members of the four major classes are called structure words, for they structure or bind together nouns, verbs, adjectives, and adverbs into sentence patterns. You might even think of them as the screws and bolts that link the big girders of language to one another.

124

The *determiners*, many of which you examined earlier, form one group of structure words. The determiners signal nouns by coming immediately before them or before adjectives modifying nouns. Common determiners are *a*, *an*, and *the*. Other words often used as determiners are *this*, *that*, *these*, *those*, *some*, *few*, *most*, *many*, *all*, *both*, *each*, *every*, *any*, *his*, *her*, *its*, *our*, *my*, and numbers (*one*, *two*, *three*, *four* . . .).

> *A* spaniel rolled in *the* grass.
> *That* spaniel rolled in *the* grass.
> *Some* spaniels roll in *the* grass.
> *Most* spaniels roll in *the* grass.
> *Our* spaniel rolls in *the* grass.

The *auxiliaries*, another group of structure words, perform a very important job. Besides signaling verbs, auxiliaries allow verbs to express exact time (tense) and shades of meaning. The most widely used auxiliaries are:

am, is, are, were	may, might
can, could	ought
do, did	shall, will
has, have, had	should, would

- Can you tell what tense is indicated by each of the auxiliaries above?

WORKING TOGETHER

A. Point out the determiners and auxiliaries in the following sentences. Give evidence for your choices.

1. Every boy will report to the gym.
2. Each girl must bring an apron.
3. Some students may collect the tickets.
4. All will meet in the playground.

5. This broken bat belongs to Jim.
6. That blue bicycle is Paul's.
7. One or two relief maps are still here on the wall.
8. Most boys and girls like this new book.
9. Those magazines in the rack are old ones.
10. Both boys arrived without their jackets.
11. Bill left his notebook in the auditorium.
12. Our class has won many awards this year.
13. Three won prizes for their essays.
14. I think this class has won the most honors.
15. I am sure few classes can match our record.
16. Some were here early.
17. Many tramped through the deep snow.
18. This bus will take you downtown.
19. These are his.
20. Any policeman will give you help.

B. Read the following sentences aloud, and specify whether the underlined words are auxiliaries or verbs themselves. Explain your choices.

1. Larry is Class President.
2. Marg is going to be elected Secretary.
3. We are singing in Tuesday's assembly program.
4. The museum was too vast to see in one day.
5. I have gone to several plays this year.
6. Jim had a toothache the day of the party.
7. May we see you this Friday?

C. Complete the following sentences by adding determiners.

1. _____ children picked _____ flowers.
2. _____ book should be returned to _____ shelf.
3. _____ daughter chose _____ color.
4. _____ armadillo has _____ armor-like shell.

On a sheet of paper, number from 1 to 5 and list structure words from this lesson that you can insert in each blank in the following sentences.

1. _____ giant sloth _____ approached _____ helpless victim.

2. Mother served Father _____ favorite dessert. Then she told him about _____ little dent she _____ put in _____ fender.

3. He _____ been absent from school so _____ days that he forgot his schedule.

4. _____ land is full of opportunity for _____ citizens.

5. _____ boots _____ lain in _____ closet for _____ years.

6 Structure Words:
Prepositions, Conjunctions, and Qualifiers

READING AND THINKING

Many of the words we use to relate the major parts of a sentence to each other belong to a subclass of structure words called *connectives*.

- After you have looked at the sentences below, explain why the term *connective* is an appropriate name for the under-lined words.

The legendary spirit dwells in the misty caverns.

The comet dropped over the horizon and disappeared.

This box of lizards arrived from my brother.

I would have looked <u>under</u> the bed if I hadn't been too frightened.

We swam <u>across</u> the bay <u>to</u> Rock Island.

- What do the underlined connectives link together?

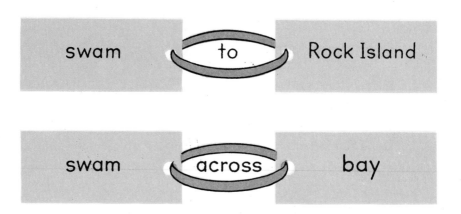

The connectives above are also called *prepositions*. The noun or pronoun that follows a preposition is its *object;* together they make up a *prepositional phrase.*

phrase

The English word *phrase* comes from the Greek *phrazein,* meaning "to explain or tell."

In English, a *phrase* is a group of words that expresses a fragment or part of a thought. Lacking a predicate, a phrase acts as a single part of speech.

What is the phrase in this sentence?

phraseology

Two special functions of prepositional phrases are illustrated in the following sentences.

Jim was hiding in the closet.
The story of Napoleon's life is fascinating.
The stuffed buffalo head hung over the fireplace.
This picture of Julius Caesar is very realistic.

- What information does each prepositional phrase give?
- What word in the sentence does each phrase modify?
- What two word groups function in the same way as these prepositional phrases?

These words usually act as prepositions:

about	beside	near
above	besides	of
across	between	off
after	beyond	on
against	by	over
along	down	round
among	during	since
around	except	through
at	for	to
before	from	toward
behind	in.	under
below	into	until
beneath	like	up

Notice that when a pronoun follows a preposition, the pronoun is in the *objective* case: to *me*, for *him*, to *us*, for *her*, for *them*.

For example, we say:

The secret was between Ben and *me*.
That package is from *him* and *me*.
The story appealed to *them* and to *us* as well.

129

The words listed below represent another important group of *connectives*, sometimes called *conjunctions*. Remember, however, that these words are not always conjunctions. Some of the words in the list can function as prepositions and adverbs as well.

after	besides	if	therefore	when
also	but	since	unless	where
although	for	so	until	whether
and	however	then	what	while
because	how	that	whenever	why

- In the examples below, how do conjunctions connect and show relationships among ideas?

We waited under a tree *until* the rain had stopped.
When the sun appeared, we decided to have lunch.
Although the sandwiches were soggy, we ate them eagerly.
We were exhausted; *however*, food revived us.
We packed our knapsacks *and* we started the hike home.
I don't know *why* the mail hasn't arrived.
Stay *where* you are *unless* I call.

Examples of still another type of structure word, the *qualifiers*, or *intensifiers*, are listed below. You can see that words in this subgroup accompany adjectives and adverbs.

He is *very* lazy	He spoke *very* lazily
rather lazy	*rather* lazily
somewhat lazy	*somewhat* lazily
quite lazy	*quite* lazily
so lazy	*so* lazily
too lazy	*too* lazily
more lazy	*more* lazily
most lazy	*most* lazily
less lazy	*less* lazily
least lazy	*least* lazily

The last group of structure words we will consider, the *interrogatives*, is represented in the sentences below.

- What do the underlined words signal?

> <u>Who</u> sits beside you?
> <u>Whose</u> gloves are these?
> <u>What</u> books are you reading?
> <u>When</u> did you begin that job?
> <u>How</u> do you like it?
> <u>Why</u> do you find it interesting?

WORKING TOGETHER

A. Construct oral sentences using the prepositions *of, in, to, for, at, on, from, with,* and *by* with the pronoun objects *me, him, her, us,* and *them.*

B. Connectives introduce each group of words below. Reading aloud, connect the groups of words with others of your own to make complete sentences.

1. since I arrived
2. although Jim tried
3. whenever I ski
4. while they watched
5. after the snow fell
6. where you travel
7. because he was ill
8. that we played
9. unless he succeeds
10. then she swam

C. As you read the following sentences aloud, fill in two connectives that can be used to link the groups of words.

1. We roasted frankfurters _____ the grill was hot.
2. We sang cowboy ballads _____ we had dinner.
3. We sat around the fire _____ it was time to go home.
4. We had pitched our tents _____ the old Indian mounds were.
5. We had a wonderful trip; _____, we were glad to get home.

A. On a sheet of paper, write five sentences using any of these qualifiers: *very, rather, somewhat, quite, so, too, more, most, less, least.* Specify whether the qualifier is followed by an adjective or an adverb.

B. Write the sentences below; then (1) circle each prepositional phrase, (2) specify its function by labeling it **Adj** or **Adv**, (3) label the subject **N** and the verb **V**. Notice that neither the subject noun nor the verb is ever found in the prepositional phrase; the prepositional phrase can be removed from most sentences and still leave a meaningful sentence.

1. The sleek train sped through the tunnel.
2. A lily hung motionless in the pond.
3. We have tickets to the new play.
4. Martha received a letter from her pen pal.
5. The wind was fierce at the top of the mountain.

qualify

The word *qualify* can mean "to be fit by training, skill, or ability for a special purpose."

As used in this lesson, the word *qualify* means "to reduce from a general to a specific form." For example, you may say, "I like games." You *qualify* this statement when you say, "I like team games."

One must be careful to qualify his remarks.
Did you qualify for the finals?

qualifier   qualification

Try to qualify the following general statements:

1. Modern buildings are ugly.
2. Americans love machines.
3. Girls are weak.
4. Winter brings illness.
5. Dogs are pests.

7   A Review

A. You have noticed in your examination of the groups of English words that words are classified in the context of sentences. While a word may be a noun in one sentence, it may be a verb in another. The groups of words in English, then, usually have *form*, *function*, and *position* characteristics.

Copy the ten sentences below. Considering all three kinds of characteristics, identify the word group to which each word belongs. Use the following labels.

N	noun	**Det**	determiner
N (pro)	pronoun	**(aux)**	auxiliary
V	verb	**prep**	preposition
Adj	adjective	**conj**	conjunction
Adv	adverb	**qual**	qualifier
		inter	interrogative

1. The boys collected the papers and placed them on the teacher's desk.

2. Our teacher settled the argument quickly, and all the students hailed the agreement.

3. We have been painting colorful posters for the dance festival in the playground.

4. It will be a beautiful performance because the students have practiced long and hard.

5. The scenery will be elaborate, with flowers and trees in the background.

6. Every student has sold two or three tickets to his parents and friends.

7. All students are looking forward eagerly to the entertainment.

8. We will beautify the fence with strands of flowers and ribbons.

9. The band will play musical selections until the program begins.

10. The chorus will be singing songs while the girls dance.

B. Read carefully the two statements below.

1. "Language is the archives of history." (Ralph Waldo Emerson)

2. "Language is the armory of the human mind, and at once contains the trophies of the past, and the weapons of its future conquests." (Samuel Taylor Coleridge)

Discuss these statements in class. Then choose one and write a paragraph on what *you* think it is saying about words and language.

C. On a sheet of paper copy the sentences below. Write **Adj** above each adjective. Be prepared to explain the clues you used to identify each adjective.

1. The committee reached a workable agreement.
2. In fact, it was a momentous decision.
3. It was the product of capable and creative people.
4. They should have a handsome and generous reward.
5. Jack has a dental appointment this afternoon.
6. The center fielder made a fantastic catch.
7. A fubless giant fought a blamsome battle.
8. The gloopful boober mooped a very scramptous bloop.
9. He was quite drumpful.
10. Most grumpments are formental.

D. Some adjectives end in *-ing*, such as *pleasing, interesting,* and *exciting*. The ending *-ing* is also a common verb ending, but only *when the verb has a helper with it*. Test *-ing* adjectives by placing them before nouns: *pleasing* manner, *interesting* poem, *exciting* adventure.

Write as many *-ing* adjectives as you can before these three nouns: <u>face</u>, <u>book</u>, <u>day</u>.

E. Some adjectives end in -*ed*, although, as you know, -*ed* is a common verb ending, too. You can tell whether *tired, bored,* and *wrinkled* are intended to act as adjectives or verbs (they can be both) by placing them before nouns: *tired* dog, *bored* class, *wrinkled* clothes. What other -*ed* adjectives can you place before these three nouns? Write them on a sheet of paper, and be ready to explain how you know they are adjectives.

F. *Interrogatives* are words at the beginning of a sentence which alert the reader or listener to a question. The most common are *who, whose, what, when, where, how,* and *why.* Write a sentence using each of these words.

G. Among the most common adverb endings are -*ly* (*quickly, easily, happily*) and -*ward(s)* (*upward, downward, forward*). List as many -*ly* and -*ward* adverbs as you can think of. Since -*ly* and -*ward*, especially -*ly*, are also adjective endings, test each adverb by writing it either before or after a verb. (For example, *ran quickly* shows that you have chosen an adverb, but *ran friendly* shows that you have not.)

H. Write ten sentences using ten different prepositions. Circle the prepositional phrase in each sentence, and draw an arrow to the word it describes or modifies. Note whether the prepositional phrase acts as an adjective (**Adj**) or an adverb (**Adv**).

I. *Qualifiers* or *intensifiers* are words which appear with adjectives and adverbs to give an extra degree of meaning to them. The most common are *very, rather, somewhat, quite, so, too, more, most, less,* and *least.* Write ten sentences using qualifiers, and specify, by means of the same abbreviations you used in **H,** whether the word following the qualifier is an adjective or adverb.

J. The passage from Alfred Lansing's book, *Endurance,* on page 137 describes one of many extraordinary experiences of twenty-eight men who made a transatlantic voyage in 1914. Read the passage and be ready to point out vivid verbs and adjectives.

136

Returning from a hunting trip, Orde-Lees, traveling on skis across the rotting surface of the ice, had just about reached camp when an evil, knoblike head burst out of the water just in front of him. He turned and fled, pushing as hard as he could with his ski poles and shouting for Wild to bring his rifle.

The animal—a sea leopard—sprang out of the water and came after him, bounding across the ice with the peculiar rocking-horse gait of a seal on land. The beast looked like a small dinosaur, with a long, serpentine neck.

After a half-dozen leaps, the sea leopard had almost caught up with Orde-Lees when it unaccountably wheeled and plunged again into the water. By then, Orde-Lees had nearly reached the opposite side of the floe: he was about to cross to safe ice when the sea leopard's head exploded out of the water directly ahead of him. The animal had tracked his shadow across the ice. It made a savage lunge for Orde-Lees with its mouth open, revealing an enormous array of sawlike teeth. Orde-Lees' shouts for help rose to screams and he turned and raced away from his attacker.

The animal leaped out of the water again in pursuit just as Wild arrived with his rifle. The sea leopard spotted Wild, and turned to attack him. Wild dropped to one knee and fired again and again at the onrushing beast. It was less than 30 feet away when it finally dropped.

Two dog teams were required to bring the carcass into camp. It measured 12 feet long, and they estimated its weight at about 1,100 pounds. It was a predatory species of seal, and resembled a leopard only in its spotted coat— and its disposition. When it was butchered, balls of hair 2 and 3 inches in diameter were found in its stomach—the remains of crabeater seals it had eaten. The sea leopard's jawbone, which measured nearly 9 inches across, was given to Orde-Lees as a souvenir of his encounter.

CHAPTER FIVE

Order in English Sentences

138

1 The Core of the Sentence

Bill's model plane crashed to the ground. "I told you it wouldn't fly with the tailpiece missing," Jerry cried.

"No wonder your recorder won't play, Jennie," exclaimed Mother. "You have the tape in backwards!"

Missing parts! Misplaced parts!

If you have watched anyone work with the parts of a car motor, a watch, a radio, or a television set, you know that every part has its place. One missing part or one part out of place and the motor or instrument will not function properly. There is a system, or pattern, to the arrangement of all the parts.

So it is with the English language. All the words in a sentence —all the parts of a sentence—must be arranged according to a pattern, or the sentence cannot do its work. Now that you know about the characteristics of words themselves, you are ready to explore the structure of English sentences—the arrangement of words in basic sentence patterns.

How does a child learn to speak his native language? The answer to this question is not simple. Scientists have devoted much research to finding the answer. We will not attempt an explanation here, but perhaps you can think about the language-learning process, and perhaps even observe a younger brother or sister learning to speak.

One fact about language learning that was suggested in Chapter One is that as a child grows, his vocabulary expands. Now you will see that as he matures, the English sentences he uses grow more complicated.

Almost from the time you began to talk you spoke in the simplest English sentence pattern.

- From the examples below, how would you describe this pattern?
- What are the names of the two main parts of the sentences?

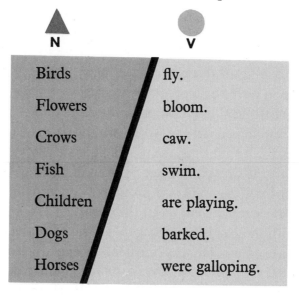

N	V
Birds	fly.
Flowers	bloom.
Crows	caw.
Fish	swim.
Children	are playing.
Dogs	barked.
Horses	were galloping.

Sometimes a determiner is used in this **N V** pattern:

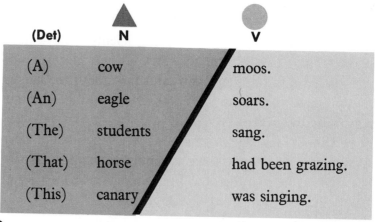

(Det)	N	V
(A)	cow	moos.
(An)	eagle	soars.
(The)	students	sang.
(That)	horse	had been grazing.
(This)	canary	was singing.

140

The pattern, however, remains the same—the basic **N V** pattern. The two major parts of a sentence can be represented by the division of the sentences into *subject* and *predicate.*

- Why do you think this pattern is the one you used when you began to speak?
- Look back at all the sample **N V** sentences in this lesson. How would you divide them according to subject and predicate?

You may wonder how subject and predicate can be found in sentences like these:

> Did you toboggan?
> Do you have a bicycle?
> Are these your skates?

To separate subject and predicate in a question, change the question to a statement:

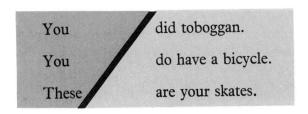

You	did toboggan.
You	do have a bicycle.
These	are your skates.

- Change other questions to statements and try to find their subjects and predicates.

Another kind of sentence which may puzzle you at first when you search for its subject and predicate is shown in the following examples.

> Look out!
> Stop!
> Pick up those skates, please.
> Please pass me my book.

The subjects of these sentences are understood even though they are not actually spoken or written. What are the subjects and predicates of the sentences below?

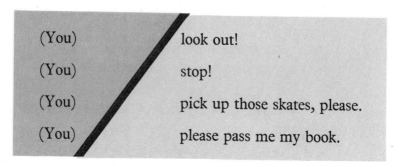

(You)	look out!
(You)	stop!
(You)	pick up those skates, please.
(You)	please pass me my book.

- How can you transform the exclamations or statements above into questions?

WORKING TOGETHER

Compose as many sentences as you can, using words from the list below as either subject nouns or verbs.

lightning	rustles
man	dew
snow	trots
glistens	ring
pencil	broke
snored	tickle
leaves	wind
fell	bells
horse	flashes
wither	feathers
fires	cough
motion	time
winter	pickle

Copy each sentence below and label it according to the **N V** pattern. Rearrange the sentence if necessary.

1. Did the phone ring?
2. His plane has left.
3. Listen carefully.
4. Has Bill arrived?
5. The pigeons cooed.
6. Come along.
7. Are you leaving?
8. Several days passed.

2 Two Linking Verb Patterns

READING AND THINKING

Two more sentence patterns you can probably find yourself using frequently contain the special kind of verb you read about on page 94. The first of these linking verb patterns is represented in the sentence below.

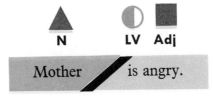

- Thinking back to your study of verbs, can you recall what **LV** represents?
- How would you label the above sentence according to the function of each word?

Examine these other sentences of the **N LV Adj** pattern:

N	LV	Adj
The leaders	were	capable.
Sparrows	were	rare.
Llewellyn	is	spoiled.
An earthquake	(aux) can be	terrifying.
(pro) He	(aux) has been	ill.

In this pattern, the word which follows the linking verb describes the subject noun. The meaning is almost the same as if you placed the adjective before the noun: *The children are happy = happy children.* Usually you can test a *predicate adjective* by seeing if the meaning remains the same when you place the adjective before the subject noun.

- Test the predicate adjectives in the five sentences above by placing them before the subject nouns.

- How would you label the following sentences according to the **N LV Adj** pattern just described?
    1. The cat seemed lazy.
    2. Two classes were late.
    3. They became restless.
    4. Mary appears calm.
    5. Several children feel ill.

- Try to test the predicate adjectives in the sentences above by seeing if the meaning is unchanged by placing the adjective before the subject noun.

144

Here is a problem for you to solve. How shall we show the pattern of "John is here"? Why won't **N LV Adj** do? The word *here* is not an adjective, but an *adverb*.

- How would you label the sentence "John is here"? Mentally label the following sentences of the same pattern.

  1. The chairman is in.
  2. Our game was over.
  3. Your gloves are there.
  4. The hotel is near.

Look at the following sentences and be ready to explain what other elements of a sentence linking verbs may connect.

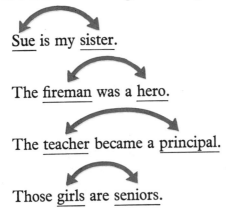

Sue is my sister.

The fireman was a hero.

The teacher became a principal.

Those girls are seniors.

- With what abbreviations would you label sentences of this pattern?

The noun in the predicate which means the same as the subject is called the *predicate noun*. Notice that in each **N LV N** sentence above the subject noun and the predicate noun refer to the same person: *Sue-sister, fireman-hero, teacher-principal, girls-seniors*. The two nouns are joined by the linking verb.

- Why is a two-way arrow used between the two nouns in **N LV N** sentences?

● How would you label the following sentences according to the **N LV N** pattern?

    1. The boy was captain.
    2. His dwelling was a cave.
    3. That ship is a schooner.
    4. She will become president.
    5. My dog is a beagle.

● What words would you connect with arrows to show that both words refer to the same person or thing?

WORKING TOGETHER

A. Practice the **N LV N** pattern by completing the following sentences with predicate nouns. You may add determiners if you wish. Tell how you would label each sentence.

    1. My father is ____.
    2. That building was _____.
    3. Those men are _____.
    4. The candidate will be elected _____.
    5. Skippy is _____.
    6. My older brother will become _____.
    7. The captain became _____.
    8. Sixth graders will become _____.
    9. She was chosen _____.
    10. We have been _____.

B. In the **N LV N** sentences below, predicate nouns are given. Complete the sentences by adding subject nouns.

    1. _____ are the winners.
    2. _____ was a sailor.
    3. _____ became a nurse.
    4. _____ was made chairman.

C. Complete the following sentences with predicate adjectives, using determiners if necessary. Using the symbols for the **N LV Adj** pattern, tell how you would label your sentences.

1. Elephants appear _____.
2. The fiddler seemed _____.
3. The gypsy chief became _____.
4. Ants appear _____.
5. The travelers looked _____.
6. That dentist was _____.
7. Winter seems _____.
8. The roller coaster ride was _____.
9. The wind became _____.
10. His eyes grew _____.

WORKING BY YOURSELF

A. On a sheet of paper copy the eight sentences below, supplying an adjective in each blank and labeling each sentence according to the **N LV Adj** pattern. Then write the sentences again, this time using a noun to fill in the blanks, and marking the sentences as **N LV N** patterns. Use determiners when necessary.

1. The book is _____.
2. That ship was _____.
3. My neighbor has been _____.
4. The reward will be _____.
5. The city is _____.
6. Her brother is _____.
7. This classroom is _____.
8. His bicycle was _____.

B. On a sheet of paper write two sentences of each of the following patterns. Be sure to label the words in each sentence with the letters to which they correspond in the pattern. You need not label determiners.

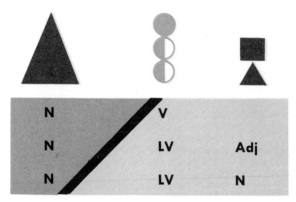

3 Sentence Patterns Containing Direct and Indirect Objects

READING AND THINKING

Below is another sentence pattern which you use frequently. How would you represent the pattern of the sentence, using the symbols **N** and **V**?

> The librarian told a story.

- How would you label the words in the sentence to indicate their functions?

You did well if you observed that in the **N V N** sentence above the familiar noun and verb pattern you have seen before was changed by the addition of a *direct object*—a word which *completes* the meaning of the verb by answering *who* or *what*. That is, if there were no object in the sentence, the meaning of the sentence would be incomplete:

The librarian told.

Told what? A reader or a listener would be left waiting for information.

- How would you label the following sentences according to the **N V N** pattern?
  1. The Hobsons entertained the governor.
  2. An observer saw a meteor.
  3. The soldier has the winning ticket.
  4. Harold did the job.
  5. The seamstress designed her dress.

If you omitted direct objects from sentences 2, 3, and 4 above, you would be left with incomplete statements. However, you have seen before in Lesson 3, Chapter One, how important the *context* of a word or words can be. In a conversation, such incomplete statements might make sense. For example:

"Who has the winning ticket?"
"The soldier has."
"Who did the job?"
"Harold did."

In written English, however, such sentences would be poor, except as statements quoted from a conversation.

Some sentences in which you find direct objects also contain another noun or pronoun, which follows the verb and comes immediately before the direct object, as in the sentence below.

Grandmother poured <u>me</u> some milk.

The noun or pronoun in this position is called the *indirect object*. One way to test for an indirect object is to insert the words *to*

149

or *for* immediately before it. If the meaning of the sentence is unchanged, the word is the indirect object. For example:

Grandmother poured (for) me some milk.

Another way to test for an indirect object is to place it in a prepositional phrase at the end of the sentence:

Grandmother poured some milk for me.

See how these tests work in another example of a sentence that contains both a direct and an indirect object:

Dad gave Laddie a bone.
Dad gave (to) Laddie a bone.
Dad gave a bone to Laddie.

It may help you to ask yourself, "What did Dad give?" Your answer will be the direct object. "To whom did he give it?" Your answer will be the indirect object.

- Look for the indirect objects in the following sentences.

    1. Aunt Stella bought me a book.
    2. We wished him a good trip.
    3. The porter called me a taxi.

- How did you test for indirect objects?
- Using the symbols **N** and **V**, how would you label the sentences above?

A. Tell how you would label the following **N V N N** sentences appropriately, asking yourself which **N** functions as direct object, and which functions as indirect object.

1. She mailed us theater tickets.
2. Dad gave me a lecture.
3. Mom baked us a cake.
4. We gave them the assignment.
5. They asked us some questions.

B. Practice the **N V N** and **N V N N** patterns by composing ten sentences of each pattern. As you discuss your sentences, explain the function of each word in the sentence. Perhaps your teacher will ask you to write your sentences at the chalkboard so that the class can discuss them easily.

WORKING BY YOURSELF

Number from 1 to 6 on a sheet of paper and list in two columns the direct and indirect objects in the sentences below. Be ready to explain your choices.

1. Mother gave Tom a camera.
2. My uncle sent me a watch.
3. I wrote him a letter.
4. He told my sister the news.
5. Dad bought our dog a leash.
6. The policeman handed the driver a ticket.

4 The Object Complement

READING AND THINKING

The basic sentence pattern you have learned to signify by **N V N N** usually contains a subject noun, a verb, an indirect object, and a direct object. However, the symbols **N V N N** also fit another kind of sentence you use occasionally. In this pattern, the first noun following the verb is not an indirect object, but a direct object; and the second noun following the verb is not a direct object, but a noun that completes some information about the object and is therefore called the *object complement*.

---

complement

The English word *complement*, which comes from the Latin *complementum*, means "something that fills up, completes, or makes perfect."

Louise's green shoes are a good complement to her outfit.

complementary   complete

Examine the sample **N V N N** sentence below, which contains a complement.

The class elected Susan president.

We would label the words in the sentence thus, according to their functions:

subject	*verb*	*direct object*	*object complement*
class	elected	Susan	president

152

● Which words are the object complements in the following sentences?

1. The team chose Toni captain.
2. We considered Harry the leader.
3. The committee named Roger their candidate.
4. Miss Willis appointed Anna the monitor.
5. They elected him treasurer.

WORKING TOGETHER

A. Read the following sentences aloud, filling in a direct object and an object complement for each, and using determiners where you wish.

1. His parents called _____ _____.
2. The teacher considered _____ _____.
3. The country elected _____ _____.
4. People thought _____ _____.
5. The school appointed _____ _____.
6. They named _____ _____.
7. The voters selected _____ _____.
8. His rival called _____ _____.
9. The librarian chose _____ _____.
10. The President appointed _____ _____.

B. Compose sentences of your own, using the **N V N N** pattern with an object complement.

WORKING BY YOURSELF

A. On a sheet of paper write ten sentences of the **N V N N** pattern explained in this lesson. Label the proper words in the sentences with the symbols **N V N N**.

B. All the following sentences are of the **N V N N** pattern, but some contain a direct and an indirect object, and some contain a direct object and an object complement. Number your paper from 1 to 10 and copy each sentence, labeling it first according to pattern, then according to function. For example:

He	passed	her	the	candy.
N (pro)	**V**	**N (pro)**		**N**
subject	*verb*	*indirect object*		*direct object.*

1. She considered him an expert.
2. The smoke gave him a headache.
3. They made themselves dictators.
4. Bill showed Terry his rock collection.
5. The class elected Steve president.
6. The planetarium sent us an announcement.
7. We appointed Tom chairman.
8. The club awarded him a medal.
9. Aunt Hilda packed me a lunch.
10. The leader made two boys guides.

MORE FOR YOU

Here is a puzzle to test your reasoning power. Notice the labels in this sentence:

N   **V**   **N**   **N**

The people thought the stunt flier a fool.

Now tell how you would label this sentence:

The people thought the stunt flier foolish.

This is a basic pattern that is almost as common as **N V N N**.

154

Change the following **N V N N** sentences to **N V N Adj**.

1. We considered Jack a hero.
2. The teacher called Mary an artist.
3. The coach considers Tom an athlete.
4. The voters thought the politician a statesman.
5. The crew considered the captain a coward.
6. His mother calls him a musician.
7. His neighbors thought the old man a miser.
8. The crowd considered the clown an acrobat.
9. Her mother considers Ann an angel.
10. The audience considered the speaker a bore.

5 Compounding Subjects and Predicates

READING AND THINKING

All sentences, even those that seem longer and more difficult, are built upon the basic sentence patterns. At first glance the sentence *The boys and girls sang and danced* may appear to be a new kind of sentence pattern, but look at it closely.

- How would you describe it according to a familiar pattern?

The sentence above differs from *The boys sang* only in that it has a *double* subject and a *double* predicate, usually called a *compound subject* and a *compound predicate*.

- Try to find the compound subjects and compound predicates in the sentences that follow.

1. The elms and maples bent and rustled.
2. My brother and sister laughed and played.
3. Betsy and Bill laughed and laughed.

compound

Our English word *compound* comes from two Latin words, *com* (together) and *ponere* (to put). We *compound* something when we put together parts to form a whole. A thing is *compound* (or a *compound*) when it is formed in the manner described. Perhaps you remember what a *compound* word is. If not, here are some examples:

steamboat, guidebook, shortbread, football

What *compound* words can you think of?
Can you explain these expressions?

compound fracture
compound interest
compound number

compose   composite   composition   composure

• What do the following sentences demonstrate about the **N V** pattern?

1. The class cheered and applauded.
2. The children and their parents cheered.
3. The children and their parents cheered and applauded.

Now notice another familiar sentence pattern. What has been added to each sentence below?

1. The children and their parents cheered and applauded the actors.

2. The children and their parents cheered and applauded the actors and the musicians.

No doubt you recognized the familiar **N V N** pattern with one or more of the three parts doubled or compounded. See the same pattern at work in the following combinations:

1. Peter dusted, swept, and scrubbed the porch.
2. Ann and Lillian sewed and pressed the costumes.
3. Jerry, Sam, and Joe built and painted the props and scenery.

- What parts of the **N V N** pattern have been compounded in each sentence above?

WORKING TOGETHER

A. Compound one part of each of the following **N V N** sentences.

1. Vince has a dog.
2. We like marshmallows.
3. Bart found a penny.
4. They know my cousin.

B. Use nouns or pronouns as compound subjects in the following sentences as you read them aloud. What pattern is each sentence?

1. _____ and _____ recited a poem.
2. _____, _____, and _____ gave a report.
3. _____, _____, and _____ conducted the meeting.
4. _____, _____, and _____ brought kites to school.
5. _____, _____, _____, and _____ wrote essays.

C. Complete the sentences below by adding compound verbs.

1. Sam, Barbara, and Jeff _____ and _____ the cupboard.
2. Mary and Polly _____ and _____ the display.
3. The class _____ and _____ the film.
4. Mother and Dad _____ and _____ the garden.

157

D. Supply compound direct objects in the sentences below.

1. Mother bought ▲__, ▲__, and ▲__.
2. The children and the librarian arranged _____ and _____.
3. The Girl Scouts made and sold _____, _____, and _____.
4. Jim and Nancy washed, polished, and arranged the _____, _____, and _____.
5. The boys and girls sketched and painted _____ and _____.

WORKING BY YOURSELF

A. Here is a familiar pattern to figure out on your own. Write each sentence, decide what pattern it follows, and label it accordingly.

1. The kittens were plump, fluffy, and frisky.
2. The skaters looked cold and hungry.
3. This bread feels hard and crusty.
4. The man became angry and noisy.
5. The boys seemed tired, downcast, and discouraged.
6. His hat was old and battered.
7. The movie was long but exciting.

B. Write the following sentences on a sheet of paper. Show the basic sentence patterns by using the familiar symbols. Place a curved bracket over the compound part of each sentence.

1. My brother plays tennis, golf, and hockey.
2. My aunt and uncle own a Ford and a Chevrolet.
3. The team and the coach discussed the game.
4. Dad sent me a watch, a bracelet, and a sweater.
5. The college students toured Europe and the British Isles.
6. The band and the orchestra played musical selections.
7. The chorus sang anthems and ballads.
8. The Pirates and the Mets played a doubleheader.

158

6 Compounding Basic Sentence Patterns

You have seen how basic sentence patterns, such as the **N V** and the **N V N**, can be varied by doubling or compounding one or more parts of the pattern. Now examine the sentence below, mentally marking it with the correct symbols.

Sally made the fudge, and Mother baked the cake.

- Did you discover a new pattern, or did you discover an old pattern dressed up?

The sentence above is made up of two parts. "Sally made the fudge" is one part, and "Mother baked the cake" is the second part. Both parts are *clauses*, for they contain a subject and a predicate. Both clauses can be written alone as meaningful **N V N** sentences; therefore, they are called *independent* clauses.

> When two or more independent clauses are joined by connectives such as *and, but,* and *or,* they form a compound sentence.

The pattern of the sentence above, then—**N V N** (connective) **N V N**—is not a new pattern, but a familiar one doubled.

Notice that a compound sentence can build on other basic sentence patterns in addition to the **N V N**:

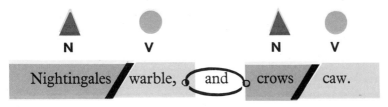

159

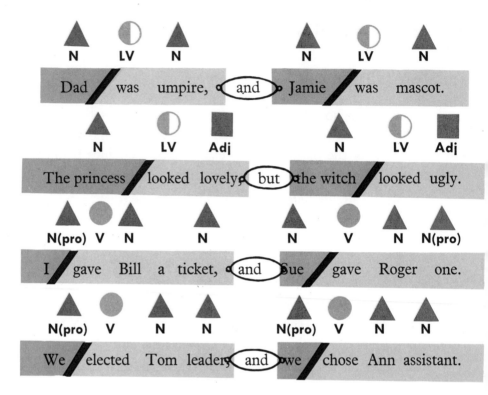

Notice that in each compound sentence, the two independent clauses are separated by a comma.

WORKING TOGETHER

A. Your teacher may choose a student to write at the chalkboard as the class composes five compound sentences and gives the labels for the words on either side of the connectives according to familiar sentence patterns.

B. Your teacher may ask several students to write simple sentences on the chalkboard, labeling the sentence patterns. Other students may then add conjunctions and independent clauses to change the sentences from simple to compound.

B. Read the following sentences aloud, combining them to form compound sentences. Choose a connective that really shows how the two ideas are related—that is, contrast or addition.

1. You bring the sandwiches. I'll bring the lemonade.
2. She is difficult to get to know. I like her.
3. We can pick you up. You can meet us there.
4. The class had a picnic. They played softball.
5. Lynn has a parakeet. She doesn't have a canary.

WORKING BY YOURSELF

Of what various combinations of basic patterns can compound sentences be composed? Copy the sentences below, label their parts, and be ready to discuss your answer to the question.

1. I'll ride my bicycle, or Father will bring me.
2. I lost my book, but I found it before class.
3. Jack seemed angry, but Mary looked pleased.
4. Tom is president, and Jane is vice-president.
5. Beth is my twin, but we look different.
6. I was there, but I have forgotten that.
7. I will be the shortstop, and Ted will play third base.

7 The Necessary Parts of a Sentence

READING AND THINKING

As you examined the sentence patterns throughout the previous lessons, you must have noticed that all sentences, regardless of pattern, must have two parts.

- What are these two parts, as represented by the color diagram below?

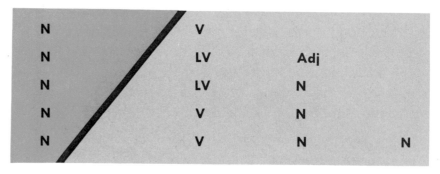

There can be no sentence without both these parts; neither one conveys a clear message without the other. Some people, however, write only fragments—pieces of sentences—when they really intend to write sentences.

One very common type of sentence fragment is caused by incorrect use of verbs, especially those ending in -*ing*. These words, such as *running, jumping, dancing, singing, coming, going, riding, laughing*—can act as verbs (or predicates) only with an auxiliary. Remembering that you must have a verb marker with an -*ing* word to make it a verb may help you to avoid this kind of sentence fragment, which lacks both an auxiliary (or verb marker) and a subject. For example:

1. The pilot was a daredevil. *Diving and looping all day.*

2. Pete almost lost his balance. *Waving his arms and swaying on the ladder.*

There are two ways to correct these fragments. One way is to give the -*ing* word a subject and an auxiliary:

1. The pilot was a daredevil. *He was* diving and looping all day.

2. Pete almost lost his balance. *He was* waving his arms and swaying on the ladder.

162

A second way is to attach the fragment to a sentence:

1. Diving and looping all day, the pilot was a daredevil.

2. Pete, swaying on the ladder and waving his arms, almost lost his balance.

Notice the punctuation required in this second way of correcting sentence fragments.

WORKING TOGETHER

Correct each of the following sentence fragments orally in two different ways.

1. Sandy hurried out the door. Whistling as he went.

2. Teddy arrived home first. Panting violently.

3. The coach gave the team a pep talk. Pointing out their mistakes.

4. Betty plunged into the pool. Springing from the high board.

5. The Panthers won the game in the ninth inning. Breaking into the lead with five runs.

6. The lightning struck suddenly. Splintering the huge oak.

WORKING BY YOURSELF

On a sheet of paper number from 1 to 8 and build the following -*ing* word groups into sentences.

1. orbiting the earth six times
2. dancing gaily across the room
3. skimming along the surface of the water
4. sparkling in the brilliant sunlight
5. erasing the blackboard
6. whispering loudly
7. watching my neighbor
8. talking on the telephone

8 Correcting Sentence Fragments by Supplying Missing Information

READING AND THINKING

Another type of sentence fragment is a word group which is introduced by connective words, such as the conjunctions *after*, *before*, *although*, *since*, and *because*, and is written alone as though it were a sentence.

- What questions do these fragments leave unanswered?

1. Although leading by three points.
2. Before saying good-by to her friends.
3. After the game was over.
4. Because I hadn't studied.

To correct this type of sentence fragment, we must provide the missing information.

1. Although leading by three points, the team had a hard game ahead.
2. Before saying good-by to her friends, Amy invited them to visit her next summer.
3. After the game was over, the team celebrated its victory.
4. Because I hadn't studied, I failed the test.

- What punctuation does each sentence require?
- Where is this punctuation placed?

WORKING TOGETHER

A. What are the subjects and predicates of each clause added to the four corrected sentences above?

B. Correct the following fragments, which are capitalized and punctuated as if they were sentences, by adding words which supply the missing information.

1. Since we saw him.
2. When the curtain fell.
3. While the band played.
4. As you know.
5. Before we opened our books.
6. After he took the test.
7. Although he succeeded.
8. Where they sailed.
9. Whenever you sing.
10. As if he knew the secret.
11. Because of her cold.
12. During the program.

WORKING BY YOURSELF

Write sentences built on the fragments below, which have been incorrectly capitalized and punctuated.

1. Although it was raining hard.
2. Before the game was over.
3. After the bell had rung.
4. Since the day was beautiful.
5. Because Mother asked us.
6. When the hurricane struck.
7. While the dog barked fiercely.
8. If you climb the mountain.
9. Before the plane lands.
10. As the farmer plows.
11. Where the road ends.
12. Since you know the way.

9   Joining Fragments to Related Ideas

You have already examined two kinds of sentence fragments and the ways of correcting them. Though we will not consider all the many types of sentence fragments, another common kind is represented below.

1. Uncle Harry gave me a new desk lamp. *For studying.*
2. My brother can do fifty push-ups. *Without stopping.*
3. Mike loves to go to the park. *To play.*

Like the sentence fragments you corrected in Lessons 7 and 8, the fragments above must be attached to independent clauses —in this instance, the sentences which go before them.

1. Uncle Harry gave me a new desk lamp for studying.
2. My brother can do fifty push-ups without stopping.
3. Mike loves to go to the park to play.

WORKING TOGETHER

Build complete sentences which include the fragments below.

1. With a mighty roar.
2. To buy a new bike.
3. With my father and mother.
4. To paint the class play posters.
5. Without even trying.
6. For fishing trips.
7. To play the guitar.
8. Near the new museum.
9. By a famous artist.
10. From cheering and yelling.

A. Build the following sentence fragments into sentences.

1. Before the ship docks.
2. Although the plane was delayed by bad weather.
3. After the teacher explained the assignment.
4. Since it was too late to catch the train.
5. Because the snow was two feet deep.
6. When the fire-drill bell rang.
7. While the orchestra played the national anthem.
8. If Father asks me to wash the car.
9. As the crowd cheered and waved pennants.
10. Although the book was very long.

B. Below is a paragraph which contains a number of sentence fragments. Rewrite the paragraph, eliminating all the sentence fragments by attaching them to sentences.

Mother and I went to the shopping center. Last Saturday in our old station wagon. We were going to buy my little brother a present. For his birthday. He said that he wanted a horn. To put on his bicycle. We bought it in Haney's Hardware Mart. Near the ice cream store. I think he'll like the horn. You can really make it toot. Without even trying. When we were at the hardware store, I pointed out a bat that I hope I get for my birthday. And a genuine leather catcher's mitt. Afterwards Mother and I stopped at the ice cream store. For sodas, and were they good! All in all, it was a successful trip.

C. Write a paragraph of not fewer than six sentences in which you describe a gift you would like very much to have or a gift you have received that has pleased you very much. Proofread carefully to be certain your paragraph contains no sentence fragments.

10 A Review

A. Write the following sentences. Above each show the basic sentence pattern by using the correct symbols, and below each write the function of each word.

1. The teacher appointed Nancy chairman.
2. The class considered her capable.
3. The choice made us happy.
4. The crowd gave the team a big cheer.
5. The principal awarded the players medals.
6. The school considers them heroes.
7. The athletic club gave them a trophy.
8. The losers sent them congratulations.
9. The captain showed us the telegram.
10. His actions made us proud.

B. Rewrite the sentences below, making the subject of each a compound subject.

1. Sam arranged the bulletin board.
2. Mary furnished the pictures.
3. Alice did the lettering.
4. Tom collected the book jackets.
5. Jerry made suggestions.

C. Rewrite the following sentences, using a compound verb in each one.

1. We made model planes.
2. The children wrote their stories.
3. David caught the fish.
4. The dogs and the cats munched their supper.
5. The boys and the girls read the lesson.
6. The teacher and the class examined the new books.
7. The scouts and their leader built the bird houses.
8. The captain and the crew inspected the plane.

168

D. Complete the following sentences by adding compound objects.

1. Mother and Aunt Jennie cleaned and polished . . .
2. Dad, Frank, and Peter sanded and waxed . . .
3. The custodian and the sixth-grade boys dusted and arranged
. . .
4. Tom and I mowed and weeded . . .
5. Boys and girls should write and proofread carefully . . .
6. At the circus we saw . . .

E. Below are two sets of sentences (or independent clauses). Match them to form compound sentences.

I	II
1. Is Tony coming to the party?	1. Uncle Henry was delighted.
2. Father seemed angry.	2. Pete was appointed manager.
3. The plane's wheels left the runway.	3. We were on our way to Athens, Greece.
4. Jeff was elected captain of the team.	4. The cake tasted stale.
5. The chocolate pie was delicious.	5. Is he going to be out of town Friday?

F. Correct each of the following sentence fragments in two different ways.

1. The Eagles won the game. Scoring a touchdown in the last minute of play.
2. Jim reached the end of the pool first. Puffing and panting.
3. Bob reached the top of the hill first. Dragging the sled.
4. The astronauts set a new space record. Orbiting the earth for 21 days.
5. We had a wonderful time. Swimming and boating.

Expanding
Sentence Patterns

170

1 Single Words and Prepositional Phrases

A sentence of the **N V** pattern can consist of only two words: *Father teaches.* But, like the flower on page 170, a sentence can grow from the seed of an idea to a much more complicated structure. Short sentences often serve our speaking and writing purposes well, but sometimes we need to add details to describe our ideas more fully and clearly. We need to expand the basic sentence patterns. Can you see how?

1. *Father teaches.*
   My *father teaches.*
   My *father teaches* at Jefferson Junior High School.

2. *Cats yowl.*
   Cats yowl every night.
   Stray *cats yowl* every night in the alley below.

3. *Swans swim.*
   The white *swans swim* gracefully.
   The six white *swans are swimming* very gracefully in the clear pond.

The words added to the basic **N V** pattern above are all *modifiers*—words which limit the meaning of the sentence by making it more specific. You can see that the pictures and information you receive in sentence 3 are much more definite than those in sentence 1. One of the chief ways by which the basic sentence patterns grow is *modification.*

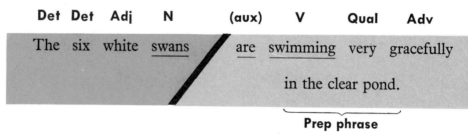

Det	Det	Adj	N	(aux)	V	Qual	Adv

The six white swans / are swimming very gracefully in the clear pond.

Prep phrase

As you see from the sample sentence above, modifiers can be single words like *six*, *white*, and *gracefully*, or they can be groups of words, like the prepositional phrase *in the clear pond*. The sample sentence also shows that modifiers, words which both expand and limit meanings, are most likely to occur around nouns and verbs. Notice how these general statements are true of the modifiers in the following sentences:

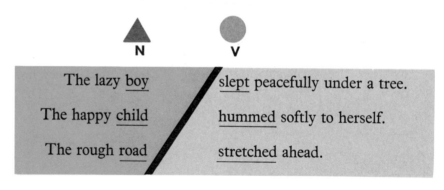

N   **V**

The lazy boy / slept peacefully under a tree.

The happy child / hummed softly to herself.

The rough road / stretched ahead.

- Find the single-word and phrase modifiers in the sentences above.
- Which modifiers modify nouns?
- What do we call them?
- Which modify verbs?
- What are they called?
- Does the addition of these modifiers change the basic sentence pattern?
- How can a modifier both limit and expand meaning?

172

In the **N V** sentences below you can see that sometimes a modifier is placed in one main part of the sentence, while the word it modifies is in the other main part. Changing the position of a modifier gives variety to sentences and can give more or less emphasis to the modifier.

                  N   **V**
The deserted <u>cabin</u>   <u>stood</u> across the lake.

                      N   **V**
Across the lake, the deserted <u>cabin</u>   <u>stood</u>.

Each of the basic sentence patterns you have studied can be expanded by modification. As you have seen, modifiers can be either single words or phrases and can be added to both nouns and verbs. These modifiers can help you to express your ideas more clearly, more definitely, and more forcefully. There are times when a short sentence is more effective than a longer one, but sometimes a basic sentence pattern alone can not express exactly what you mean. See how familiar sentence patterns have been expanded in the examples which follow.

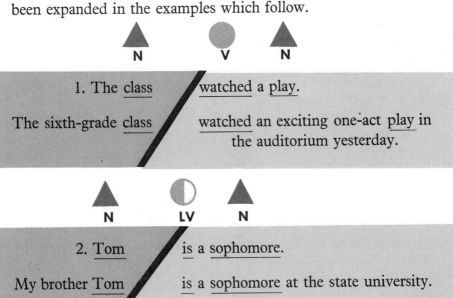

          N   **V**   **N**

1. The <u>class</u> / <u>watched</u> a <u>play</u>.

The sixth-grade <u>class</u> / <u>watched</u> an exciting one-act <u>play</u> in the auditorium yesterday.

          N   **LV**   **N**

2. <u>Tom</u> / <u>is</u> a <u>sophomore</u>.

My brother <u>Tom</u> / <u>is</u> a <u>sophomore</u> at the state university.

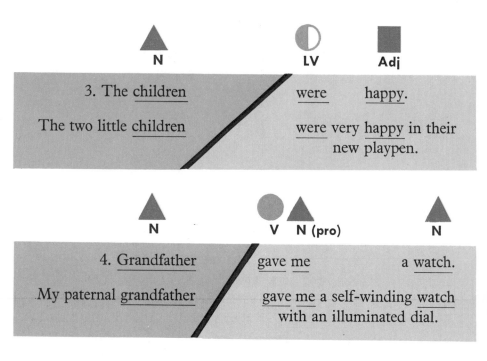

- Can any sentence pattern be expanded?
- What kinds of modifiers have been added above?
- Which single-word modifiers expand nouns?
- Which single-word modifiers expand verbs?
- Which words do the prepositional phrases modify?
- Try changing the positions of the modifiers and notice how your changes affect the sentences.

WORKING TOGETHER

A. Construct ten sentences using prepositional phrases to expand either the **N** or the **V** part of the sentences. Decide what sentence patterns you have used and discuss which parts of the patterns you have expanded. Then try adding variety to your sentences by changing the positions of the modifiers.

B. Expand the following sentences, using the single–word modifiers—adjectives and adverbs—and the phrase modifier—the prepositional phrase—you have seen in operation in this lesson.

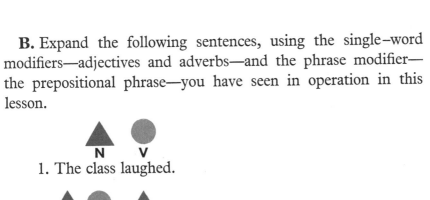

1. The class laughed.

2. Jack saw a robin.

3. The captain became discouraged.

4. Trish bought her brother a kite.

5. Tennis is a game.

        N   LV   Adj
6. Snowshoeing is exhausting.

        N   V   N
7. Martha expressed gratitude.

        N   V   N
8. They capsized the boat.

        N   LV   Adj
9. The plane looked full.

     N LV Adj
10. Jim got angry.

          N   LV   N
11. Mr. Peterson was the owner.

A. Write each sentence below on a sheet of paper. Identify the sentence pattern by placing the correct symbols above the key words, and circle and label each modifier. For example:

Adj   N   V   Adv   Prep phrase

Some (wild) ponies raced (madly) (across the plain)

1. Six big diesel trucks rumbled noisily along the highway.
2. The great ocean liner moved slowly into the harbor.
3. A huge jet roared down the runway.
4. An old battered station wagon chugged slowly up the hill.
5. We bought Mother a big cake with pink icing.
6. Most sixth-grade girls wore Bermuda shorts to the picnic.
7. My oldest sister is a sophomore at our state college.
8. Her classmates elected her president of the class.
9. Our new little puppy is very frisky and playful.
10. My father has built a walnut bookcase for me.

B. Add an adjective or an adverb and a prepositional phrase to each sentence below. Label each sentence according to pattern and be prepared to tell how each modifier functions in your sentences.

1. The chorus sang.
2. The team played baseball.
3. Mr. Smith is the principal.
4. The custodians gave the boys instructions.
5. The men are resurfacing the playground.
6. Mrs. Jenkins sent Janet.
7. Jeremy bought a guitar.
8. Father is a salesman.
9. The snake slithered.
10. Mother drove.

176

2   Appositives

Another way to expand nouns in the basic sentence patterns is through the use of appositives, as shown in the following sentences.

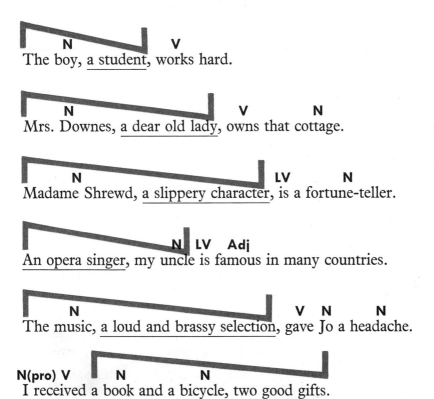

The boy, a student, works hard.

Mrs. Downes, a dear old lady, owns that cottage.

Madame Shrewd, a slippery character, is a fortune-teller.

An opera singer, my uncle is famous in many countries.

The music, a loud and brassy selection, gave Jo a headache.

I received a book and a bicycle, two good gifts.

- Which groups of words are the appositives? Notice that each appositive contains a noun.
- How are the appositives set off from the basic sentence patterns?
- What positions can the appositives occupy?

appositive

The word *appositive* comes from a Latin word, *apponere*, which means "to place near."

In English, an *appositive* is a noun or a word group containing a noun that refers to the same thing as another noun in the sentence. The appositive is always placed next to the noun it equals, usually following it, occasionally preceding it.

The appositive, our Treasure Chest word in this lesson, is usually easy to find.

apposition

WORKING TOGETHER

All the following sentences contain appositives. Read each sentence aloud and identify the appositive. Tell how you would punctuate each sentence.

1. We sent the documents to my brother a certified public accountant.

2. Dr. Samson a stubborn man would not give up his research.

3. The dog a Labrador retriever was extremely intelligent.

4. A gentle person he would not become involved in the argument.

5. He mailed the crate a bulky load.

6. Mrs. Christopher a good cook brought us some molasses cookies.

7. A good driver Bob never passes when the yellow line is in his lane.

8. Scott appointed Richard a good organizer chairman of the program committee.

9. People never believe me when I tell them about my pet a boa constrictor.

10. My aunt a resident of Cheyenne, Wyoming invited me to visit her and see the rodeo.

WORKING BY YOURSELF

Copy the following sentences on a sheet of paper, inserting an appositive in each. Label the sentence according to pattern, punctuate it properly, underline the appositive, and draw an arrow from the appositive to the noun it modifies or expands. For example:

The cat climbed a tree.

N **V** **N**
The cat, a Siamese, climbed a tree.

1. The dog sat yelping at the base of the tree.
2. Mrs. Jones waved her broom at the dog.
3. Mr. Smith stood laughing on his back porch.
4. Jeff coaxed the dog out of the yard.
5. Captain Moore climbed a ladder and rescued the cat.
6. My father will buy a car this spring.
7. I still like Bert's old jalopy.
8. Our television set is almost worn out.
9. That building was once an old inn.
10. This book is an exciting one.
11. Brian walked home from school.
12. Every morning I feed my pets.
13. My sister annoys me.

3 Participial Phrases

Another type of phrase used to expand nouns through modification may already be familiar to you. The participial phrase is one you worked with in correcting sentence fragments. Remembering the typical endings of participles, try to find the participial phrases in the following sentences.

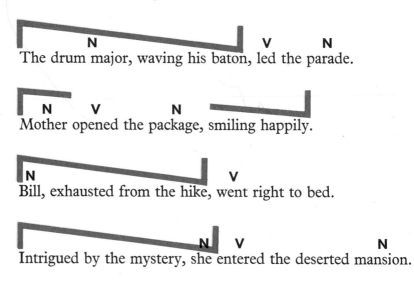

The drum major, waving his baton, led the parade.

Mother opened the package, smiling happily.

Bill, exhausted from the hike, went right to bed.

Intrigued by the mystery, she entered the deserted mansion.

- What two kinds of participles are represented above? You may wish to refer to the verb chart on page 98.
- What noun does each participial phrase modify?

Notice that although participial phrases are formed from verbs, they act as adjectives in that they modify nouns.

- What positions can participial phrases occupy in a sentence?
- How are sentences containing participial phrases punctuated?

Compose 10 sentences in which you use the participial phrases below to expand nouns.

1. whirling in the wind
2. studying his notes
3. shaken with laughter
4. prepared for the task
5. tapping his foot
6. hoisting the mainsail
7. whisked into the fire
8. withered with age
9. painting the fence
10. whispering his answer

WORKING BY YOURSELF

Copy the following sentences on a piece of paper, inserting in each blank a participial phrase which gives added information about the subject noun in each sentence.

N   V   N

1. Timmy, _____, slammed the door.
2. The campers, _____, pitched their tents.
3. The quarterback, _____, hurled a long pass.
4. The center fielder, _____, snagged the long drive.
5. Susan passed the examination, _____.
6. Bill, _____, built a birdhouse.
7. The hikers, _____, finally reached the mountain top.
8. _____, Dad mowed the lawn.
9. _____, Sally washed the dishes.
10. Bobby adjusted his camera, _____.

4 Relative Clauses

Another word cluster used to expand the basic sentence patterns is the *relative clause,* a group of words always introduced by one of several relating or connecting words. Before you see relative clauses in action, let your Treasure Chest remind you of what a clause is. Notice how a clause differs from a phrase. You may want to review the definition of a phrase on page 128 of Chapter 4.

clause

Our word *clause* is a derivation of a Latin word, *clausus,* which means "to close."

Groups of words known as clauses are closed units in the sense that they contain subjects and predicates.

When you read this sentence, you will find two clauses.

claustrophobia

See how the following basic sentence patterns have been expanded by adding relative clauses.

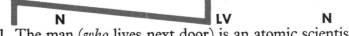

1. The man (*who* lives next door) is an atomic scientist.

2. The job (*which* he has) is an important one.

182

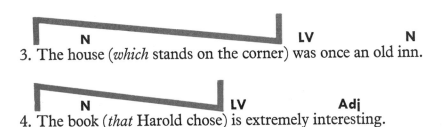

N   **LV**   **N**

3. The house (*which* stands on the corner) was once an old inn.

N   **LV**   **Adj**

4. The book (*that* Harold chose) is extremely interesting.

N   **V**   **N**

5. The girl (*whose* collie won the blue ribbon) has five dogs.

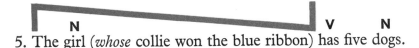

N (pro) V   **N**

6. I   have a mongrel (*that* is the smartest dog in town.)

- Which words relate or connect the expanding clause to the rest of the sentence?
- Which words do the relative clauses describe or modify?

Notice that the relative clauses would not be written alone as statements. However, the words that remain in sentences 1 to 6 when the relative clauses are removed, are *independent clauses.* They could be written alone as meaningful statements.

WORKING TOGETHER

Add a *who, which, that,* or *whose* clause to tell more about the underlined nouns in the following sentences. Tell what symbols you would use to show the basic sentence patterns.

1. A jet liner made an emergency landing.
2. The battered old rowboat looked unsafe.
3. The sleek canoe was made of fiberglass.
4. The old stone fort stood on the highest hill in town.
5. Aunt Ruth came to visit us.

6. A big trailer <u>truck</u> lurched dangerously toward our car.

7. The <u>statue</u> was carved of marble.

8. My roller <u>skates</u> were left on the train.

9. The new <u>turnpike</u> will provide for twice as many cars.

10. The steel suspension <u>bridge</u> was beautiful at night.

WORKING BY YOURSELF

A. Build sentences in which you use the following groups of words as relative clauses.

1. who owns the drug store
2. who directs traffic at the busy intersection
3. which he bought in New York last summer
4. which she values greatly
5. that was torn down
6. that is the most difficult
7. that has withstood every storm
8. which is the most beautiful building in town
9. whose sister goes to the state university
10. whose home is two blocks down this street

B. Construct a *who* clause of your own. Build it into a sentence. Do the same with a *which* clause, a *that* clause, and a *whose* clause.

C. Copy the following sentences. Show the basic sentence patterns by using the correct symbols. Draw a line under the word that relates the two clauses.

1. The girl who won the prize deserved it.
2. Washington has an art gallery that owns one of the finest collections of paintings in the country.
3. The actor who plays the lead role is very talented.
4. The vase which stands on the shelf is very valuable.
5. The man who owned the house showed us his garden.

184

5 Adverb Clauses

The adverb clause is a modifying word cluster which can be used to expand the verb part of basic sentence patterns. Introduced by such words as *when, while, although, because,* and *after,* adverb clauses usually have something to add about *when, why,* or *how* an action takes place in the independent clause, or main part of the sentence.

Examine the adverb clauses in the sentences below:

                       N **V**   **N**
1. When the news came, Jeff called his mother.

                            N **V**   **N**
2. While Fred mixed the paint, Dick sanded the wood.

                           N **V**   **N**
3. Although he disliked the job, Paul scrubbed the porch.

                    N (pro) V   **N**
4. After the storm passed, we spread our lunch.

   N **V**   **N**
5. Jill left the store because she had forgotten her money.

                         N   **V**
6. When everyone had arrived, the meeting began.

- What question does each adverb clause answer?

When an adverbial clause comes first in a sentence, it is usually followed by a comma.

We would use a comma in the following sentence. For example:

comma

When I saw the deserted house, I stifled a scream.

We would not, however, use a comma in the sentence below:

no comma

I stifled a scream when I saw the deserted house.

If the adverb clause is introduced by *although* or *though*, it is set off from the rest of the sentence by a comma, whether or not it comes first. For example:

comma

Though we knew him well, we didn't recognize him.

comma

We knew him well, though we didn't recognize him.

WORKING TOGETHER

A. Attach a *when, while, although,* or *after* clause to the main parts of the sentences below. Tell how you would label the pattern of each main clause. For example:

                        N   V   N

When Tom reached the hilltop, he could see the river bend.

Explain the punctuation of each sentence.

1. _____, the boys arranged the books on the shelves.
2. Dad and Jim polished the car (,) _____.
3. _____, Mother and Sue baked cookies.
4. _____, we played volleyball on the playground.
5. The Army scouts pitched camp (,) _____.

186

6. _____, the students assembled in the auditorium.

7. _____, we are going to the World's Fair.

8. My sister is going to camp this summer (,) _____.

9. _____, Billy will deliver newspapers.

10. The little skiff reached port safely (,) _____.

B. Attach the following adverb clauses to sentences.

1. although I hate to dry dishes

2. when the snow begins to fall

3. while the teacher explained the assignment

4. after we finished our homework

5. although I enjoy watching television

6. when the principal announced the plans

7. while Dad polished the car

8. after I finished cleaning my room

9. when Mother asks me to do something

10. while Susie played the piano

WORKING BY YOURSELF

Combine each of the following pairs of sentences into one sentence by using adverb clauses. Remember that the clauses will be introduced by such words as *when, while, although, because,* and *after.*

1. It was snowing hard. The boys decided to hike to the planetarium.

2. Sandy read the directions. Bobby fitted the pieces together.

3. The storm was over. The umpire yelled, "Play ball!"

4. Their players were much taller. We won the game.

5. This book is quite long. I enjoyed reading it.

6. The fire bell rang. The students marched quietly from their rooms.

7. School was dismissed early. We dashed to the playground.

8. Kitty tried on several sweaters. She decided to buy the maroon one.

9. We have had several dogs. I think Laddie is the smartest.

10. The climbers reached the summit. They were tired and hungry.

6 Substitutes for Nouns

READING AND THINKING

Jane and Larry never know exactly what to expect from their mother, Mrs. Phillips. She bakes their favorite chocolate cake every week, but always surprises them by substituting some new ingredient. Sometimes she adds nuts, sometimes chocolate chips, shredded coconut, or different kinds of jam. Mrs. Phillips keeps Jane and Larry interested, even though they know the basic ingredients of their weekly treat.

We can follow Mrs. Phillips' example in our speaking and writing, both by using modifiers like those we have seen in action, and by *substituting* certain words or groups of words for what are usually nouns in the sentence patterns. For example:

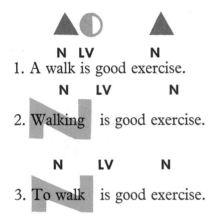

    N LV   **N**
1. A walk is good exercise.

     N   **LV**   **N**
2. Walking is good exercise.

     N   **LV**   **N**
3. To walk is good exercise.

In sentence two, you may recognize the *-ing* form, or present participle, of the verb *walk*. The present participle of a verb can be used as a noun; it can appear in a noun position and perform a noun function. When the present participle of a verb is used as a noun, it is called a *gerund*. Find the gerunds below.

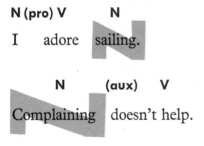

N (pro) V   **N**
I   adore   sailing.

     N   **(aux)**   **V**
Complaining doesn't help.

- What are the noun functions of *sailing* and *complaining*?

If you look back at sentence 3 on page 189, you will see that another substitute for the noun *walk* is *to walk*. The simple form of any verb, with the word *to* before it, is called an *infinitive*, and can also be used as a noun. Notice the infinitives in the sentences below:

N (pro) V   N

I   love   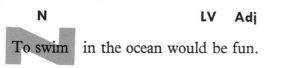to sail.

- What is the function of *to sail?*

N   LV   Adj

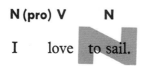To ask   is sufficient.

- How do you know *To ask* acts as a noun?

N   LV   Adj

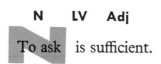To swim   in the ocean would be fun.

- How does *To swim* function in the sentence?

WORKING TOGETHER

Read the following sentences aloud. Then substitute either an infinitive or a gerund for a noun in the sentence. Omit other words when necessary.

1. The flight was exciting.
2. I like a swim now and then.
3. A hike in the mountains is invigorating.
4. An argument never solves anything.
5. The climb up Mt. Baldy was hard work.
6. A walk around the pond is pleasant.

WORKING BY YOURSELF

A. On a sheet of paper write a sentence for each of the gerunds and infinitives listed below.

1. tattling
2. judging
3. to decide
4. experimenting
5. to daydream

6. to tease
7. skiing
8. to sing
9. whispering
10. working

B. On your paper copy the sentence patterns and sample sentences below, leaving two lines under each example. For each sample write two sentences in which you substitute different gerunds or infinitives for the italicized words, keeping the remainder of the sentence exactly like the sample.

1. (**N LV Adj**) *To succeed* is satisfying.
2. (**N LV N**) My favorite activity is *fishing*.
3. (**N V N**) *Gossiping* annoys me.
4. (**N V N Adj**) *Giving* makes me happy.
5. (**N V**) *Worrying* doesn't help.

C. Use gerunds or infinitives in sentences to accompany the pictures below. Label the pattern of each sentence.

7 Clause Substitutes for Nouns

READING AND THINKING

Try to use your knowledge of basic sentence patterns, word groups, and substitution to decide what substitution has been made in each sentence below.

1. I know *whose dog that is.*

2. *What you say* is certainly true.

3. He could not determine *which brother it was.*

4. They know *how football should be played.*

5. *Who will win the prize* is evident.

6. I can't understand *why you will not come.*

7. We hope *that the play will go on.*

- What basic sentence patterns are represented above?
- How does each italicized group of words function in the patterns?
- Is each italicized group of words a phrase or a clause? Why?

The groups of words you have examined in the preceding sentences are called *noun clauses*, as perhaps you could predict. Each group of words contains a subject and predicate. The entire clause acts as a noun and can function as subject, direct object, or object of a preposition.

In the seven sample sentences on page 192 you will notice that the noun clauses are joined to the rest of the sentences by connectives—the words *who, whose, what, which, how, that,* and *why*.

WORKING TOGETHER

Be ready to read the following sentences aloud, substituting a noun clause with a connective for the underlined words in the sentences. Following each sentence are some connective words you may wish to use. For example:

I doubt it. (that, what)

I doubt that he will come.

I doubt what he says.

1. I can't believe it! (that, what)
2. How do you know that? (that, who, what, why)
3. Jay explained his plan. (how, that)
4. You will never discover it. (what, who, where, how)
5. This will not go unnoticed. (that, who, how, why)
6. Find it on the map. (where, what, how)
7. Last week I learned it. (what, who, how, why)
8. Because of that, he won't speak to me. (what)
9. It is a tragedy. (that, where, how)
10. He imagined it. (that, what)

A. On a sheet of paper number from 1 to 15 and complete each group of words below with a noun clause. Remember that the noun clauses will usually begin with the words *who, that, which, what, whose, why,* or *how.*

1. I couldn't hear _____.
2. _____ was unexplained.
3. Wilbur asked _____.
4. The librarian told the children a story about _____.
5. Let us know _____.
6. _____ the judge could not discover.
7. Nancy imagined _____.
8. He saw _____.
9. _____ is impossible to discover.
10. She learned _____.
11. I do not accept _____.
12. We couldn't decide _____.
13. _____ is my wish.
14. Madge doubted _____.
15. Opening the cookie jar, Mother wondered _____.

B. Use the following as noun clauses in sentences.

1. why he whistled
2. that she was wrong
3. how he had learned to swim
4. who shouted the answer
5. what the assignment is
6. which man was the winner
7. what flavor to choose
8. that he had been late

Check your work to see that you have used each clause as a *noun.*

194

8 Question and Passive Transformations

READING AND THINKING

You have studied sentences that follow the **N V** pattern, as in *The dog barked*, or the **N V N** pattern, as in *The dog chewed the bone*. These structures can be changed to express slightly different ideas. In the sentence *Is the dog barking?*, for example, the original **N V** sentence has been changed from a statement to a question. In the sentence *The bone was chewed by the dog*, the original **N V N** sentence has been changed from active (a direct statement in which the verb carries the action to the object: *chewed → the bone*) to passive (a more indirect statement in which the subject is acted upon by the verb: *bone ← was chewed*). Study the samples below.

Statements	*Questions*
The dog is barking.	Is the dog barking?
The dog barks.	Does the dog bark?
The dog has barked.	Has the dog barked?
The dog barked.	Did the dog bark?
The dog can bark.	Can the dog bark?
The dog will bark.	Will the dog bark?
The dog should bark.	Should the dog bark?

195

English usually constructs questions in this way: The subject comes *after* the helping verb (*is, was, does, did, can, will, should*) and *before* the main verb (*chew, chewing, chewed*). This is true also when questions are introduced by signal words, such as *when, why, what,* and *how:*

When did you arrive?   What was she saying?

Why have you done that?   How is the work progressing?

- Study the following sentences. What has been done to the verbs in the sentences in the second column?

Active	*Passive*
The dog is chewing the bone.	The bone is being chewed by the dog.
The dog chewed the bone.	The bone was chewed by the dog.
The dog has chewed the bone.	The bone has been chewed by the dog.
The dog will chew the bone.	The bone will be chewed by the dog.
The dog can chew the bone.	The bone can be chewed by the dog.
The dog should chew the bone.	The bone should be chewed by the dog.

English changes, or transforms, the active form of the verb to the passive form by using the past participle of the verb (*chewed*) with a form of *to be* (*is, was, is being, was being, has been, will be*).

Now look at the nouns in the sentences below. What change in position occurs when the verb becomes passive?

Active

The *dog* chewed the *bone.*

The *class* appointed *Tom.*

Mary read the *book.*

Sally wrote the *report.*

The *band* played *"America."*

Passive

The *bone* was chewed by the *dog.*

Tom was appointed by the *class.*

The *book* was read by *Mary.*

The *report* was written by *Sally.*

"America" was played by the *band.*

The direct object of the first sentence has become the subject of the second sentence. The subject of the first sentence has become the object of the preposition *by*. However, not all passive constructions end in the *by* + **N** pattern:

Adv
"America" was played beautifully.

197

A. Using the question *Did John come?* give as many additional questions as you can by changing *did* to another helping verb.

B. Rewrite the sentences below, using the verb form in brackets.

1. Sam wrote a fine book review. [*was written*]
2. Martha read the poem beautifully. [*was read*]
3. The class chose a new chairman. [*was chosen*]
4. The chorus sang "America the Beautiful." [*was sung*]
5. The teacher related a funny story. [*was related*]
6. The team has played a good game. [*has been played*]
7. The class will read the poem aloud. [*will be read*]
8. The secretary should give a report. [*should be given*]
9. Uncle Peter bought the tickets. [*were bought*]
10. The class should write a thank-you note. [*should be written*]

C. Change the following sentences from active to passive.

1. The chorus gave a concert recently.
2. The chorus will give a concert soon.
3. The chorus has given several concerts this year.
4. The chorus should give a concert for our parents.
5. The chorus can give a fine concert.
6. The chorus had given only one concert last year.
7. The chorus is giving a fine concert today.

WORKING BY YOURSELF

A. Write five statements and then change each of them to a question, following the pattern described at the top of page 196. For example:

> The sun rose at 5:10 this morning.
> Did the sun rise at 5:10 this morning?

B. Write five sentences in which the verbs are active. Then rewrite the sentences, making the verbs passive. For example:

> We received the news.
>
> The news was received by us.

9 Other Types of Transformations

Although English follows a few basic sentence patterns, it is possible to create many arrangements within these patterns. These arrangements and rearrangements of words enable us (1) to tighten and tie together more clearly related ideas, and (2) to give variety and emphasis to what we say and write.

- Notice how the two short sentences in each example below have been combined into a single sentence which avoids useless repetition and ties together the two ideas.

1. Ted went to the store. Jerry went to the store.
   Ted and Jerry went to the store.
2. Sally sang a song. Mary sang a song.
   Sally and Mary sang songs.
3. Jack built a bird feeder. Jack put it in the elm tree.
   Jack built a bird feeder and put it in the elm tree.
4. Roger hit a grounder. Roger was safe on first base.
   Roger hit a grounder and was safe on first base.
5. I boarded the airplane. I sat by the window.
   I boarded the airplane and sat by the window.
6. Mother called my brother. Mother called me.
   Mother called my brother and me.

Another way to tie together ideas that belong in one sentence is to construct a relative clause which modifies the noun used as subject or as direct object of the sentence. Look at the relative clauses in the sentences below.

7. The boy is my brother. The boy has the measles.

The boy who has the measles is my brother.

8. My grandmother lives in the house. The house has awnings.

My grandmother lives in the house that has awnings.

9. The problem was difficult. I solved the problem.

The problem which I solved was difficult.

Constructing a sentence with an appositive—a word or group of words which follows a noun and means the same person or thing as the noun—also brings into a tighter, clearer relationship ideas that belong in one sentence.

10. Mary Jane is a teacher. Mary Jane is my cousin.

Mary Jane, my cousin, is a teacher.

11. We have a new puppy. The puppy is a beagle like Snoopy.

We have a new puppy, a beagle like Snoopy.

12. My uncle sent me this belt. My uncle is a Marine.

My uncle, a Marine, sent me this belt.

- How has the first sentence in each pair below been reconstructed to give emphasis to the *where, when, why,* or *how* part of the sentence?

13. We missed the plane yesterday.
    Yesterday we missed the plane.
14. My cousin will be here in an hour.
    In an hour my cousin will be here.
15. I left the house when Jean arrived.
    When Jean arrived, I left the house.

- What kind of word or word group is the movable part of sentences thirteen to fifteen?

WORKING TOGETHER

A. Combine each pair of sentences below into a single sentence by compounding whatever parts you can. In some cases, you may decide to form a compound sentence from the pair of sentences.

1. Lucy read the poem. Ted read the poem.
2. Joe cleaned the aquarium. Joe fed the fish.
3. Roddy studied the plans. Jack actually built the plane.
4. Mother swept the hall. Mother swept the porch.
5. Sue collected tickets at the play. I seated guests.

B. Combine the following pairs of sentences into single sentences by changing the second sentence to a relative clause and inserting it in the first.

1. The book is fast-moving. I read the book last week.
2. Phil is very popular. Phil scored the winning point.
3. I will meet you near the house. The house is bright yellow.
4. The boy rides a bicycle. The boy delivers newspapers.
5. The principal introduced the talented boy at an assembly program. The boy won the art award.

C. Combine the following pairs of sentences into single sentences by changing the second sentence to an appositive and inserting it in the first.

1. Laddie wagged his tail wildly. Laddie is an enthusiastic dog.
2. Officer Ross directs traffic at that dangerous intersection. Officer Ross is our favorite policeman.
3. The clock was decorative. The clock was an antique.
4. Adepto made the woman disappear. Adepto was a magician.
5. That building is a tourist attraction. That building is a science museum.

D. Reconstruct the following sentences, moving the adverbial modifiers to positions of greater emphasis.

1. The plane went into a nose dive suddenly.
2. The car plunged into a ditch.
3. The tiger leaped out of the cage.
4. We raced for cover when the storm broke.
5. The crowd cheered wildly when Mays hit the home run.

WORKING BY YOURSELF

A. Rewrite each of the following pairs of sentences as single sentences, changing the second sentence to an appositive and inserting it in the first.

1. His sister is charming and attractive. His sister is an airline stewardess.
2. Luke is a law student. Luke is my favorite cousin.
3. Curly lies asleep in the sun for hours. Curly is a lazy old poodle.
4. The principal sent for me. The principal is Mr. Hill.
5. Violets are blooming in my window box. Violets are delicate flowers.

202

B. Using the second sentence of each pair below as a relative clause, combine the pair into a single sentence.

1. He is an actor. He performed last night.
2. This is the book. I read it for my report.
3. Danny is on the Olympic team. Danny swims so well.
4. The film won an award. I enjoyed the film.
5. Fred is on a hunting trip. Fred is my older brother.

C. Rewrite the following sentences, placing the movable adverbial modifiers in positions of greater emphasis.

1. The vast plains stretched for miles to the west.
2. The batter strode from the plate angrily.
3. The frightened boys crept into the dark cave.
4. They looked around cautiously.
5. They raced for home when daylight came.
6. They climbed the stairs wearily.

10   A Review

A. To each of the sentences below, add an adjective or an adverb and a prepositional phrase.

1. The crew launched the rocket.
2. The sixth grade won the contest.
3. That girl is my cousin.
4. This boy will be the leader.
5. That man has been a pilot.
6. Those girls were cheerleaders.
7. Mother baked us a cake.
8. The usher handed us a program.
9. The policeman called the boy a hero.
10. The committee may elect Jennie chairman.

B. Use each word group below as an appositive.

Example: Mr. Wright, <u>our scoutmaster</u>, taught us this song.

1. a big diesel
2. the tallest building
3. a battered old station wagon
4. our mailman
5. their shaggy puppy
6. an old jacket
7. the zoo keeper
8. a giant liner
9. a beautiful place
10. my favorite hobby

C. Attach a participial phrase to the subject of each of the following sentences in the two ways shown below.

Examples: <u>Whistling loudly</u>, the boys hurried past the old deserted house.

or

The boys, <u>whistling loudly</u>, hurried past the old deserted house.

1. The crowd leaped to its feet.
2. The swimmers reached the old raft.
3. Our team won a great victory.
4. The band strutted down the street.
5. The old man slumped into the rocker.
6. The rocket roared from its pad.
7. The ship crashed onto the rocks.
8. Mr. Culpepper scrambled up the ladder.
9. The audience applauded the antics of the clown.
10. Laddie dashed to greet his master.

D. Use each word group below as a relative clause.

Example: My dad, <u>who teaches chemistry</u>, has helped me with the experiment.

1. who lives down the street
2. who won first prize
3. who practiced hardest
4. which requires courage and skill
5. which occurred last year
6. that was painted red

7. that was just constructed
8. that stands on the corner
9. whose father is a mechanic
10. whose courage we admire

E. Expand each sentence below by adding an adverb clause:

Example: <u>When the plane landed</u>, the crew praised the captain's skill.

1. I hurried to answer the phone.
2. We applauded the actors' fine performances.
3. The passengers disembarked in an orderly fashion.
4. Relatives crowded around the gate to greet them.
5. Sam agreed to wax the floor for his mother.
6. Mary finally finished her painting for the contest.
7. The boys decided to go to the mountain to ski, anyway.
8. They discovered that the snow had melted.
9. The team dejectedly walked to the dressing room.
10. Tom immediately went to help the old lady.

F. Use each word group below as a noun clause.

Example: When asked about his failure to turn in his assignment, James explained <u>that an elephant had eaten it.</u>

1. which man was guilty
2. how to change a flat tire
3. that I would try
4. whose cat this is
5. why I prefer a good book to a television program
6. what Mrs. Peabody was saying
7. who can eat the most watermelon
8. how much I enjoy skating
9. which player had been injured

G. Write five sentences following the **N V N** pattern. Then expand each sentence by adding single-word modifiers, phrases, or clauses.

CHAPTER SEVEN

Writing Paragraphs

1 Paragraph Structure and Design

Two men stand on a hilltop, looking at the sky. One is a scientist, the other an artist. What do they see and talk about? The scientist sees and talks of the stratosphere, of light-years, of orbital paths, of the solar system. The artist sees and talks of blue and turquoise and purple seas, of puffy, snowy sails, and of slim, golden ships. Are they looking at the same sky? How is it they see different things? The first emphasizes scientific marvels; the second, artistic marvels. One sees system and order; the other sees form and beauty. Together they give a more nearly complete description of the sky than either would give alone.

Language may be compared to the sky in the story above, since our words also have two important traits that must be combined if we are to use language well. One trait is the orderly structure which the language scientist, or *linguist* observes; the other is the beautiful flow of words which concerns the language artist, or *writer*. We must try to be both linguists and artists. We must observe and create both order and beauty in our own language.

- What other examples can you give of the working together of order and beauty in nature?
- How many situations can you think of in which you would be less successful as a speaker or writer if you used *only* the scientist's or *only* the artist's approach to language?

Since written language is more carefully structured and designed than oral language, learning to write well is a major step in our mastery of language.

207

Listen as the following two paragraphs are read aloud. Find the topic stated at the beginning of each paragraph.

A. Otters are extremely bad at doing nothing. That is to say that they cannot, as a dog does, lie still and awake; they are either asleep or entirely absorbed in play or other activity. If there is no acceptable toy, or if they are in a mood of frustration, they will, apparently with the utmost good humour, set about laying the land waste. There is, I am convinced, something positively provoking to an otter about order and tidiness in any form, and the greater the state of confusion that they can create about them the more contented they feel. A room is not properly habitable to them until they have turned everything upside down; cushions must be thrown to the floor from sofas and armchairs, books pulled out of bookcases, wastepaper baskets overturned and the rubbish spread as widely as possible, drawers opened and contents shovelled out and scattered. The appearance of such a room where an otter has been given free rein resembles nothing so much as the aftermath of a burglar's hurried search for some minute and valuable object that he has believed to be hidden. I had never really appreciated the meaning of the word ransacked until I saw what an otter could do in this way.

From RING OF BRIGHT WATER, by *Gavin Maxwell*

B. When I was a boy, there was but one permanent ambition among my comrades in our village on the west bank of the Mississippi River. That was, to be a steamboatman. We had transient [temporary] ambitions of other sorts, but they were only transient. When a circus came and went, it left

us all burning to become clowns; the first Negro minstrel show that came to our section left us all suffering to try that kind of life; now and then we had a hope that, if we lived and were good, God would permit us to be pirates. These ambitions faded out, each in its turn; but the ambition to be a steamboatman always remained.

From LIFE ON THE MISSISSIPPI, by *Mark Twain*

DISCUSSING

A. Is each sentence in the two preceding paragraphs related to the sentence before it? How?

B. Do all the sentences develop the topic of the paragraph? How?

C. What is the general purpose of each paragraph?

D. Are the paragraphs successful? Why?

E. Some people's thoughts when set on paper look like the house below—a jumble of poorly related, misplaced words which build a structure that does not fulfill its purpose of communication. Knowing how to structure a paragraph according to a basic construction plan will help you set your thoughts in order so that others will understand what you write. What would you say about the person who built this house?

210

Sometimes charts of paragraphs help you test their structure. The sample chart below has been used to outline the paragraph by Mark Twain which begins on page 208. Study the outline, and then go on to use the same kind of chart to outline the paragraph by Gavin Maxwell on page 208. Write the topic of the paragraph in the proper place; then, on the lines growing out of the topic, write the main words of the sentences that develop the topic. Use subheadings as in *a*, *b*, and *c* below if necessary.

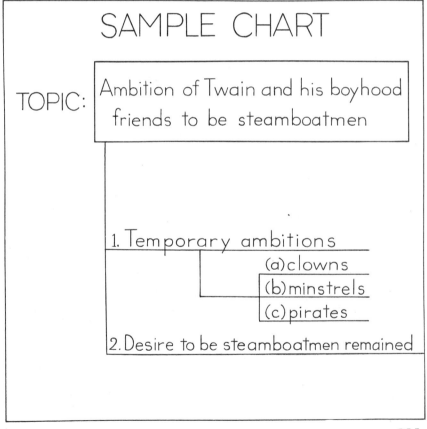

SAMPLE CHART

TOPIC: Ambition of Twain and his boyhood friends to be steamboatmen

1. Temporary ambitions
   (a) clowns
   (b) minstrels
   (c) pirates
2. Desire to be steamboatmen remained

2 Topic Sentences

The crumbling house you saw on page 210 needs sturdy walls and strong beams to hold it together; without both, it will not stand. As another kind of structure, a paragraph also needs several parts working together to support the whole. Every sentence you write in a paragraph must work to support the entire paragraph.

An important part of a paragraph is the sentence which informs a reader *what* he will find discussed—the *topic sentence* of the paragraph. The topic sentence is the foundation on which the structure of the paragraph is built; therefore, most good paragraphs need a topic sentence. In a long piece of writing with many paragraphs, not every paragraph will have a topic sentence, but until you have considerable writing experience, a topic sentence will help you to remember clearly what you want your paragraph to explain or describe. From the examples below you can see that a topic sentence usually has two clearly stated parts.

The library	is an active place in our school.
Good writing	can improve all school work.
Visiting the zoo	is a good Sunday afternoon project.

- What does each part of the topic sentences above tell you?
- What convincing details might you include in paragraphs built on the topic sentences given above?

Topic sentences state the *topic* of a paragraph and the writer's *main idea about the topic.* Topic sentences are statements which give a sum total to which all other sentences in a paragraph should add up.

212

> (Topic)   (Main Idea)
>   *TV* | *can be a valuable teacher*
>   (Details)
> (1) *shows us faraway people, places*
> (2) *lets us see news happen*
> +(3) *introduces us to new ideas*
> _____
>   *TV can be a valuable teacher.*

WORKING TOGETHER

Form topic sentences from each of the following phrases by adding a main idea.

Topic	Main Idea about Topic
1. The school orchestra	
2. Our auditorium	
3. Singing in the chorus	
4. Good conduct in the halls	
5. Our school newspaper	
6. Birthday parties	
7. Space exploration	
8. TV commercials	
9. Machines	
10. Big game hunting	

What other names have we given the two parts of sentences? How do the two sentence parts, *subject* and *predicate*, correspond to the two parts of a topic sentence? Can you find the **N** and **V** parts of the sentences you have formed?

A. Write topic sentences for paragraphs about eight of the topics listed below. Be sure your topic sentence states not only the topic but the main point you wish to make about it.

1. The duties of the Safety Patrol
2. My neighbor
3. The importance of arithmetic
4. The values of the library
5. Activities in the art room (gym, music room, or lunch room)
6. What to do during a fire drill
7. Riding the bus
8. Enjoying the playground
9. The joys of water skiing (fishing, painting, sewing)
10. Watching television
11. Getting up in the morning
12. Doing homework
13. Foods I dislike
14. My favorite animal

B. Choose one of the eight topic sentences you wrote. Make a list of all the details which could support the topic and the main idea about the topic. Using the following pattern, make a work-sheet from which you could build a paragraph.

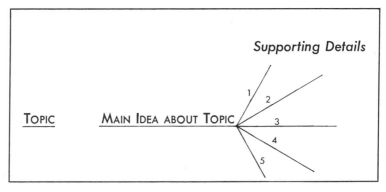

3   Developing a Paragraph

READING AND THINKING

When you read a statement such as "The Giants are the best team in baseball" or "Playing in a band is more fun than playing football," you may have the urge to say, "Prove it." Although a topic sentence does not always raise an argument, its main idea does need to be supported; you must prove or explain at least why *you* feel as you do about the topic.

You know that the major ingredients of a sound paragraph are the sentences which *develop* the general statement of the topic sentence by providing specific details.

- How many specific details can you think of to support the following topic sentence?

TOPIC	MAIN IDEA ABOUT TOPIC
Visiting a museum (farm, TV station, newspaper)	is a valuable experience.

Before you begin to write a paragraph, a good plan is to make a worksheet that looks like this:

TOPIC	MAIN IDEA ABOUT TOPIC
_____	_____

Details as Proof

1. _____
2. _____
3. _____
4. _____
5. _____

Details to explain or prove the topic sentence "The library is a valuable part of our school" might be:

1. encyclopedias, atlases, and biographies as references for reports
2. all kinds of magazines for information and pleasure
3. good fiction books to read
4. card catalogues for finding material
5. quiet place to work on assignments
6. colorful exhibits and book jackets

- How will you decide which details to include?
- How many details do you think are desirable—just a few or as many as possible?
- Look at the details you have chosen to include. What kinds of proof are they?

WORKING TOGETHER

Mention at least *three* details to prove each of the following topic sentences.

1. Give me city life; the country is for the birds!
2. People-watching provides the strangest sights.
3. It was the most beautiful _____ I ever saw.
4. I never want to see another chocolate dream sundae.

WORKING BY YOURSELF

Write a topic sentence for one of the following topics and list as many details as you can to support it.

1. My room reflects my personality
2. My visit in outer space
3. Life on Mars
4. Jobs for students

5. Earth—2000 A.D.
6. Dogs I have known
7. How to make enemies
8. How to get along with parents

From your list of details choose three you would include in a paragraph to develop the topic sentence you have written. Be ready to explain why you have selected these three details. Decide in what order you would place them and be ready to explain your reasons for this order.

4 Concluding a Paragraph

READING AND THINKING

Imagine watching a good television program. Suddenly sound and picture fade away and you cannot see or hear how the program ends! You are left asking yourself who won the crucial battle, or if the hero reached his goal. In fact, you can miss the whole point of the program if you miss the concluding two or three minutes.

The end of your paragraph can be just as important as the end of a TV program. Don't leave your reader sitting on the edge of his chair, scratching his head in bewilderment. To be complete, a paragraph with a good beginning sentence and strong supporting details needs an effective concluding sentence that summarizes the point of the paragraph. Sometimes the concluding sentence is the high spot of the paragraph, the peak toward which all preceding details have been building; it is like a parade band's final crash of cymbals and drums. Notice how this is true of the concluding sentence in the paragraph on page 218.

Snow-splotched woods and fields when the sun shines on them are full of color. Shadows that fall dark on dead leaves and grass grow faintly purple on the snow. Thick green moss hides the base of a jagged black stump, and pale lichens cover grey tree trunks with a delicate tracery of silvery green and blue. In a sunny opening free from snow, fresh mullein leaves grow around withered stalks. The white trunk of the sycamore is mottled with green as pale as the mullein leaves, and with the mauve and grey of shadows. Willows by the river catch the sunlight on their burnished branches, and red buds and twigs of brush left by the woodcutters gleam as brightly as the bitter-sweet berries in the thicket near by. Frayed yellow bark hangs from the birches growing at the bend of the road. Faint yellow tinges the frozen river, deepens over snowy fields to a shimmering film of purple, and gradually fades above the distant hills into the gray haze of the horizon. Beyond the river, over the white field, a vivid streak of red marks the flight of a cardinal.

Student theme, from the University of Pittsburgh

Sometimes the concluding sentence of a paragraph serves as a bridge which leads to the paragraph that follows.

People of one country come into contact with people of other countries in many different ways. They travel and trade; they exchange ideas about art, science, and religion. No language is completely isolated from all other languages, especially today with our modern communication systems. Whenever two languages come into contact, they borrow words from each other.

Words borrowed from another language are loan words. Such words are called the "milestones of history" because they reveal the wanderings of peoples with their possessions, ideas, and languages. Through all its history, English has been an eager borrower of words from other languages. Today hundreds of words of non-English origin are so firmly knit into English that only the historian of language knows their foreign sources. English has been exposed to foreign languages in two main ways: by a succession of invaders and immigrants, and by world commerce.

Jean Malmstrom

From LANGUAGE IN SOCIETY, by *Jean Malmstrom* © 1965 by Hayden Book Co., Inc., New York, N.Y. Reprinted with permission.

- How do you think a third paragraph might begin?

Many times, especially when a paragraph stands alone and says all that the writer intends to say about his topic, the concluding sentence strengthens the paragraph by *restating* or *summing up* the topic. The concluding sentence truly *concludes*, or *completes*, the paragraph.

- How did the paragraphs by Mark Twain and Gavin Maxwell on pages 208 and 210 conclude?
- Read the paragraph on page 220 and examine the concluding sentence.

The only permanence is change. Whether we like it or not, all things change. The only way to stop change in language is to stop its life. A language that is "dead" is stiffened into changelessness. As long as it exists in the mouths of men, it will change.

From LANGUAGE IN SOCIETY, by *Jean Malmstrom*

WORKING TOGETHER

Read the paragraph below. Make a worksheet like the one on page 221 that will show (1) the topic sentence with its topic and main idea, (2) the details which support the topic sentence, and (3) the concluding sentence. Discuss other details that might have been used. Are any details unnecessary?

As I open the door to our garage, I love the mingled smell of spilled gasoline, discarded paint, pine sawdust, and drying herbs. This room, which was planned by an orderly architect for two cars and some storage space, has become the center of all my activities. At one end is my father's battered workbench that by now is barely visible under the jumble of greasy screwdrivers, rusty pipes, a dismantled vacuum cleaner, and a lisping radio of 1929 vintage. Above this hang drying herbs, long forgotten by my mother, which send down a light snow of basil, thyme, and dill with each vibration of the opening and closing of the automatic overhead door. Under the bench lies our garden hose, coiled and ready for the first sign of summer. A dental drill, used by my uncle in Guadalcanal during World War II, stands, formidable, in a corner beside my father's newest noisemaker, a circular saw. In this room I am completely surrounded by a comforting, masculine disorder. The room is my retreat as well as my laboratory.

Student theme, from the Pittsburgh Public Schools

A. Make a worksheet patterned after the following sample for one of the topics listed below.

Topic	Main Idea about Topic
Details as Proof	
1. _____	
2. _____	
3. _____	
4. _____	
5. _____	
Concluding Sentence	

1. A hobby that helps me in science class
2. Why I enjoy my art class
3. Music is fun
4. My favorite school subject
5. The smartest dog (cat, parakeet) I know
6. A teacher's problems
7. Places I like to visit
8. How much homework?
9. A quality I admire in _____ (Mother, Father, a sister, a brother)
10. The sport I most enjoy

B. Develop a paragraph from your worksheet. Is every detail you have used in your paragraph related to the topic? Are the details you have chosen the best ones possible to prove the point of the paragraph? Does your concluding sentence truly complete your paragraph?

5 Using Reasons as Proof

1. *A cheetah makes a better pet than a dog or a cat.*
2. *A cheetah, which has been clocked at 70 miles per hour, is the fastest of all land animals.*

How much do you remember about a subject we discussed in relation to our oral work, such as speeches before the class? If you remember Lesson 5 in Chapter Two, you will be able to see the basic difference between the two statements above and the different ways they would be developed in paragraphs.

- Examine the following paragraph worksheet and decide what the writer's *reasons* are based on.

	TOPIC	MAIN POINT ABOUT TOPIC
Topic Sentence	Our town	is the ideal place to live.
Proof	1. beautiful river	
	2. wide streets	
	3. parks	
	4. historic square	
	5. friendly neighbors	
	6. good school	
	7. library	
	8. museum	
Concluding Sentence	I want to see the world some day, but I know this is where I'll always want to live.	

The writer's town may offer scenic beauty, historic sites, fine schools and museums, and friendly people, but a reader may feel that his own town does, too. He may even argue that a farm is a far better place to live than a town. It is really unimportant, however, whether or not we agree with the writer. What *is* important is that he give well-founded reasons for his opinion, and that we understand why he feels as he does.

- How does the following paragraph outline differ from the one you have just seen on page 222?

TOPIC	MAIN IDEA ABOUT TOPIC
Williamsburg, Virginia	is one of the most historic places in the United States.

Proof

1. Capital of Virginia in 1699
2. Site of William and Mary College, founded in 1693, the second oldest American college
3. Location of the House of Burgesses, Raleigh Tavern, and Bruton Church, where ideas that became parts of the Declaration of Independence and the Bill of Rights were debated
4. Scene of Patrick Henry's "Give me liberty or give me death" speech

Concluding Sentence

Williamsburg, now rebuilt, makes it possible to relive some of the important events of Colonial America and "meet" many of the men who founded our nation.

- Why is it essential to be able to see the difference between *fact* and *opinion?*

The two kinds of reasons you may use to develop topic sentences in your writing are the same ones you learned about in supporting spoken statements: (1) reasons based on opinion, and (2) reasons based on fact—other ways of providing the *details* which will prevent your reader from saying to himself, "Prove it!"

DISCUSSING

A. Discuss the opinions that might be offered as proof for each of the following topic sentences.

1. Summer is the best time of the year.
2. There is no game as exciting as basketball.
3. Hamsters make the best pets.
4. The Village Mart is the most unusual store in town.
5. Families should spend less time watching television and more time getting to know each other.
6. Playgrounds could be improved.
7. A train ride is more interesting than a plane ride.
8. I vote for school vacation in winter instead of in summer.
9. Girls (Boys) make the best school officers.
10. Every school should have an auditorium.

B. Discuss the kinds of reasons you would need to develop the following topic sentences.

1. San Francisco is one of our great American seaports.
2. Detroit is the automobile capital of the United States.
3. John F. Kennedy International Airport is one of the busiest air terminals in the world.
4. Florence Nightingale earned the title "The Lady with the Lamp."

224

5. The _____ is the fastest aircraft in the skies.
6. Douglas MacArthur was a great military leader.
7. The _____ is the finest ship afloat.
8. Of all the rivers in the world the Nile is the most famous.
9. The world owes one of its largest debts to Thomas Edison.
10. The Grand Canyon is one of the wonders of the world.

WORKING BY YOURSELF

Choose one of the topic sentences from the preceding exercise, find the facts necessary to prove it, and draw up a worksheet for it, following the examples in this lesson. Working in pairs or in small groups, share your information with your classmates.

6 Arranging the Details: Time Order

READING AND THINKING

"I just can't make any sense of this jigsaw puzzle the way you've put it together, Gary," said Sarah.

"Why not? All the pieces are there!" Gary answered.

The pieces of Gary's jigsaw puzzle must be in the proper places in relation to each other for Sarah to understand what the whole puzzle represents. The same need for order applies to paragraphs and, finally, to your longer pieces of written work.

In telling about an experience or in explaining something, sometimes it is important to present events in an order that shows which happened first, next, and so on. This arrangement of details is called *chronological* or *time* order. Observe the chronological order of details in the following worksheet.

Topic sentence	What began as just the annual wiener roast for our class suddenly turned into a terrifying adventure.
When and where *Time order of* *events*	On Brown's farm at sunset . . . 1. Sky suddenly blackened . . . 2. Then wild gusts of wind . . . 3. Crashes of lightning followed . . . 4. Soon power lines toppled . . . 5. Next trees snapped . . . 6. Before long the bridge washed out 7. By seven o'clock marooned in blacked-out farmhouse . . . 8. Finally jeeps got through to us . . .
Concluding *sentence*	Every time I see a hot dog I think of that wild night.

- What words showing passage of time link the separate events in the above outline?

226

Notice how Anne Morrow Lindbergh links sentences together in the paragraph below by using time-order words to show how the sentences are related.

The spray sluiced over the windshield as we started to take off—faster now—we were on the step—we were trying to get off the water. I held my breath after each pounding spank as the pontoons skipped along from wave to wave. Weighed down with its heavy load of test fuel, the plane felt clumsy, like a duck with clipped wings. It met the coming waves quivering after each effort to rise. Now the spanks were closer together—quick, sharp jolts. I put my hand on the receiving set. It was shaking violently. Suddenly all vibration smoothed out. Effortlessly we rose; we

were off; a long curve upward. The squat ferry boats below plowed across our wake, and great flat barges carrying rectangular mounds of different colored earth like spools of gold and tawny silk. I found the little black mass of people on the pier where we had been. Small and insignificant it looked, now I could see the whole life of the river: many piers and crowded ferry boats, ships and roofs and fields and barges, dredges and smokestacks and the towers of New York. We looked insignificant, also, and small to them, I knew, now that our bulk on the end of the pier no longer blocked the horizon. It had become simply a boat in the river of many boats; then a plane in the sky with other planes; now, only a speck against the blue, easily mistaken for a gull.

From NORTH TO THE ORIENT, by *Anne Morrow Lindbergh*

- What words signal the time sequence of the sentences in the paragraph above?
- What time-order words can you find in the following paragraph by Stephen Crane?

When the correspondent again opened his eyes, the sea and the sky were each of the gray hue of the dawning. Later, carmine and gold was painted upon the waters. The morning appeared, finally, in its splendour, with a sky of pure blue, and the sunlight flamed on the tips of the waves.

From THE OPEN BOAT, by *Stephen Crane*

After you have gathered details for a paragraph and listed them on a worksheet, you will be ready to consider the best arrangement for them. As you can see from the paragraphs above, a chronological arrangement is one good way to bring order to your paragraph.

WORKING TOGETHER

Read aloud the paragraph below. Note the time-order words. From this description list the steps in baking a loaf of bread.

When I was a little girl I used to sit in the kitchen and watch Mother bake bread. I loved to watch her throw the dough on the board, grasp it with her large, sure hands, and knead it. The dough came up between her fingers as she squeezed it. When it was just right, she smoothed it into a big flat mass and cut it into pieces. The dough went down— and then came up again as if it were breathing. She molded one part after another into loaves, dropped them into buttered pans, patted the tops with melted butter, and then popped them into the oven. I always waited breathlessly for her to open the oven door, and when she did I was always excited by the miracle of the little white loaf growing so quickly into a big, golden-brown loaf. Then after what seemed to me almost forever, the bread was baked. When it had cooled a little, Mother often cut off a brown, crisp heel for me and spread it with butter. My mouth waters now when I think of its crispiness, its softness inside, its sweet nutlike richness.

Carole Mitry, Pittsburgh Public Schools

WORKING BY YOURSELF

A. Use at least five of the following linking words in a paragraph to describe an event or to give directions, organizing details in proper time order.

after	finally	next
at last	first	soon
before	last	then
during	later	while

B. On a piece of paper write the following pairs of sentences, using linking words to show the time relationship of each pair of sentences. You may place the linking words anywhere in the sentences, but do not use any linking word more than once.

1. John broke Mr. Grumply's window. Mr. Grumply informed John's father.

2. I blew on the coals. A flame began to grow.

3. Rhoda had to eat all her spinach. She could have strawberry shortcake for dessert.

4. The firemen spotted smoke. They discovered the burning warehouse.

5. Ray exercised his dog. Dick phoned to ask about the homework.

6. Jay hit a single. Ron struck out.

---

chronological

The English word above is composed of two combining forms which come from two Greek words. The English combining form *chron-* or *chrono-* originates from the Greek *chronos,* or "time," and has the same meaning. The combining form *-logy,* which means "an oral or written expression," derives from the Greek *logos,* which means "word". A chronological arrangement, then, is one which expresses time, or the order of events.

Are the following events in chronological order?

The Boston Tea Party
The Civil War
The Declaration of Independence

7 Arranging the Details: Space Order

Especially useful when you write descriptive paragraphs is the plan of organizing details according to *space order*, for example, far to near, left to right, or above to below.

- What space order does Walter D. Edmonds use in the following brief description of a room in his book, *Drums along the Mohawk?*

The inside of the store was a long room with a fireplace at the end and a bed in the corner. There were rough shelves along one wall and storage chests along the other. There were two benches set end to end down the middle of the floor. The benches were made of split basswood logs with hickory legs let into them. Two windows allowed some sunlight to filter through the fly specks.

---

space

The English word above is a descendant of the Latin word *spatium*, which means "area." A *space* in English is usually a limited area, though we may also speak of the *space* beyond the earth's atmosphere. This "outer space" has no limits. *Spatial*, the adjective, means "relating to space," as we have defined it, and *spacious* means "vast in area."

The entrance hall of the castle was an immense, cold space.

spatial   *spacious*

A. Listen as classmates read aloud the following paragraphs. Note words that help steer your view of the scenes described.

1. The trail dropped quickly, staggering among broken rock. At the bottom of the slope there was a dark crease, thick with brush, and on the other side of the crease a little flat, in which a grove of oak trees grew. A scar of green grass cut across the flat. And behind the flat another mountain rose, desolate with dead rocks and starving little black bushes. Pepé drank from the bag again for the air was so dry that it encrusted his nostrils and burned his lips. He put the horse down the trail. The hooves slipped and struggled on the steep way, starting little stones that rolled off into the brush. The sun was gone behind the westward mountain now, but still it glowed brilliantly on the oaks and on the grassy flat. The rocks and the hillsides still sent up waves of the heat they had gathered from the day's sun.

From FLIGHT, by *John Steinbeck*

2. Beneath the blades of our skates the creek gurgled peacefully, winding its way through the depths of the ice. Behind us over the creek bank the stubble of the field stretched away in frosty stillness under the January moon, like a forest of crystals. But our attention was centered in front of us, on the cliff that faded away into dimness on either side, as it followed the crooked course of the creek. Above the bulky outline of the cliff, fifty feet up, the forest began, black trunks plastered white with snow. Behind the trees, starkly silhouetting them, the moon rose, brushed by transient clouds. Above this peaceful scene the stars, Capella and Rigel and Algol, slowly wheeled on their endless journeys through space.

Jeff Buckwalter, Pittsburgh Public Schools

3. The pond is about a mile and a half south of Concord, just after you cross Route 2 that goes into Boston. As you drive up to the hallowed ground, the property on the left is almost a commercial slum. I remember the trailer park, the soft-ice-cream stand, and a sort of pavilion. We pull off the road to the right and park in a special area from which we can see most of the lake. Right below us is a scarred area where the Concord supervisors started to build another swimming beach. Public opinion stopped them, and the slope has been replanted in grass and trees. I suppose in another twenty years nobody will be able to recognize the slash. Straight ahead and to the left is the public beach and bathhouse. At this time in the afternoon it's always deserted, and the rustic brown wood and the white concrete walls and walks have started to fade into the shadows.

Student theme

From DEVELOPING WRITING SKILLS by *William W. West* © 1966 by Prentice-Hall, Inc., Englewood Cliffs, N.J. Reprinted with permission.

B. Your teacher may choose one member of the class to take notes at the chalkboard as a classmate describes how to reach your school, using as a starting point a place familiar to everyone in your class. Then judge how accurate the directions have been.

C. Discuss how you would describe the room diagramed below, using a space order which moves from nearest to farthest. Assume that you are standing at X, looking into the room. List on the chalkboard all the space-order words you use in your description.

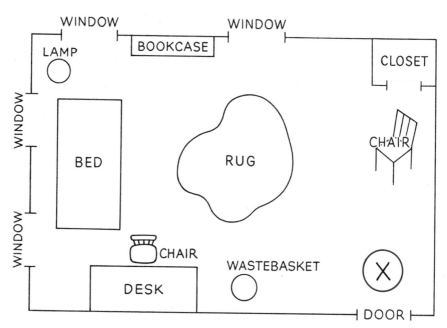

WORKING BY YOURSELF

A. Choose a place such as the kitchen of your home, the window or corner of a drug store, or a section of a supermarket. Outline your topic following the pattern on page 235 and re-arrange the proof until you are satisfied that it is in the best possible order. (Note that the kind of space order you choose may be different from the counterclockwise order in the pattern.)

TOPIC SENTENCE: I think that the art room is the most attractive room in our school.

DETAILS:

on the right
1. cluster of tent-like easels
2. bright jars of tempera paint on the shelves
3. rainbow stacks of poster paper

straight ahead
4. cork boards covered with gay watercolors and brilliant murals

along the side wall
5. table of three-dimensional wire and clay objects

on the left
6. shining chrome sinks

toward the rear
7. green metal clay bins

CONCLUDING SENTENCE: In every part of the room there are interesting and colorful things to see.

B. Develop your outline into a paragraph and be ready to work in pairs, evaluating each other's use of space order. How accurate is the picture your classmate's paragraph gives?

8 A Review: Polishing Paragraphs

In the first seven lessons of this chapter you learned ways to build paragraphs—to organize details so that a firm structure resulted. This lesson will help you polish paragraphs so that they are interesting and attractive as well as strong.

A. *Proofreading*

Though you may think the writer's job is over as soon as he writes a concluding sentence for his paragraph, a very important part of his work remains to be done. Even the best-planned paragraph can be ruined by mistakes in sentence construction and in spelling.

- How can you weed mistakes and weaknesses out of your writing?
- Why is it a good idea to read your work aloud when proofreading it?

Some kinds of writing weaknesses that proofreading may help you correct are rough, awkward, or faulty sentence structure; punctuation mistakes; misspelled words; misused words; flat, dull expressions; and monotonous sentence structure.

Find the mistakes and weaknesses in the following paragraph and tell how you would correct them.

I have wanted to be a firemen ever since I could walk. If I heard a siron I would run and see if the fire engines was coming passed our house. This went on so much that by the time I was four I could tell whether it was a hook and ladder, a pumper, a ambulance, a police wagon, or a police care. I can still tell the differents. Also, even if I didn't go to where the fire was at I could still tell whether it was a false alarm or a real fire. I always wanted to help. Then my chance came. It was a Tuesday. My brother and I was coming home from

236

Haller's Field from playing softball with the other kids when we seen grass burning nearing Stankey's garage. We ran over to start putting it out and then the fire engines come. I knew right away it was a pumper. After the engine backed into the driveway the firemen started grabbing hoses and brooms and they told my brother and I to help. We all helped to put the fire out and I felt real proud. All this explains why when I grow up I want to be a fireman.

B. *Attaining Sentence Variety*

Often you will find that your sentences need variety. They may be too short and choppy or too long and rambling. Sometimes they may be just limp and lifeless, showing little action or feeling. Can you point out such sentences in the theme above?

- How do the following sentences avoid being lifeless?

    I crept down the stairs in the dark. On the landing I stopped and listened. Was that a creak in the hall? Huddled against the railing, I . . .

    The ball shot at our second baseman, who stepped on second and fired to first for the final out. What a roar went up from the bleachers!

- What do you notice about word order in the different kinds of sentences above?

Rewrite the following statements as questions. Then build a paragraph around one of your questions.

  a. I wondered where the key was.
  b. We hoped he would arrive in time.
  c. We thought the train would never stop.
  d. I thought I saw a snake.
  e. The tree blew down.
  f. We wondered who was there.

C. *Using Concrete Words*

Words are paint with which you make pictures for your reader. Well-chosen words, especially verbs and adjectives, can help your reader see color, shape, and motion. Some can even make him hear sound. But carelessly chosen words paint no pictures, re-create no sounds. They leave your reader with a picture as dull and fuzzy as an old, faded snapshot.

1. Read the following paragraph, paying special attention to the picture-making words.

It is always cool and fresh under the old stone bridge. The bridge, with its moss-covered keystone, arches the creek below the bend, where the willows come right to the water and birch and honeysuckle hang from the bank. The willows never let the sunlight come under the bridge, and it is there that the long pike lie and stare at the glistening walls and minnows loaf under the black rock that sticks its slippery surface above the water. On hot days, the cool breeze jostles the weeds that line the walls, and in the sand nearer the water, crabs hide under rocks. The sand is damp and loose; water quickly fills a footprint or hollow where a stone has been. Snails and salamanders are there, and cool, flattish pebbles tinged with green. Dragonflies dart in and out of the heat but do not stay long. Water trickles from the walls that arch above the stream and drips into the lazy current with sudden, metallic plops. And, sometimes, a floating leaf will eddy near the black rock before it sails out into the sunlight.

Student theme, University of Pittsburgh

a. What words help you see the bridge and its surroundings?
b. What words describe movement?
c. What words describe coolness, freshness, or laziness?

238

2. Read the following paragraph and decide what makes the description vivid.

Standing on the cobbles at the bottom of Kenova Street, I am aware of a foggy grayness that has settled on everything. There are thirteen houses on the street, and they all have cold gray cement steps leading up to rickety porches. Cars parked close to the broken curb have a slippery gloss to them after the rain. The strong odor of creosote from the telephone poles is mingled with the aroma of frying chicken that the wind brings. The top of Kenova Street is a dead end where rotted guard rails, an old tire, weeds, and a cement foundation of an abandoned building have become permanent eyesores. In the foggy distance, a river boat whistles. The usual racket of baying dogs, kids playing tag in the street, and the rumble of traffic from downtown Pittsburgh seems muffled by the fog. The hammering on a house being built in the next street echoes in dull thuds through the neighborhood. A brown and white cat slips through a hedge and flees under a parked car.

Luan Adams, Pittsburgh Public Schools

239

a. The writer describes a city street. What details of *sight, smell, color,* and *sound* has she used?

b. What words can you think of that describe the general mood—the general appearance—of the scene? Does the detail about the cat fit the scene?

c. How would you improve "I am aware" and "is mingled with the aroma"?

3. Read the following paragraph, in which the author describes an army encamped on a hill.

The cold passed reluctantly from the earth, and the retiring fogs revealed an army stretched out on hills, resting. As the landscape changed from brown to green, the army awakened, and began to tremble with eagerness at the noise of rumors. It cast its eyes upon the roads, which were growing from long troughs of liquid mud to proper thoroughfares. A river, amber-tinted in the shadow of its banks, purled at the army's feet; and at night, when the stream had become of a sorrowful blackness, one could see across it the red, eyelike gleam of hostile campfires set in the low brows of the distant hills.

From THE RED BADGE OF COURAGE, by *Stephen Crane*

a. What words help you see the enemy across the stream?

b. What words help you see the time of day?

c. What words help you see the road and river?

d. What words help you know how the soldiers felt?

4. List the following words and after each write as many words as you can that will concretely describe size, shape, color, or movement.

1. building	5. trees
2. bicycle	6. birds
3. road	7. rain
4. clouds	8. bus

5. Write as many words as you can that will concretely describe the sound of the following:

1. water	3. wind	5. tires
2. bells	4. thunder	6. doors

D. *Analyzing Paragraph Organization*

Below are paragraphs built on some of the structures you have learned. What can you discover about their strengths and weaknesses?

1. I like to watch a storm gather. At first, the signs are faint. The sunshine cools, and soon the sun goes out of sight in thickening clouds that scrape the top of Black Hill and race on toward Old Baldy. The air scarcely moves, yet out on the river the smoke from Smith Brothers' barge flattens out on the water and hugs the rising swells that roll upstream. On the banks and near the shore, clumps of slim, pliant sawgrass test their blades. A chill runs through the hills; the leaves turn pale. Birds flutter restlessly. Far over on Cottage Hill, in the gathering haze, a washing is jerked away, white piece after white piece. Then the tempo quickens. A gust of sand from the alley curls along the backyard fence, sprinkling the flags and hollyhocks and spreading itself over the moist retaining wall by the garage. Down on Third Street, cars whiz by on self-made tracks. The maple in the yard bends and creaks. The lid on Stanley's garbage can clatters to the ground. A cat speeds past. A door slams. A window is shut emphatically. A milk bottle rolls across Hellers' porch and bumps down the steps. Over in the next block, a woman's voice, tremulous and high-pitched, calls, "Jim-e-e-y," and ends on a half note. The insistent clamor of two robins by the cherry tree swings my attention back to our own yard. There, half-hidden in the grass, lies a crushed blue egg.

Student theme, University of Pittsburgh

a. What order has the writer used to arrange his details?

b. Why do you think he did not use a concluding sentence that restated his topic sentence? What special qualities must a concluding sentence such as this have?

c. What details has he used to describe the wind?

d. How do you know that the rain has begun?

e. Why are the few sentences beginning with "A cat speeds past" so short?

2. For a hunter who is out at sunrise on a freezing March morning there are many things to hear and see. Then, when the first grey begins to come, the world is full of sounds. In the frosty quiet is the grinding of an ice gorge and the sharp crack of the twigs of some willow or maple whose low hanging branches have been frozen into the moving ice. A crow in the top of a cottonwood caws sleepily; a mallard that has stood guard all night calls his mates, now, to go for their morning feed. And as the light grows clearer, the hunter sees the ducks begin their flight. First the blue-wing teal sweep along and are quickly past. Then the mallards come soaring above the decoys, the slanting rays of the sun brightening their big green heads. After these fly the smaller ducks—pintails, bluebills, blackjacks, and the rest. But the flying of the first duck breaks up the sunrise mood. Then begins the real business of the hunter's day.

Student theme, University of Pittsburgh

a. What order has the writer used here?

b. How do you know the kind of paragraph which might follow this one?

c. The writer tells you that there is much to see and hear. What details describe sights and sounds? What details could you add? Are there any verbs or adjectives you would substitute for those the writer has used?

3. At five o'clock in the morning, a secluded inlet of the lake in Raccoon Creek State Park has a relaxing atmosphere. As my fishing companion and I anchor our rowboat along a steep shore, the first rays of the midsummer sun break through the thick, white mist that shrouds the lake. Although the mist cuts off the distance, we hear the sharp rapping of a woodpecker drilling into a tree and the cawing of flying crows. From the stump along which we fish, six or seven twisted roots jut into the water and form a shelter for a school of sunfish. To the right of the boat, darting minnows, which try desperately to escape from a hungry bass, break the surface of the water. Three chipmunks scamper on the shore, picking acorns and other seeds and storing them away for the winter season. Farther down the shore, a wood duck in the lake, followed by nine ducklings, swims in a straight line. Along the stump, the red and white bobber dips silently under the calm surface of the water as a fish seizes the minnow that is impaled on the hook.

Ronald Chetlin, Pittsburgh Public Schools

a. What order has the writer used to arrange his details?
b. If the concluding sentence does not satisfy you, how would you rewrite it or what would you add?
c. Do all the details support a "relaxing atmosphere"?

4. Write a paragraph about the sights and sounds *you* observe in the early morning or in the late evening, either in the country or in the city.

- Use one of the methods of paragraph organization we have studied, either chronological or spatial order.
- Be sure you have a good topic sentence and concluding sentence and that you have chosen vivid details.
- Be ready to point out the words in your paragraph which link sentences together.

243

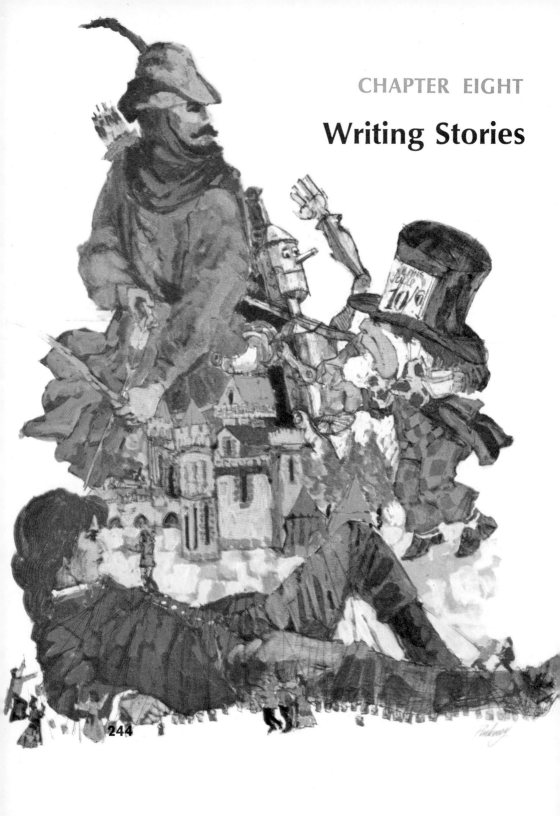

CHAPTER EIGHT

Writing Stories

244

1   Sharing Your Experiences

READING AND THINKING

Most of us remember stories like *Snow White*, *The Wizard of Oz*, *Homer Price*, *Pinocchio*, *Alice in Wonderland*, *Rabbit Hill*, and *Dr. Dolittle*—stories that we read or had read to us in earlier years. We remember them because we enjoyed them.

Books and magazines are not the only sources of enjoyable stories; sometimes very good short stories result when boys and girls write about some of the unusual, funny, exciting, or interesting things that actually happen to them or to people they know. Few people can expect to write with as much skill as professional writers do, but if they remember some of the ways these authors present material, beginning writers can create entertaining stories. Just as professional writers often draw upon experiences in their own lives for their stories, so, too, can boys and girls find much in their own lives worth writing about.

Good stories—good accounts of our own experiences—can be interesting to others if we are aware of what makes such stories interesting. Read the following story written by a sixth-grader and be ready to discuss the questions which follow it. Pay special attention to the paragraphs and how the writer leads from one to another by the use of connective words.

Mighty Hunters

Hunting is not for me, except on television and in movies and books. I made up my mind about this last weekend, which I spent with my brother Dick, a counselor at Camp Crestview.

Dick had agreed to take all the new campers—and me—on a snipe hunt. If we were successful in catching one, we were to have the rare treat of snipe brew at midnight around the campfire.

Out we started about nine o'clock, bundled up in jackets and boots, armed with lanterns and sticks, and carrying laundry bags—to bag the snipe. We stumbled for miles, it seemed, through thick underbrush and over slippery, jagged rocks. Since there was no moonlight, it was so dark we could hardly see one another, even with the lanterns. Sometimes we got tangled in low tree branches that seemed to reach out and grab us. Once several of us tripped and slid into marshy ground up to our knees. By this time most of us were so cold and jittery we would gladly have returned to camp without a snipe.

Then suddenly Dick shouted, "There's one! I've got him!" And he grabbed my laundry bag and stuffed the snipe into it.

As we scrambled around him, Dick yelped, "Ow! He bit me!" And sure enough, there was blood all over his hand. But Dick was brave, all right. "Don't worry, fellows," he said. "I'll manage somehow. I'll get you back to camp okay. Just stick close."

We were a scared lot as we huddled together, fighting our way through the dark to the mess hall, Dick moaning and groaning and warning us not to let the snipe out of the bag. My hands were shaking so I could hardly hold it, and the thing seemed to be thrashing around inside it.

While Dick was being bandaged and the cook was preparing the stew, we were sent to our cabins for dry clothes. Later, as we were herded around the campfire, the cook told us what a battle he had had with the snipe before slitting its throat and putting it in the kettle. Somehow, we all had trouble swallowing that brew. And we imagined other

246

snipes lurking in the shadows of the campfire waiting for revenge. The croaking of frogs down by the creek and the shrill cries of the locusts in the bushes all around us sounded like an army of snipes ready to pounce on us.

Afterwards, Dick and the cook told us the snipe was only a sock stuffed with cotton, the blood ketchup, and the brew sassafras tea. But we had had enough big game hunting for a while. However, by the time next summer comes around, it might be fun at that to take the new campers on a snipe hunt.

DISCUSSING

A. Discuss the following questions about the story "Mighty Hunters" with your classmates.

1. Was I interested from the very beginning?
2. Was I still interested when I finished?
3. Could I actually see the places described?
4. Did I feel I was there, taking part in what happened?
5. Did I care how things turned out?
6. Could I retell the story?

B. Decide whether or not "Mighty Hunters" follows the suggestions given below for writing a story.

Storywriting Suggestions

1. Choose a title that will arouse interest at once.

2. Plan a beginning sentence that will hold the reader's interest and lead him into the story.

3. Tell as soon as possible whom the story is about, when and where the action takes place.

4. Include conversation occasionally to make the people in the story seem real and alive.

5. Tell things in the order in which they happen. This will help you avoid giving away the ending.

6. Use good descriptive details—action verbs and vivid adjectives and adverbs—to paint as clear a word picture as possible.

7. Don't add unnecessary details that may drag out the story.

C. In what ways could you improve "Mighty Hunters?"

D. Discuss how the paragraphs are organized and linked together in "Mighty Hunters."

WORKING BY YOURSELF

Choose a story from your reader and see if it follows the suggestions above. Write the title and the author of the story and list your comments. If the story differs from any of the above suggestions, what do you think was the author's purpose in choosing to write his story the way he did?

2   Giving First Impressions

Even before you began to read "Mighty Hunters," you probably formed some impression about the story.

- What led you to form a first impression?
- Which one of each of the following pairs of stories would you rather read? Why?

1. "The Snipe Hunt" or "Midnight Brew"
2. "A Thrilling Ride" or "Ceiling Zero"
3. "An Embarrassing Moment" or "I Squirm to Recall"
4. "Lost in Chicago" or "One in a Million"
5. "A Scary Night" or "When the Clock Struck Midnight"
6. "An Exciting Game" or "One Second to Go"

A catchy title arouses interest at once, but so must your opening sentences if you are to *keep* your reader's interest.

- What is effective about the following story openings? Notice how each arouses your interest.

1. "A bee with a long purple tail chased me!" shrieked Janie, flinging open the door.

249

2. "A stitch in time" I always say, but . . .

3. "Where is my fishing tackle?" roared Father as he stared into the empty car trunk.

- Sometimes a story begins by telling *when* the action is to take place. Perhaps the time of day or the season of the year is especially important to the story. For example:

1. The pale sun rose slowly above the gray, bleak mountain range. We scrambled . . .

2. The moonlight seemed to edge the leafy branches and the roof tops with silver. It was . . .

- What kind of information do the following opening sentences give the reader? Are the sentences effective?

1. The ruin of an old stone bridge sprawled across the creek just below the dam. Here we climbed . . .

2. A gnarled, twisted oak tree arched itself over the iron gate. We stopped to . . .

3. The place was strange. I had never seen anything like it.

4. The mill was a rambling, one-story, brown frame building standing just at the edge of the river. It was here that . . .

5. The shack, weatherbeaten and deserted, was hidden from the road by shaggy, overgrown bushes. We decided to . . .

DISCUSSING

A. What questions, quotations, or unusual statements might have been used to begin "Mighty Hunters"? Compose as many different opening sentences as you can for "Mighty Hunters."

B. Reword these titles to make them arouse greater interest:

1. A Visit to the Planetarium
2. Bicycling in Traffic
3. An Exciting Sled Ride
4. Our Hike up Mount Nittany
5. When Our Cat Fell into the Well
6. The Day Our Canoe Capsized
7. A Frightening Experience
8. My Best Friend

Remember that prepositions and the determiners *a*, *an*, and *the* are not capitalized unless they are at the beginning of a title.

C. Some of you have read and enjoyed *The Good Master* by Kate Seredy. Perhaps you will remember some of Miss Seredy's descriptive details that helped you see where Kate and Jancsi lived and played. Point out adjectives and verbs that make the word pictures clear and interesting in the following paragraphs from *The Good Master*.

The apple tree was in full bloom. White strawberry blossoms covered the edge of the pastures. The farmyard was teeming with new life. Baby chicks swarmed in the grass, pink piglets squealed in an enclosure. Mali, the cow, had a brown-and-white calf, marked like a chestnut. It was tottering and tumbling after Mali, getting in everybody's way. . . . The fresh green plants were standing in even rows, like so many pert little green soldiers. Swallows darted between the squatty white pillars of the porch, repairing their nests.

251

There were large wheat and rye fields on both sides. Narrow paths forked out of the main road, leading to white cottages nestling under shade trees. From the distance they looked like small white mushrooms under their heavy thatched roofs.

The road led through a small forest of acacia trees. Their branches were heavy with clusters of white flowers. The air was drenched with their sweet, heady perfume. White petals drifted in the breeze, covering the ground like snow.

WORKING BY YOURSELF

A. Write an opening sentence of your own to describe the weather, the place, or the time of an incident that happened to you. Then try combining details about time and weather in an opening sentence.

B. Giving attention to size, shape, and color, write a description of one of the following places.
1. A lake, river, or stream
2. A school, library, church, or store
3. A factory, warehouse, or railroad station
4. A ball park, playground, or skating pond
5. A yard, field, meadow, or woods
6. A camp, fairground, or picnic area
7. A subway car or bus

C. Choose at least three interesting beginnings from stories in your reader. Be ready to read them in class and tell why you think they are especially good.

D. Write a good opening sentence for each new title you composed in exercise *B* on page 251. Be ready to compare your opening sentences with those written by your classmates to see which ones are most effective in arousing interest.

3 Making Your Characters Live

Writing about our experiences usually means we write about other people as well. A truly difficult part of writing about people is making the characters seem real, for no matter how well *we* know them, they are mysteries to a reader unless we can bring them to life in our writing.

Notice the way Charles Dickens describes an old man at his workbench:

A broad ray of light fell into the garret,[1] and showed the workman with an unfinished shoe upon his lap, pausing in his labour. His few common tools and various scraps of leather were at his feet and on his bench. He had a white beard, raggedly cut, but not very long, a hollow face, and exceedingly bright eyes. The hollowness and thinness of his face would have caused them to look large, under his yet dark eyebrows and his confused white hair, though they had been really otherwise; but, they were naturally large, and looked unnaturally so. His yellow rags of shirt lay open at the throat, and showed his body to be withered and worn. He, and his old canvas frock, and his loose stockings, and all his poor tatters of clothes, had, in a long seclusion[2] from direct light and air, faded down to such a dull uniformity[3] of parchment-yellow,[4] that it would have been difficult to say which was which.

From A TALE OF TWO CITIES, by *Charles Dickens*

[1] *garret:* attic; room just under the roof
[2] *seclusion:* separation
[3] *uniformity:* sameness
[4] *parchment-yellow:* the color of a writing material made of sheepskin

- In the paragraph on page 253 what does Charles Dickens tell you about the appearance of the old man?
- What other physical traits might it be important to include in a description of a person?

Remember that the descriptive details you choose to include should be those which really distinguish one person from everyone else.

WORKING TOGETHER

A. A person's facial expression is an important feature of his appearance. Mention several ways you might describe the expression on a person's face. Your teacher may ask a student to list some of your ideas at the chalkboard.

B. Perhaps a person's build and posture are striking enough to set him apart from others. You might use such words as *sturdy*, *stooped*, *scrawny*, or *husky* to describe build and posture. Discuss what other adjectives describe build and posture. It may help you to visualize people you know well; how would you describe their way of standing, sitting—their *bearing?*

C. Suggest a good sentence to describe each of the following: *height, posture, build, hands.*

D. Discuss words that could be used to describe the appearance of some famous person familiar to the class, such as an actor or a politician.

WORKING BY YOURSELF

Hair, eyes, smile, and complexion are important parts of a person's appearance. List as many descriptive words as you can to picture each of these. Then develop a paragraph describing one of these physical traits for a specific character.

4 Using Descriptive Language

Creating pictures or images in words demands careful, concentrated effort from a writer. Yet, vivid descriptions of people and places will become much easier for you if you try to use some of the methods explained in this lesson and the ones that follow.

Two special kinds of descriptive language are *similes* and *metaphors*. Both these forms of expression draw comparisons between two things which are unlike in almost all respects, except for the similarity you wish to bring out in your comparison. For example, we do not usually think of people as being like birds, yet notice what likeness Charles Dickens brings out in this simile describing one of his characters in the book *David Copperfield:*

Mr. Chillip laid his head a little more on one side, and looked at my aunt like an amiable bird.

- How are Mr. Chillip and the bird alike?

Similes, like the one you have just examined, always use the words *like* or *as . . . as* to compare two things. You can see from the following example that a simile can describe a scene as vividly as it can a person:

. . . The elms bent to one another, like giants who were whispering secrets, and after a few seconds of such repose, fell into a violent flurry, tossing their arms about, as if their late confidences were really too wicked for their peace of mind . . .

From DAVID COPPERFIELD, by *Charles Dickens*

- In the simile above, how are the two parts of the comparison alike?

255

The simile in the following description is of the *as . . . as* type. Notice that *as* is used twice, since a comparison is made between two things.

The old man was thin and gaunt with deep wrinkles in the back of his neck. The brown blotches of the benevolent skin cancer the sun brings from its reflection on the tropic sea were on his cheeks. The blotches ran well down the sides of his face and his hands had the deep-creased scars from handling heavy fish on the cords. But none of these scars were fresh. They were as old as erosions in a fishless desert.

From THE OLD MAN AND THE SEA, by *Ernest Hemingway*

Metaphors, like similes, are means of describing vividly through comparison. However, they *suggest* similarity between basically unlike things, whereas similes actually state the likeness by using *like* or *as . . . as.* Read the following passages and try to explain what two things are compared in each metaphor or simile.

The girl's eyes beamed affection under her mother's caress. Then she straightened up, folded her white hands in her lap, and became a splendid iceberg.

From THE GILDED AGE, by Mark Twain

Up to now he had merely been an interested spectator, taking a keen interest from a professional point of view, for a good fight is meat and drink to a bull terrier. Now a look of pure, unholy joy appeared in the black-currant eyes, and he tensed his stocky, close-knit body, timing his spring with a mastery born of long practice. A white, compact bundle of fighting art shot like a steel projectile to the collie's throat.

From THE INCREDIBLE JOURNEY, by Sheila Burnford

- Did you find any metaphors or similes in the paragraphs above? If so, you are ready to read the third sample below, which is taken from a narrative poem called "The Highwayman," by Alfred Noyes.

The wind was a torrent of darkness among the gusty trees.
The moon was a ghostly galleon tossed upon cloudy seas.
The road was a ribbon of moonlight over the purple moor.

- How would you explain the comparison made in each of the three metaphors from "The Highwayman?"

- Be ready to give some metaphors or similes which you use in your everyday speech. Some similes are so familiar that they are overused and uninteresting. Can you think of substitutes for such overworked comparisons as: *quick as a fox, teeth like pearls, thin as a rail?*

WORKING TOGETHER

A. Compose original metaphors and similes to describe any five of the following:

1. a ballerina
2. a pigeon
3. a spaceship
4. an old man's head
5. a grizzly bear
6. a drop of dew
7. a worn catcher's mitt
8. a dachshund
9. a snake
10. a train

B. Look through the poems in your reader to find examples of five similes and five metaphors. Discuss the two parts of each comparison and decide whether or not the similes and metaphors create vivid pictures.

WORKING BY YOURSELF

Expand one of the similes or metaphors you composed into a paragraph. What method of paragraph development from Chapter Seven will you be using?

MORE FOR YOU

A. In the description of Mr. Chillip quoted on page 255, Charles Dickens uses a word that tells us Mr. Chillip is a friendly bird, not a frightening one, such as a hawk. What word gives us that information?

B. What words might you use in the following comparisons?

1. as _____ as an eagle
2. as _____ as a peacock
3. as _____ as an ostrich
4. as _____ as a canary
5. as _____ as a buzzard

C. In the description from *The Old Man and the Sea*, what word tells us that the old man's skin cancer is not harmful?

Let your Treasure Chest help you check your answers.

amiable

From the Latin word for "friend," *amicus*, we get our English word *amiable*, which means "having a friendly disposition."

Arthur is so amiable that he will make a good member of the team.
His amiability makes him a popular fellow.
He behaves amiably in his dealings with other people.

amiable   amiability   amiably

benevolent

The two Latin words—*bene*, "well," and *volere*, "to wish"—give us the English word *benevolent*, which means "well-wishing." A person who is *benevolent* wishes to do good. A thing that is *benevolent* is harmless.

The benevolent ruler improved the living conditions of his people.
The ruler's benevolence won him his subjects' love.

benevolent   benevolence

5 Choosing Words Carefully

READING AND THINKING

Whether you are setting a scene or giving life and individuality to a person in your story, choosing words carefully and precisely will help you to write vivid descriptions. For example, verbs are strong words, yet they become weak and vague if you use them in a lazy way. What picture do you get from the sentence *The man walked down the road?*

- What verb can you substitute for *walked* to show precisely how the man was walking?

If chosen with precision, adjectives too can create vivid pictures. Some adjectives, however, have been used so often and so carelessly that they have ceased to have real picture-making value. *Nice*, *good*, *wonderful*, and *great* are just a few of the vague, overworked adjectives.

- What more specific adjectives can you substitute for the ones above?

An exact noun often eliminates the need for an adjective. If you wanted to create a clear picture in the sentence *The old woman lived in a house*, you might need to insert an adjective. For example:

The old woman lived in a <u>huge</u> house.

However, more careful thought might provide you with a noun that is at once more precise and concise (brief):

The old woman lived in a <u>mansion</u>.

- What other specific nouns can you substitute for *house?*

260

WORKING TOGETHER

A. Substitute for each of the following verbs as many verbs as you can that show more exact motion or sound.

1. fell   2. knocked   3. ran   4. rang   5. threw

B. Add to each word group below as many picture-making verbs as you can.

1. The waves _____.
2. The thunder _____.
3. The wind _____.
4. The clouds _____.
5. The train _____.
6. The airplane _____.
7. The boy _____.
8. The chimpanzee _____.

C. Mention adjectives to describe each of the following:

1. bacon	5. worm	9. stream
2. bell	6. dog	10. street
3. face	7. lake	11. storm
4. cat	8. school	12. tree

WORKING BY YOURSELF

Without using adjectives to help out, substitute more exact and descriptive nouns for the ones below.

1. boat   4. field
2. building   5. plant
3. car   6. street

Write each noun in a sentence and then combine as many sentences as you can into one paragraph. Add as many others as you need to create a well-developed paragraph.

6 Actions and Words Reveal Character

What is there about the following passages from *A Tale of Two Cities,* by Charles Dickens, that makes the two characters real and easy to picture?

Now that he had no work to hold, he laid the knuckles of the right hand in the hollow of the left, and then the knuckles of the left in the hollow of the right, and then passed a hand across his bearded chin, and so on in regular changes, without a moment's intermission.

★   ★   ★

Mr. Stryver sucked the end of a ruler for a little while, and then stood hitting a tune out of his teeth with it, which probably gave him the toothache.

- What characteristic actions—perhaps unusual ones—can you think of to describe someone you know?

Another way to help your readers *see* the people in your story is to make them say as well as do things that will show the kinds of people they are. For example, the *direct* quotation "*Just wait, I'll fix 'em,*" *muttered Bob* shows that Bob is angry and is planning some way to get even. It tells more than simply saying Bob was angry or even saying Mary said Bob was angry (*indirect* quotation). The direct quotation "*Bring the bird in here. Perhaps I can fix his wing,*" *urged Ann* shows you more about Ann than simply saying that Ann is a kind person or even that Ruth said Ann is a kind person.

When you use direct quotations to indicate something about the character of the speaker, sometimes you can use a more vivid word than *said* to describe voice and manner of speaking. Look

262

at the two direct quotations in the preceding paragraph and notice how *muttered* and *urged* reveal something about Bob and Mary. We all know that there are many tones of voice and attitudes with which to say the same words, and that the way we say words depends upon our mood at the time. Use this fact to convey more about the people in your stories.

WORKING TOGETHER

A. Be ready to read the following bits of conversation aloud. Listen carefully to the tone of voice and to the words which receive emphasis as each is read. Perhaps your teacher will ask two or three students to read each remark, so that you can decide whose reading sounds most real to you. Then go on to discuss the kind of person you picture saying each of the quotations.

1. "I'll be glad to help you. Call me any time."
2. "I beg your pardon. I wasn't watching where I was going."
3. "Let me carry that. It must be very heavy."
4. "Take mine. I have plenty—more than I need."
5. "Of course you can play with us."
6. "Go on home. We were here first."
7. "You should see *my* camera."
8. "You pushed me. You did it on purpose. Just you wait."
9. "Give me back my book. I'll never speak to you again."

B. Speak a few lines of conversation that will show:

1. An angry policeman
2. An unselfish girl
3. A thoughtful person
4. A disappointed person
5. A bully
6. A hot-headed boy
7. A boastful person

C. Sometimes conversation is used to show how a character in the story feels about another person. For example, the direct quotation *"If I ever get into a jam, Pete will try to help me out"* describes Pete and how others feel about him more clearly than saying that everybody likes Pete or that Pete is a good friend. Suggest a few lines of conversation in which one person describes another as one of the following:

A grouchy person	A stingy person
A good sport	A trustworthy person

Your teacher may ask one student to write some of your suggestions at the chalkboard.

D. What words can you think of to describe voice and manner of speaking, as *muttered* and *urged* do on page 263? Use four such words in sentences.

E. Use each of the following verbs in a sentence to describe gesture or motion: *crouches, slumps, stoops, sprawls, shakes, swaggers, tosses, waves, stomps, wrings, jerks.*

WORKING BY YOURSELF

A. Another way to make people seem real is to describe their manner. You get a picture of a person's manner through words like *cocky, bristling, hesitant,* and *shy.* List four other words that can be used to describe manner and write each in a sentence on a sheet of paper.

B. Write a *dialogue* between two persons in one of the following situations or in the situation pictured on page 265.

1. They have just learned that they are related.
2. They have just had an automobile collision.
3. They share a secret.
4. A boy shows his father a poor report card.

dialogue

The prefix *dia-* and the combining form *-logue* are joined to make the English word, *dialogue*. *Dia-* is a Greek prefix, which means "through" or "across." The combining form *-logue* derives from the Greek word *legein*, meaning "to speak." A *dialogue*, then, is a conversation, either written or oral, between two or more persons.

We heard a heated dialogue between Edna and Jan.

7 Punctuating Dialogue

READING AND THINKING

Using direct quotations to develop characters in your stories requires first that you be certain about what a direct quotation is, and then that you know how it must be punctuated. In the following examples, the *direct* quotations are underlined. Aside from punctuation, what differences can you see between a *direct* and an *indirect* quotation?

Lauren asked us to call for her at six.
<u>"Call for me at six, will you?"</u> asked Lauren.

Terry warned that it looked like rain.
<u>"It certainly looks like rain,"</u> warned Terry.

Jeff yelled that the boulder was beginning a slide.
<u>"Watch that boulder! It's beginning a slide!"</u> yelled Jeff.

Once you recognize the difference between direct and indirect quotations, you need only remember certain punctuation patterns in order to write direct quotations correctly. You probably know that quotation marks are used to enclose the exact words of the speaker, but you must also know how and when to use commas, periods, and question marks in quotations. Perhaps you can decide by studying the following examples.

"My dad's taking me to the game on Saturday," said Paul.
"Wow! You sure are lucky!" exclaimed Ted.
Jerry asked, "What time are you planning to leave for the stadium?"

- What punctuation marks are placed *inside* the quotation marks?
- When are separate paragraphs begun?

Examine the following conversation, paying special attention to the use of periods and commas.

"We're leaving at one o'clock," answered Paul, "but that should give us plenty of time to get there."

"I wish I could go, too," said Ted. "My father has to work on Saturday, though."

"Will you bring me a score card?" asked Jerry. "I'd like to have it for my collection."

- What phrases interrupt the speakers' remarks?
- How many sentences are there in each speaker's comment?
- When do we use a period after an interruption in the speaker's words? When do we use a comma?

WORKING TOGETHER

Explain how you would punctuate the following conversation correctly.

1. It was a great game exclaimed Paul
2. Tell us all about it cried Jerry who won
3. I watched it on TV said Ted but that wasn't the same as being there
4. Did you have good seats asked Pete I've never seen the stadium
5. Did you bring me a score card asked Jerry I hope you didn't forget it
6. Be quiet interrupted Ted and let Paul tell us about the game
7. We missed the first ten minutes said Paul my sister made us late as usual
8. Too bad said Pete you should have left her at home
9. Yeah grumbled Paul because of her we missed the first touchdown
10. Next time Jerry suggested leave your sister and take me

Write a short word sketch of someone you know well, using conversation and describing appearance, gestures, voice, and manner of speaking. Make the person seem real. You might describe the person in one of the following situations:

1. father at the breakfast table
2. mother in the kitchen
3. big brother doing his homework
4. big sister drying dishes

You might begin something like this:
Dad is grumpy at breakfast. You can hardly see him behind his newspaper, but . . .
Sally hates to dry dishes. She slouches over the sink and . . .

8 Unraveling the Plot

READING AND THINKING

Stories, like paragraphs, are strengthened by an effective arrangement of details. In planning a story, a good writer arranges events in a sequence which carries his plot forward. Many writers arrange the events of their stories by *time*, in the order in which events occur. They build from a struggle, conflict, or problem to events of more and more suspense and tension until a deciding point or climax is reached, and finally to a conclusion which resolves or settles the original conflict.

- What familiar books or stories that you have read show the kind of plot development just described?

One type of story that illustrates the plot development described is the *myth*. Myths are stories created by ancient or primitive peoples to explain various things about the world and nature which they could not account for in any other way. For example, a myth might explain thunder and lightning as the fury of the gods. Today, however, we would explain the same natural events scientifically.

In the myth which follows, the ancient Greeks attempted to explain the daily journey of the sun through the sky. You should find the story an exciting one, and you may see in it a method of plot development which you can use in your own stories.

Read the myth of Phaëthon first for enjoyment. Then read it again, paying particular attention to the way the events are arranged—the way the plot is developed.

Phaëthon

(*fā′ə thən*)

The palace of the Sun was a radiant place. It shone with gold and gleamed with ivory and sparkled with jewels. Everything without and within flashed and glowed and glittered. It was always high noon there. Shadowy twilight never dimmed the brightness. Darkness and night were unknown. Few among mortals could have long endured that unchanging brilliancy of light, but few had ever found their way thither.

Nevertheless, one day a youth, mortal on his mother's side, dared to approach. Often he had to pause and clear his dazzled eyes, but the errand which had brought him was so urgent that his purpose held fast and he pressed on, up to the palace, through the burnished doors, and into the throne-room where surrounded by a blinding, blazing splendor the Sun-god sat. There the lad was forced to halt. He could bear no more.

Nothing escapes the eyes of the Sun. He saw the boy instantly and he looked at him very kindly. "What brought you here?" he asked. "I have come," the other answered boldly, "to find out if you are my father or not. My mother said you were, but the boys at school laugh when I tell

270

them I am your son. They will not believe me. I told my mother and she said I had better go and ask you." Smiling, the Sun took off his crown of burning light so that the lad could look at him without distress. "Come here, Phaëthon," he said. "You are my son. Clymene[1] told you the truth. I expect you will not doubt my word too? But I will give you a proof. Ask anything you want of me and you shall have it. I call the Styx[2] to be witness to my promise, the river of the oath of the gods."

No doubt Phaëthon had often watched the Sun riding through the heavens and had told himself with a feeling, half awe, half excitement, "It is my father up there." And then he would wonder what it would be like to be in that chariot, guiding the steeds along that dizzy course, giving light to the world. Now at his father's words this wild dream had become possible. Instantly he cried, "I choose to take your place, Father. That is the only thing I want. Just for a day, a single day, let me have your car to drive."

The Sun realized his own folly. Why had he taken that fatal oath and bound himself to give in to anything that happened to enter a boy's rash young head? "Dear lad," he said, "this is the only thing I would have refused you. I know I cannot refuse. I have sworn by the Styx. I must yield if you persist. But I do not believe you will. Listen while I tell you what this is you want. You are Clymene's son as well as mine. You are mortal and no mortal could drive my chariot. Indeed, no god except myself can do that. The ruler of the gods cannot. Consider the road. It rises up from the sea so steeply that the horses can hardly climb it, fresh though they are in the early morning. In midheaven it is so high that even I do not like to look down. Worst of all is the descent, so precipitous that the Sea-gods waiting to

[1] klim′ə nē   [2] stiks

receive me wonder how I can avoid falling headlong. To guide the horses, too, is a perpetual struggle. Their fiery spirits grow hotter as they climb and they scarcely suffer my control. What would they do with you?

"Are you fancying that there are all sorts of wonders up there, cities of the gods full of beautiful things? Nothing of the kind. You will have to pass beasts, fierce beasts of prey, and they are all that you will see. The Bull, the Lion, the Scorpion, the Great Crab, each will try to harm you. Be persuaded. Look around you. See all the goods the rich world holds. Choose from them your heart's desire and it shall be yours. If what you want is to be proved my son, my fears for you are proof enough that I am your father."

But none of all this wise talk meant anything to the boy. A glorious prospect opened before him. He saw himself proudly standing in that wondrous car, his hands triumphantly guiding those steeds which Jove himself could not master. He did not give a thought to the dangers his father detailed. He felt not a quiver of fear, not a doubt of his own powers. At last the Sun gave up trying to dissuade him. It was hopeless, as he saw. Besides, there was no time. The moment for starting was at hand. Already the gates of the east glowed purple, and Dawn had opened her courts full of rosy light. The stars were leaving the sky; even the lingering morning star was dim.

There was need for haste, but all was ready. The seasons, the gatekeepers of Olympus, stood waiting to fling the doors wide. The horses had been bridled and yoked to the car. Proudly and joyously Phaëthon mounted it and they were off. He had made his choice. Whatever came of it he could not change now. Not that he wanted to in that first exhilarating rush through the air, so swift that the East Wind was outstripped and left far behind. The horses' flying feet went through the low-banked clouds near the ocean as through a

272

thin sea mist and then up and up in the clear air, climbing the height of heaven. For a few ecstatic moments Phaëthon felt himself the Lord of the Sky. But suddenly there was a change. The chariot was swinging wildly to and fro; the pace was faster; he had lost control. Not he, but the horses were directing the course. That light weight in the car, those feeble hands clutching the reins, had told them their own driver was not there. They were the masters then. No one else could command them. They left the road and rushed where they chose, up, down, to the right, to the left. They nearly wrecked the chariot against the Scorpion; they brought up short and almost ran into the Crab. By this time the poor charioteer was half fainting with terror, and he let the reins fall.

That was the signal for still more mad and reckless running. The horses soared up to the very top of the sky and then, plunging headlong down, they set the world on fire. The highest mountains were the first to burn, Ida and Helicon, where the Muses dwell, Parnassus, and heaven-piercing Olympus. Down their slopes the flame ran to the low-lying valleys and the dark forest lands, until all things everywhere were ablaze. The springs turned into steam; the rivers shrank. It is said that it was then the Nile fled and hid his head, which still is hidden.

In the car Phaëthon, hardly keeping his place there, was wrapped in thick smoke and heat as if from a fiery furnace. He wanted nothing except to have this torment and terror ended. He would have welcomed death. Mother Earth, too, could bear no more. She uttered a great cry which reached up to the gods. Looking down from Olympus they saw that they must act quickly if the world was to be saved. Jove seized his thunderbolt and hurled it at the rash, repentant driver. It struck him dead, shattered the chariot, and made the maddened horses rush down into the sea.

Phaëthon all on fire fell from the car through the air to the earth. The mysterious river Eridanus,[3] which no mortal eyes have ever seen, received him and put out the flames and cooled the body. The naiads,[4] in pity for him, so bold and so young to die, buried him and carved upon the tomb:—

> Here Phaëthon lies who drove the Sun-god's car.
> Greatly he failed, but he had greatly dared.

His sisters, the Heliades,[5] the daughters of Helios, the Sun, came to his grave to mourn for him. There they were turned into poplar trees, on the bank of the Eridanus,

> Where sorrowing they weep into the stream forever.
> And each tear as it falls shines in the water
> A glistening drop of amber.

By *Ovid*

Retold by *Edith Hamilton* in Mythology

[3] i rid'ə nəs   [4] nā'ads   [5] hi li' ə dēz

DISCUSSING

A. Discuss the characters in the myth, deciding who the most important character is. Give reasons for your choice.

B. In one or two sentences state the struggle or conflict that the main character faces.

C. When does the climax of the story occur? Explain why you think a particular event is the climax. Mention the events you think lead up to the climax.

D. What is the conclusion of the myth? How is the struggle or conflict settled? What moral, if any, do you think the myth contains? Point out specific words in the myth that seem to you to present a moral.

WORKING BY YOURSELF

A. A reader of your stories is aided in seeing the relationship of paragraphs to one another by guide words such as those below.

accordingly	however	on the contrary
consequently	in addition to	similarly
finally	moreover	therefore
furthermore	nevertheless	thus

Write each of the words or phrases above in a sentence which illustrates the use of each word as a means to show the relationship between one idea and another. For example:

> We were drenched and exhausted. *Nevertheless,* we were happy to have made the climb.

B. The ending of a story is especially important because it is the ending that makes the final impression on the reader. You can improve your stories by avoiding trite, overused endings and those which trail off like weak, uncertain voices.

Number from 1 to 8 on your paper and evaluate the following story endings according to GOOD, TRITE, UNCERTAIN or WEAK. Be ready to compare your answers with your classmates'.

1. Then we went home and that's how it all turned out. And I guess I'll never forget that experience. It sure was exciting.

2. Everything worked out fine. I was really worried, though, and Joe said he was plenty worried too.

3. All's well that ends well.

4. We were a sadder but wiser group.

5. Dad finally broke into a grin. We knew everything would be all right. "Good night, astronauts," he said, as he flipped the light switch.

6. Water, water everywhere! After that night the Sahara would look like paradise to me.

7. Next time we go mountain climbing, we'll check with the weatherman first.

8. When we got home, exhausted by our climb and wet to the skin, we couldn't decide whether we felt more like astronauts or aquanauts.

C. Locate several stories in your reader that you think have especially good endings and be prepared to tell why you think they are effective.

9 A Review

Many good writers take more time to think about and plan their writing than they use in the actual writing of their stories. The guide on page 277 will help you both in planning and in writing your stories as you follow it throughout the year.

Storywriting Guide

1. Choose an experience that you have really enjoyed or found especially interesting, unusual, or exciting.

2. Choose carefully the details that will recapture the experience. Too few details will make it hard for others to "see" the events. Too many may confuse the reader or cause the story to drag. Decide on the most *important* details.

3. Arrange your details thoughtfully in outline form, and determine the best sequence, or order, to use.

4. Set the stage carefully. The reader will want to know *when, where,* and *why* things happen. Paint him a clear and interesting word picture.

5. Decide on the most interest-catching title and opening sentence you can think of.

6. Decide when the use of conversation will help the people in the story come "alive."

7. Plan carefully a concluding sentence, perhaps one that will sum up what the experience meant to you or one that will end the action the moment the outcome is reached. Don't let your story end with a dull thud.

8. After you have written your story, *read it aloud* to (a) weed out unnecessary details, (b) see how the conversation really *sounds,* (c) see if the ending is clear and satisfying. Then look over your paper carefully to make sure sentence structure, spelling, punctuation, and capitalization are correct.

A. Write a story about an experience that has meant a great deal to you. Perhaps some of the suggestions below will jog your memories:

1. An event that happened while you were skating, hiking, picnicking, delivering papers, swimming, shopping, or doing a chore.

2. An event that happened to you and a pet, a friend, a member of your family, or another relative.

3. An event that happened at a camp, circus, zoo, fair, park, store, school, or an airport.

4. An event that frightened you, pleased you, surprised you, embarrassed you, or taught you a lesson.

B. Perhaps you would like to write an original story—not one based on an experience that actually happened to you.

1. Sometimes original stories grow out of events that have occurred in history. For example, you might pretend that you are a cabin boy on the *Santa Maria*. You sight land first and call Christopher Columbus to check your discovery. Here are some other suggestions:

a. You are a stable boy the night Paul Revere rides to Lexington and Concord.

b. Your mother keeps an inn at which Washington and his generals plan the crossing of the Delaware.

c. Your house faces the wharf and you witness the Boston Tea Party.

d. Your father takes you to hear Abraham Lincoln at Gettysburg.

e. You arrive at Plymouth with your parents on the *Mayflower*.

f. You are a member of Admiral Richard E. Byrd's expedition to Antarctica.

g. You are on board the recovery ship which picks up astronaut Alan B. Shepard after his historic flight.

2. What events in the lives of these famous people might you tell as though you had been there with them?

Betsy Ross	Stonewall Jackson
Robert E. Lee	Lewis and Clark
Robert Fulton	Benjamin Franklin
Eli Whitney	John Paul Jones
Pocahontas	Thomas Jefferson

C. Sometimes original stories have been told to explain why animals have certain characteristics or to explain certain wonders in nature. You probably remember stories which explain why the bear has a stumpy tail, why the elephant has a trunk, why the sunflower faces the sun, or why we have four seasons of the year. Choose one of the following subjects and write a story to develop it:

1. How dogs learned to wag their tails
2. Why parakeets can talk
3. How the lion got his mane
4. How the bee got his sting
5. How the giraffe got his long neck
6. Why weeping willows weep
7. Why Old Faithful is so reliable
8. How the cat got his purr
9. Why corn grows in ears
10. Why roses have thorns

EVALUATING YOUR STORIES

Working either in pairs or in small groups, read aloud the stories you have written and let your classmates evaluate them according to the Storywriting Guide on page 277. Your teacher may then ask you to share the best stories with the entire class.

CHAPTER NINE

Reports and Reviews

1 Limiting Topics

If you were asked to write a report on "Our School," many of you would say, "Oh, that's easy." It *would* be easier than writing a report on "Zymosis" because "Our School" is a subject you know a good deal about—a necessary condition before anyone can write about anything. You know so much about your school that the difficulty of planning such a report might lie in deciding where to begin and what to include. Every subject is made up of a number of parts—subdivisions that are really topics in themselves. For the topic "Our School," for example, you might think of such subdivisions as *appearance, activities, subjects taught, teachers, students,* and *grades,* all of which are parts of your school. Since you could not tell everything about your school in your report, you would have to limit yourself to perhaps three or four subdivisions of the topic.

Limiting a topic involves moving from a broad, general subject to a narrower, more specific one. We might compare the process to the movement of a television camera from a view of an entire stage filled with dancers to a closer and closer view of three or four dancers, then one dancer, and finally, the feet of a single dancer.

- How would you arrange the following items in order from most broad and general to most limited and specific: *Ford, four-wheeled vehicle, transportation, automobile, red Ford convertible, vehicle, Ford convertible?*

WORKING TOGETHER

A. Imagine that you are moving in for a closeup of the following topics. How might you limit them?

1. Space travel
2. Baseball
3. Television
4. South America
5. Insects
6. Electricity

B. A topic such as *Cities* might be limited to *Cities of the United States*, further limited to *Cities of the Southwestern United States*, further limited to *Cities of Arizona*, and still further limited to *Flagstaff, Arizona*. A report on *Flagstaff, Arizona*, would include subdivisions which would narrow the subject still further. On the chalkboard list possible subdivisions for a report on your town. You may find that some subdivisions are broad enough to serve as report topics themselves or that some subdivisions might be effectively combined.

WORKING BY YOURSELF

Copy the following list of topics on a piece of paper. Place a check beside those which you think are limited enough to be covered in a brief oral report to the class. Beside each topic which you find too broad, write your suggestion for limiting, or narrowing, the topic.

1. Fish
2. Do Dolphins Talk?
3. Famous Scientists
4. Life in the Desert
5. Volcanoes
6. Schools in Japan
7. How a Vaccine Is Made
8. Unusual Animals
9. Food from the Sea
10. Plastic
11. Chewing Gum
12. Musical Instruments
13. Webs—The Art of a Spider
14. The Uses of the Laser
15. Advertising
16. The Basenji—A Barkless Dog

282

2 Outlining

A good report writer limits his general subject to a topic he can handle and makes a sketch outline, or working outline—a listing of points he thinks he wants to write about—as he gathers information. Before he can write his report, however, he must decide upon his main points and the order in which he plans to present them. One of the best ways to plan the arrangement of important points is to make an outline.

Perhaps you have studied *topic outlines* in previous years. If so, you realized that you were beginning to construct a topic outline when you worked out on the chalkboard the subdivisions of a report on your town.

Read the article below and study the two types of outlines that follow it.

PROJECT SURVEYOR:
America's First "Soft" Landing on the Moon

Reprinted from *U. S. News & World Report*, published at Washington. (June 13, 1966)

The Surveyor:

A three-legged spacecraft—actually an aluminum frame with antennas, TV cameras, rotating mast, solar panels, fuel tanks, rocket engines, sensing devices, guidance equipment.

All this was folded up inside the nose shroud of an Atlas-Centaur rocket at blast-off. Actual landing weight on moon: 620 pounds. With legs and antennas extended, Surveyor stands 10 feet.

Trip to the Moon:

Lift-off from Cape Kennedy at 10:41 a.m. Eastern daylight time Monday, May 30. At an altitude of 111 miles

above earth, Surveyor separated from its rocket while racing toward the moon at 24,562 miles an hour. Speed gradually slowed to 3,000 miles an hour while "coasting" between earth and moon.

During most of the journey, Surveyor was "locked" for power and guidance onto the sun and Canopus, brightest star in the Southern Hemisphere. Several intricate maneuvers, on radio command from earth, helped keep Surveyor on exact course.

Speed increased to 6,000 miles an hour as the craft was drawn into the moon's gravitational field. Some 2,000 miles and 41 minutes away from the moon, Surveyor broke its lock on the sun and Canopus and twisted around, on radio command from the ground, to point its feet toward the target area. It started picking up speed . . .

The Soft Landing:

An electronic brain sensed when Surveyor was 60 miles above the moon's surface and automatically fired three small adjustment engines and a large braking rocket to slow the craft from 6,000 miles an hour to 250 miles an hour. The larger rocket stopped firing at 25 miles' altitude and fell away. Three small engines continued to slow the speed. Fourteen feet above the surface, all engines shut off and Surveyor fell the rest of the way, setting down at about 8 miles an hour—with less than the landing jolt felt by a parachutist.

Impact at 2:17 a.m. EDT Thursday, June 2, was cushioned by foot pads of aluminum honeycomb. Time from lift-off to landing: 63 hours 36 minutes.

Surveyor hit with pinpoint precision near lunar equator in the Ocean of Storms, possible touchdown area for the first U.S. astronauts two or three years from now. Mission: to determine if that region is suitable for manned expeditions.

Taking the Pictures:

A special TV camera, directed from earth, went right to work. First photographs received showed Surveyor's own circular feet, indicating that the spacecraft survived the landing with no damage and did not sink deep into the lunar surface.

When a high-gain antenna was raised to permit clearer pictures, earth observers began to make out pebbles, rocks and boulders, even small fragments. Said one scientist: "It is more like rough asphalt, but it's still pretty smooth. I'll bet the scientists who predicted a heavy layer of dust are committing hara-kiri about now."

Surveyor was equipped to send thousands of photos—from many angles—during the 12 days following its landing. Once lunar night falls—equivalent to 14 earth days—the spacecraft can survive only a few hours in the moon's nighttime temperatures of 260 degrees below zero, and will cease functioning.

Project Surveyor (Topic Outline)

I. Trip to the Moon
   A. Lift-off
   B. Guidance system
   C. Speed
II. Landing on the Moon
   A. Slowing the craft
   B. Impact
III. Taking Pictures
   A. Camera equipment
   B. Kinds of photographs
   C. Number of photographs

Project Surveyor (Sentence Outline)

On June 2, 1966, Surveyor made a soft landing on the moon to photograph its surface.

I. In 63 hours and 36 minutes Surveyor lifted off from Cape Kennedy and traveled the distance to the moon.
   A. At 111 miles above the earth, Surveyor separated from its rocket while traveling at a speed of 24,562 miles per hour, and then it coasted at 3,000 miles per hour.
   B. Surveyor was kept on course by the Sun, Canopus, and radio commands from the earth.
II. Surveyor made a "soft" landing on the moon.
   A. When Surveyor was 60 miles from the moon, an electronic brain began slowing the craft.
   B. Surveyor settled softly upon the Ocean of Storms.
III. Surveyor began photographing the surface of the moon.
   A. A TV camera will send photographs back to earth.
   B. Scientists will learn new information about the surface.
   C. When lunar night falls, Surveyor will cease operating.

Notice that the *sentence outline* contains topic sentences for the report. In the final writing of the report, the writer may decide to revise some of the sentences, but generally the report becomes an expansion of the sentence outline, strengthened by facts that support the key sentences.

WORKING TOGETHER

Roger M. Latham, in *Mammals of Pennsylvania*, begins a report on the river otter with the following introduction:

Sleek as an otter, playful as an otter, graceful as an otter, smart as an otter—he's earned them all. This large-sized aquatic weasel is one of the most delightful of mammals.

Discuss what you think each of the four paragraphs following the introduction might stress. Discuss how the following main points of a topic outline might be rewritten for a sentence outline.

The River Otter

I. Appearance
II. Temperament
III. Movements
IV. Intelligence

A. Develop the following topic outline into a sentence outline. Your teacher may then ask you to work in pairs, comparing your outline to a classmate's.

Our School

I. Physical Facilities
    A. Size and type of building
    B. Number and kinds of classrooms
    C. Other important areas

II. Personnel
    A. Principal and assistants
    B. Teaching staff
    C. Secretarial staff
    D. Custodial staff
    E. Number of pupils

surveyor

The word *surveyor* means "one who looks over, views, or examines." A surveyor usually views land in order to determine its condition or to measure it for size, shape, boundaries, and position.

Why is *Surveyor* a good name for the spacecraft described in the article on page 283?

The surveyor set up his instruments and began to survey the road.

survey   surveillance

B. Make a topic outline of the following report written by a sixth-grader.

The Amazing Honeybee

One of the best-equipped workers on earth is the honeybee. His tiny body contains remarkable equipment for gathering nectar and pollen from flowers and for transporting them back to the hive. Even more remarkable is the honeybee's ability to communicate. A scientist named Karl von Frisch, after years of study, discovered "the language of bees."

Before the worker bees leave the hive each morning, they must have a flight plan. They learn the location of blossoming flowers from scouts who fly out first and return with information for the other bees. A scout reports to his fellow workers by means of a weaving dance which tells the other bees what direction to fly in relation to the sun, how far away the flowers are, and how many flowers he has found. If he hasn't found many flowers, he dances lazily, and only a few bees follow his flight plan, while the others wait for another scout with a different report. Speaking his dance language, the scout runs in a straight line and then circles back to the starting point, repeating this pattern several times. The direction of the line indicates the direction of the flowers, and the number and speed of the circles indicates the distance from the hive. The bees can even tell what kind of flower to look for from the scent of the pollen on the scout's body.

Once the flower is located, the honeybee puts his nectar and pollen gathering tools to use. He sucks nectar through his tongue and stores it in a nectar sac, or honey stomach, inside his body. A bee's body is covered with soft hairs which the pollen clings to when he dives into a flower and rolls around. Even on their eyes bees have hairs which collect pollen.

After the bee, covered with pollen, leaves the flower, he uses other specially designed tools: the brushes on his legs for scraping pollen from his body, a comb with bristles to catch the scrapings, and a rake to pull the pollen from the comb into a press formed by his knee joint. Adding a little nectar to make the pollen stick together, the bee forms two balls which are carried in the bristle-lined troughs on his hind legs. Curved hairs help to hold the cargo in place as the bee flies back to the hive. No wonder we say "busy as a bee!"

3 Written and Oral Reports

READING AND THINKING

Some reports are prepared as written reports, others as oral reports. Though the two kinds of reports have much in common, each has its own special features and methods. These are outlined for you in chart form below and on the following pages, according to three main stages in reporting—the planning stage, the coordinating, or putting-together stage, and the polishing stage.

Planning the Report

Choosing a Topic

1. Choose a topic in which you are interested.
2. Choose a topic about which you are informed.
3. Subdivide the topic into its parts to determine which part or related parts you plan to use.

(*Continued on Page 291*)

Written Reports	Oral Reports
4. Make a sketch outline to guide you in gathering information. Revise this working outline as you discover more about your topic.	4. Make a sketch outline to guide you in gathering information. Put each point on a separate note card so that you can turn easily from one point to the next as you speak.

5. Write a topic or sentence outline of the main points you plan to write about:
 	
Topic of report
I.
  A.
  B.
II.
  A.
  B.
 	
Summarizing sentence
	5. Do not write points and details in full sentences. Write just parts of sentences containing facts and figures that will remind you of what you want to say.

6. Be sure your chief points are arranged in a logical order, usually by *time* or *importance*.	6. Check your information carefully. Be sure it is accurate and in the order in which you want to present it.
	7. Try to find diagrams, maps, illustrations, or objects that will make your explanation clearer.

Putting the Report Together

Written Reports

1. Be sure to write a topic sentence that will state your topic and your main idea about it.

2. Recheck your outline to be sure each chief point will develop the topic sentence and that the points are in their proper order.

3. Develop each point by writing clear, complete sentences.

4. Be sure to weave the points together by connecting them with such linking words as *next, later, finally, therefore,* and *however.*

5. Write a concluding sentence that drives home the main idea of the report.

Oral Reports

1. Plan a topic sentence that will state your topic and your main idea about it. Although you do not want to memorize every word of your talk, try to fix the topic sentence so clearly in mind that it will launch your talk successfully.

2. Sort your note cards according to the order in which you wish to present each point. Review each point carefully so that it is firmly fixed in your mind. Then you will be able to speak with confidence.

3. Plan a good summing-up sentence that will clinch your talk and leave your audience satisfied.

Polishing the Report

Written Reports	Oral Reports
1. Look carefully at each word to be sure it says what you want it to say.	1. Make a list of all the words that you are planning to use that are not usually a part of your everyday speech. Check each word for correct pronunciation.
2. Read your report aloud to be sure that the meaning of each sentence is clear. Reading aloud may help you decide if the punctuation is correct.	2. Practice your talk before a friend or member of your family. Ask him to help you rate yourself on (a) posture and poise, (b) volume and pace, (c) grammar and usage.
3. Check each word carefully for correct spelling.	

WORKING TOGETHER

When reports are given orally, each student has two jobs to perform—one as speaker and one as listener. Discuss the following guide questions to help you rate yourself as a *listener*.

1. Do I look at the speaker and give courteous attention?

2. Do I listen carefully to what he is saying so that I can learn from his report and question what I do not understand?

3. If questions are called for, do I ask thoughtful and courteous questions that show my interest in his topic?

4. If suggestions for improvements are called for, do I praise the good features of the talk and make kind but helpful suggestions on organization, voice, and diction?

Prepare and discuss good guide questions to rate yourself as a *speaker*. What might you ask about posture, voice, enunciation, pronunciation, use of note cards, and audience contact, for example? Look back at your Speaking Guide on page 47 for help.

WORKING BY YOURSELF

In your notebook construct a chart based on the following questions that will enable you to evaluate yourself and others.

Written reports

1. Was the report well-organized, following a careful plan?
2. Were the details related to one another by guide words such as *then, next, finally, therefore,* and *however?*
3. Was the report carefully proofread to weed out spelling, punctuation, and grammatical errors as well as vague or trite words?
4. Was the report written legibly and neatly?
5. Was the report informative?

Oral reports

1. Was the report well-organized?
2. If new or unusual words were used in the report, were they explained to the audience?
3. Were any pictures, charts, diagrams, or objects used by the speaker to make his explanations and descriptions clearer?
4. Was the speaker prepared to answer questions about his topic?
5. Did the speaker look at members of the class and speak directly to them?

6. Was the speaker's voice clear, pleasant, and easily heard?

7. Did the speaker stand with ease and confidence? Did he handle his note cards quietly and naturally?

8. Was the speaker enthusiastic about his topic?

9. Was the speaker free from mispronunciations, usage errors, and "uh's" and "and-a's?"

10. Was the audience courteous and attentive?

4 Books

READING AND THINKING

Not all reports are based on material you find in encyclopedias, atlases, and other reference sources. Some reports are about your own experiences with books, magazines, television, and movies. One of the greatest pleasures in reading can be found in stories about real or imaginary people, and you can increase that

pleasure if you can discuss books in such a way that your friends will share your enjoyment. One way to share reading enjoyment with classmates is to write or give orally a book review. Below is a list of points which may help you decide what to include in a book review. Perhaps you can think of other points which you would add to or substitute for those listed. Decide which items best apply to the book you have read.

1. Title and author.
2. Kind of book (mystery, adventure, travel, animal story, biography).
3. Time and setting(s) of the story.
4. Important characters and their relationships to one another.
5. The main character's chief problem or goal. How does he solve the problem or reach the goal?
6. Important events in the main character's life. Do they reveal anything about what kind of person he is? Does he change as a result of them?
7. What new ideas or understandings came to you from reading the book?
8. Would you or would you not recommend the book to others? Why?

WORKING TOGETHER

A. Listen as a classmate reads aloud the book review on page 297. Then discuss the review, pointing out the statements that give you information suggested in the guide above. Suggest any changes you might make to improve the review.

A Review of *I, Juan de Pareja*

I, Juan de Pareja, by Elizabeth Borton de Treviño, is a novel based on a few known facts about the lives of several people who actually lived in Spain in the seventeenth century.

The main character, Juan de Pareja, was a Negro slave who became the servant of the famous artist, Diego Velasquez, when the woman Juan served in Seville died of the plague. Juan was then sent to Madrid, where he learned from Velasquez the art of grinding colors for paints, stretching canvases, and building frames. Though most of the story takes place in Madrid, where Velasquez had his studio, the setting shifts twice to Italy, where Juan journeyed with Velasquez.

One of the best qualities of this book is the way the reader gets to know the main characters. Since Juan himself tells the story, the reader gets to know him best—his loyalty, gentleness, sense of pride, and personal courage. The master, Diego Velasquez, is a serious and devoted artist, kind, but sometimes thoughtless. A third main character is Bartolomé Esteban Murillo, a gay and friendly man who comes to study with Velasquez, and is a valuable friend to Juan.

The major problem that Juan de Pareja has to overcome is being a slave. By Spanish law, slaves were not allowed to practice the arts. However, Juan had been such a good student while he served Velasquez that he had been painting secretly, using methods he had observed from the master artist. Though Juan knew he had to follow his urge to paint, his conscience troubled him. He felt he was deceiving Velasquez. When Juan's paintings are revealed, the book reaches a dramatic conclusion.

I would recommend this book to any boy or girl who enjoys reading a good story about life in the past, and who enjoys experiencing a character's sorrow and his happiness.

Using the guide on page 296 or one your teacher suggests, prepare a book review, oral or written, to share with your classmates.

MORE FOR YOU

A. Tell or write why your book would make a good motion picture or television play.

B. Tell or write about the character you would like to have for a special friend.

C. Make a drawing of an event in the book and tell the class about it.

D. If you would change the ending, explain how and why.

E. If you think the book helped you face or solve any difficulty or problem, explain how.

F. Find a proverb that fits your book and explain how it sums up the main idea of the story.

5 Magazine Articles

READING AND THINKING

Much of the reading that you do now probably is in magazines in which you find articles of interest. As you grow older you are likely to use magazines even more for pleasure and information. You are likely, too, to want to share your enjoyment of magazine articles with friends. Casual conversations about your reading will not call for formal reports, but in the classroom carefully planned reviews can acquaint you and your classmates with

articles from a greater variety of magazines than you would be likely to encounter on your own. The following questions may guide you in preparing for such a report.

1. Did I read thoughtfully and carefully so that I can arrange in the best order the points I want to discuss?

2. Do I have names, dates, and places (if these are important) accurately in mind or accurately recorded on notes?

3. Do I have an accurate record of the magazine title, the date of the issue, the article title, and the author?

4. Since I cannot retell or rewrite the entire article, what are the important points I want to discuss?

Consider carefully the information given in each paragraph or point in the guide that follows:

Introduction

Name and date of magazine, name of author, title of article, and main point you want to make about it

Development by Details

Development of main point by giving details from article which you found interesting

Conclusion

What others might learn or enjoy from reading the article

If you are writing your review, remember that the title of the magazine is underlined and the title of the article is placed within quotation marks. All words in titles are capitalized except prepositions like *in*, *from*, and *for*, and determiners like *the*, *a*, and *an*, unless such words are the first or the last in the title.

WORKING TOGETHER

A. Prepare a list of magazines you can find on your school library rack. Discuss the subjects each magazine deals with and to what special interests each magazine would appeal.

B. Bring to class as many examples as you can of each of the following magazines: sports magazine, science or mechanics magazine, nature magazine, news or current events magazine, hobby magazine.

Be prepared to compare magazines of each type and discuss points they have in common and points on which they differ.

300

C. Read the following review of the magazine article that appeared in Lesson 2 on page 283. Then evaluate the review in terms of the guide on page 300.

Can you change any words or phrases to improve the review? Would you change the organization of ideas in the review?

A Magazine Article Review

In an article called "Project Surveyor: America's First Soft Landing on the Moon," the June 13, 1966, issue of *U.S. News and World Report* brought out how dramatic life in the space age can be.

The article gave an explanation of the major events that happened between the Surveyor's lift-off on May 30, and its landing on the moon 63 hours and 36 minutes later. Next, the article went on to mention some of the facts the Surveyor's photos have revealed about the moon.

One fact we have learned is that the moon's surface is hard enough to support a landing vehicle, since upon landing the Surveyor did not sink. As a result of other photos taken by the Surveyor, one scientist was able to say about the lunar surface, "It is more like rough asphalt, but it's still pretty smooth." How exciting to live at a time when we can find out such information!

Anyone who lives in this age of space exploration would enjoy reading the article in *U.S. News and World Report* and knowing about the Surveyor's amazing journey.

WORKING BY YOURSELF

Share a magazine article with your classmates. Prepare a review, oral or written, following the guide suggested on page 300. Working in pairs, evaluate each other's reviews and select the most interesting ones to share with the rest of the class.

6 Motion Pictures

READING AND THINKING

Most of us enjoy movies and like to discuss them with our friends, though movies are not easy to discuss well. They are usually one to two hours in length, often cover wide ranges of time and setting, frequently have many characters, and employ techniques most of us know little about. To give some direction to your discussion of movies, consider these questions:

1. What type of movie is it? A Western? A historical picture? A musical? Some other type?

2. Who are the important characters—their names, occupations, and relation to one another?

3. Are the characters presented as all good or all bad, or do they seem as complicated as all human beings, with both good *and* bad characteristics?

4. Is the film intended to be humorous or serious?

5. What part of the movie did you enjoy most?

6. For whom is the movie most suitable? Adults? Teenagers? Sixth graders?

7. Was the movie worth seeing? Why? For entertainment? Good story? Fine acting? Fine photography?

8. How did the movie make you *feel?* What contributed to the effect it had on you? Color? Music? Other devices?

9. What differences might there have been if the story had been presented as a play or as a novel? What can a film do that plays or novels cannot?

10. Did the film help you understand yourself or other people any better?

WORKING TOGETHER

A. Discuss standards for judging a film. Consider these topics in arriving at standards: (1) photography, (2) casting of characters, (3) dialogue and action, (4) story, (5) acting. Perhaps you can think of others.

B. Compile a list of what you consider the five best movies of the year. As you share your list with your classmates, be prepared to justify each choice.

C. Explain to your class something you learned about from a film, such as a new part of the world, a new period in history, a new occupation, new information about animals or nature, new uses of tools or machines, or a way to solve a problem.

D. Find some pictures that would help you describe the setting, characters you liked, or some of the action in a film. Show them to the class and explain how they relate to the film.

WORKING BY YOURSELF

Using the questions at the beginning of this lesson as a guide, prepare an oral review of a motion picture you have seen.

A. Many people cooperate in the making of a film: director, editor, cameraman, set designer, actor, scriptwriter, makeup artist, creator of special effects, musical director, and costume designer, among others. Find out what each contributes to the finished film, and report your findings to the class.

B. If you have seen a film based on a book you have read, compare the movie and the book.

7 Television Programs

READING AND THINKING

Few boys and girls need to be urged to talk about their favorite television programs. Great as your enthusiasm for certain programs may be, however, you may find friends or classmates interested in knowing more about the program than just the fact that you liked it. The following points may help you to organize your thoughts in preparation for a review.

> 1. *Type of program.* Is it a story, a travelogue, a variety show, a telecasting of an important event?
>
> 2. *Performers.* Are they actors, commentators, singers, comedians? Do they perform well?
>
> 3. *Purpose.* Is it to instruct, to inform, to entertain? Does the program accomplish its purpose?
>
> 4. What was the most interesting, entertaining, or informative part of the program?

DISCUSSING

A. What questions in the guide for movie reviews on pages 302 and 303 would apply to a television play as well? What points would apply to any kind of program?

B. Discuss TV programs scheduled for the next week. Which will probably be worth watching? Why? Which will give the viewer the best balance of entertainment and information?

C. Nominate a TV actor or program for an "Emmy" award. What are the reasons for your choice?

D. Discuss TV commercials. Ask yourself which ones seem particularly original or clever and to what kind of audience they appeal. Would they make you buy their product? Why? Why not?

WORKING BY YOURSELF

A. Plan an oral report on a news telecast. Be sure to explain who takes part and why you like to listen to the commentator.

B. Plan an oral report on a sports telecast. If the program is an interview, tell who takes part and mention some of the most interesting comments made. If it.is a televised game, mention the accuracy of the reporter's descriptions and the work of the camera crew in picking up the action. Avoid trying to do a play-by-play account yourself. You might discuss the differences between watching a sports event on television and actually being there.

MORE FOR YOU

Imagine yourself a TV producer, interested in presenting a program or series that you believe will truly benefit a large number of people.

Describe the kind of program you would produce, the kind of audience you think it would benefit, and how it would benefit that audience.

Your teacher may ask you to exchange ideas in a discussion, or to present your ideas in writing.

8 Visits or Travels

READING AND THINKING

Often we like to discuss our visits to friends and relatives, but the reports that are usually of most interest to others are those we make about unusual places we visit. Such reports require careful organization. Before outlining the report, review these questions:

1. Where, when, and why was the visit made? Who was present?

2. What was the most interesting thing I saw or did? Single out the most important point, since you cannot tell everything you saw or did.

3. Why do you recommend that others make such a visit? What will they learn and enjoy?

In reporting on a visit to a certain place, always remember that your reader or listener may never have been to such a place. You will need to be clear and accurate in your descriptions. It will help if you use a *time order* or a *space order* in giving a general description of the place. For example:

Time Order—First we saw the reptiles . . .
Next we went to the elephant house . . .
After that we visited the big cats . . .
Finally, we had a chance to see a baby lemur . . .

Space Order—On our left was a jade vase . . .
Behind it stood a totem pole . . .
Over to the right we saw a brass gong . . .
Just above, from a large platform, a ceremonial mask glared down at us . . .

In her book, *San Francisco*, Jean Fritz describes the special personality of that city. Read the following passage from her book, paying particular attention to the specific and colorful details she includes in her description of one area of San Francisco which she especially enjoyed visiting.

In the shadow of the downtown hills, there are many worlds—bits of Europe and Asia side by side; mementos of old San Francisco; and modern, sophisticated centers of fashion. Almost from block to block, the city presents a different face. And never is it more diverse than it is at the

foot of Nob Hill, on the mile and a half span of Grant
Avenue that begins among luxurious stores, within a few
blocks becomes the main street of Chinatown, and then
takes you into the heart of "Little Italy."

Chinatown, which is the largest Chinese community in
the Western world and the home of 35,000 Chinese, is,
perhaps, the most picturesque of all the city's varied communities. A short walk down from the luxury hotels of Nob
Hill and you are suddenly in the midst of pagoda-roofed
buildings. The streets are lined with long, vertical signs
and the air is permeated with the smell of Chinese food
just as it is in every city and town of China itself.

Go inside the newspaper office of the *Chinese World* and
you will find typesetters picking out sticks of type from
thousands of Chinese characters. At the soda fountain in

the Fong Fong Bakery, ginger ice cream, a specialty of the house, is sold to the Chinese high school crowd; moon cakes are sold in the Eastern Bakery during Moon Festival season.

There are shops where herbs that look like dried centipedes hang in the window, and other shops filled with lacquer trays and tables, porcelain dishes with red roosters on them, blue and white rice bowls, vases with green dragons crawling up their sides. There are tiny models of wedding processions, bolts of brocaded material, ivory-carved rickshas, and lions' heads of papier maché . . . .

The Chinese population today is a highly respected group that has merged old traditions with new and contributes a great deal, both collectively and individually, to the life of the city. Although many of the Chinese have been born in

San Francisco and most now wear American clothes, they still preserve many important aspects of their own culture. After regular public school is out in the afternoon, their children attend Chinese school and can be seen late in the afternoon going home, each with his red schoolbag. Many Chinese attend Christian churches, but some go to their own temples where the smoke of incense curls beside their altars. The sing-song chant of Chinese music occasionally mingles with rock and roll records. Near modern movie houses there are still Chinese theaters where all-male casts give performances on stages bare of scenery and where musicians sip tea when they are not performing.

Chinatown's biggest event of the year is the celebration of Chinese New Year which falls some time in late January or February. It used to be that bowls of Chinese lilies, carefully forced so they would blossom on this day, stood in every window. Long ropes of firecrackers hung to the ground from the roofs of shops and laundries; they made a wonderful crackling when set off. There are still firecrackers, and although old-time San Franciscans say that Chinese New Year is not as spectacular as it used to be, it is something none of them would miss. Performances of Chinese operas and folk dances take place, but the climax is the parade led by a fierce-looking block-long dragon which snakes down Grant Avenue on the backs of scores of young men in tennis shoes. "Gung hay fat choy!" Chinese call to one another and the New Year has begun.

- What specific details in Jean Fritz's description tell you what you might see in Chinatown?
- Which details tell you what you might taste, smell, or hear?

9 A Review

A. Prepare either an oral or written review of an assembly program that was presented at your school during the year. Follow whichever review guide best applies to the program you choose. Be ready to meet with several of your classmates to evaluate each other's reviews.

B. In a daily newspaper or magazine, find a review of a book, a movie, a TV program, or a play. Read the review carefully, and then evaluate it either orally or in writing, according to the review guides established in this chapter. If possible, clip out the review so that you can add it to a bulletin-board collection of current reviews.

C. Write a review of whatever type you choose—book, movie, TV show, or visit. Your teacher will then ask you to meet in groups, evaluate each other's reviews, and choose the outstanding review from each group. Share these four or five reviews with the rest of the class.

D. Plan a report on a TV travelogue. Discuss the place visited, giving specific details about customs, houses, transportation, or geographical features.

E. Describe a visit you have made, including specific details which might interest a reader or a listener. The description of Chinatown by Jean Fritz should give you ideas for making your own report effective. You might describe a visit to an observatory, a newspaper plant, a TV station, an airport, a museum, a weather station, a city hall or court house, a place of historical interest, a farm, a dairy, or a similar place.

Remember to begin with a sentence or two that will tell *when, what, who, why,* or *where.* Conclude with a sentence that will sum up your main feeling about the experience.

CHAPTER TEN

Poetry: A Special Use of Language

1 Rhythm

READING AND THINKING

The sea laps against the shore; the seasons pass from one to another and back again; the sun rises and sets, giving way each night to the moon. In the world about us there is a natural rhythm of events—a rhythm evident, too, in man, as he regularly, repeatedly, breathes, eats, and sleeps. Since rhythm is such a part of him and of the surrounding world, man finds it natural to sing and dance, to rock an infant gently to sleep, and to read and write poetry. Even in our everyday speech we can find rhythms, although we are so used to these rhythms we usually do not notice them. Listen to the rhythms of the following words.

BUMblebee   TELescope   AStronaut   PROPaGANda
bruNETTE   teleSCOPic   asTRONomer   CLASsifiCAtion

The language of poetry can create many rhythms. Some poems have simple rhythms, like:

> JACK and JILL went UP the HILL
> To FETCH a PAIL of WAter.

Other poems may not set our toes tapping, but we feel their rhythm, nonetheless. Listen to the natural speech rhythm of the following lines from a poem by Walt Whitman.

> On the beach at night,
> Stands a child with her father,
> Watching the east, the autumn sky.

Combinations of words, like combinations of musical notes, can make rhythms that skip, dance, gallop, or march in many different speeds. As you read the lines on the following pages, try to identify the rhythms the poet creates.

THE FLAG GOES BY

Hats off!	1
Along the street there comes	2
A blare of bugles, a ruffle of drums,	3
A flash of color beneath the sky:	4
Hats off!	5
The flag is passing by!	6
Blue and crimson and white it shines,	7
Over the steel-tipped, ordered lines.	8
Hats off!	9
The colors before us fly;	10
But more than the flag is passing by:	11
Sea-fights and land-fights, grim and great,	12
Fought to make and to save the State:	13
Weary marches and sinking ships;	14
Cheers of victory on dying lips;	15

Days of plenty and years of peace;   16
March of a strong land's swift increase;   17
Equal justice, right and law,   18
Stately honor and reverent awe;   19

Sign of a nation, great and strong   20
To ward her people from foreign wrong: 21
Pride and glory and honor—all   22
Live in the colors to stand or fall.   23

   Hats off!   24
Along the street there comes   25
A blare of bugles, a ruffle of drums;   26
And loyal hearts are beating high: 27
   Hats off!   28
The flag is passing by!   29

Henry Holcomb Bennett

- Which lines skip, march, or gallop?
- If you were to move across the room in step with the rhythm of these lines, how would you go?
- What is the "flash of color" in line 4?
- Explain the meaning of "steel-tipped, ordered lines" in line 8.
- How would you interpret line 11 of the poem?
- How does the rhythm of the lines suit the subject described?
- Explain the meaning of "strong land's swift increase" in line 17.

WORKING TOGETHER

A. Your teacher may ask the class to read aloud "The Flag Goes By," to feel the rhythm of the poem. She may assign some lines for solo parts.

B. Several students may be asked to read aloud the poem below. As you listen, decide which reading is most effective. Discuss your choice and your reasons for it with your classmates.

A VAGABOND SONG

There is something in the autumn that is native to my blood—
Touch of manner, hint of mood;
And my heart is like a rhyme,
With the yellow and the purple and the crimson keeping time.

The scarlet of the maples can shake me like a cry
Of bugles going by.
And my lonely spirit thrills
To see the frosty asters like smoke upon the hills.

There is something in October sets the gypsy blood astir;
We must rise and follow her,
When from every hill of flame
She calls and calls each vagabond by name.

Bliss Carman

C. Notice the different line lengths in "A Vagabond Song." How does the length of lines in a poem affect its rhythm? How does rhythm, in turn, affect the mood of "A Vagabond Song"?

D. Decide what kinds of rhythm would be suitable for a poem about: *city traffic, a waterfall, a turtle, a hummingbird, a horseback ride, anger, joy, death, loneliness.*

WORKING BY YOURSELF

The lines that you have read show only a few of the many kinds of rhythm poets can create through word combinations. Look through collections of poems in the library and find poems that have other kinds of rhythms. Find some that have slow, solemn rhythms. Look for some that create the rhythms of ships and waves, of wind and clouds, of brooks and streams, of people weary, lazy, sad, or gay. Prepare to read to your classmates one of the poems you find.

Being well-prepared when you read your poem will help make your oral reading effective. The suggestions given below may help you prepare to read a poem orally.

1. If you are uncertain about the meaning or pronunciation of any words in the poem, use a dictionary to give you the necessary information.

2. Decide what you think the poem means. Then decide which words in each line are most important to the meaning of the poem. These are the words you will emphasize, both by stress and by the tone of your voice. All poems do not have the singsong rhythm of "JACK and JILL went UP the HILL." Don't try to force every poem to fit this up-and-down rhythm pattern.

3. Practice reading the poem aloud several times. Be sufficiently familiar with the poem so that you can glance up at your audience as you read.

2 Sounds in Poetry

Much of the pleasure to be found in poetry lies in *hearing how it sounds;* like music, it is really meant to be heard. The rhythms of poetry make it pleasant to hear, but there is another element in poetry that contributes to the poem's effect when we listen to it read aloud. Read the following poem silently and then aloud.

- What quality of poetry do you think you can appreciate more if you hear the poem read aloud?
- What specific words create certain sounds in the poem?
- How do sounds contribute to the total effect of the poem?

CROSSING

STOP   LOOK   LISTEN
as gate stripes swing down,
    count the cars hauling distance
    upgrade through town:
        warning whistle, bellclang,
        engine eating steam,
        engineer waving,
            a fast-freight dream:
            B&M boxcar,
            boxcar again,
                Frisco gondola,
            eight-nine-ten,
            Erie and Wabash,
            Seaboard, U.P.,
                Pennsy tankcar,
            twenty-two, three,
            Phoebe Snow, B.&O.,

318

thirty-four, five,
Santa Fe cattle
shipped alive,
red cars, yellow cars,
orange cars, black,
Youngstown steel
down to Mobile
on Rock Island track,
fifty-nine, sixty,
hoppers of coke,
Anaconda copper,
hotbox smoke,
eighty-eight,
red-ball freight,
Rio Grande,
Nickel Plate,
Hiawatha,
Lackawanna,
rolling fast
and loose,
ninety-seven,
coal car,
boxcar,
CABOOSE!

Philip Booth

WORKING TOGETHER

A. Plan a choral reading of the poem "Crossing." Decide what lines, if any, you think would be suitable for solo parts, and perhaps your teacher will assign solo readers for them. Decide how you can best create the sounds of the poem, and where you will pause in your reading. Then read the poem aloud, perhaps for another class, or as part of an assembly program.

B. Be prepared to read aloud the following poems by Carl Sandburg. Remember to read according to the rhythm of the poem—not in sing-song fashion, but letting the punctuation of the poem guide you. For example, do not pause at the end of a line unless punctuation indicates a pause. Use the tone and pitch of your voice to convey the *ideas* of the poem, as you would to convey your ideas in conversation.

SPLINTER

The voice of the last cricket
across the first frost
is one kind of good-by.
It is so thin a splinter of singing.

Carl Sandburg

UNDER A TELEPHONE POLE

I am a copper wire slung in the air,
Slim against the sun I make not even a clear line of shadow.
Night and day I keep singing—humming and thrumming:
It is love and war and money; it is the fighting and the tears, the work and
    want,
Death and laughter of men and women passing through me, carrier of
    your speech,
In the rain and the wet dripping, in the dawn and the shine drying,
        A copper wire.

Carl Sandburg

C. You may have concluded from these two poems that rhyme is not necessary in a poem. Which of the poems you have read thus far rhyme? How does rhyme generally affect a poem?

D. Discuss the ideas of the two poems by Carl Sandburg and point out words that create specific sound effects.

E. Try substituting other words in "Splinter" for *across, frost, thin,* and *splinter,* and decide whether you like the poem as well without the sounds of these words.

320

F. If you were able to see and hear and feel the sound and movement of the freight train, you should be able to experience the soaring of a plane, as described in the following poem by a nineteen-year-old World War II pilot. Listen to the sounds and the rhythm of the poem as it is read in class.

HIGH FLIGHT

Oh, I have slipped the surly bonds of earth,
And danced the skies on laughter-silvered wings;
Sunward I've climbed and joined the tumbling mirth
Of sun-split clouds—and done a hundred things
You have not dreamed of—wheeled and soared and swung
High in the sunlit silence. Hov'ring there,
I've chased the shouting wind along and flung
My eager craft through footless halls of air;
Up, up the long delirious, burning blue
I've topped the wind-swept heights with easy grace,
Where never lark, or even eagle, flew;
And, while with silent, lifting mind I've trod
The high untrespassed sanctity of space,
Put out my hand, and touched the Face of God.

    Pilot-Officer *John Gillespie Magee, Jr.*, R.C.A.F.

G. Point out the words that describe the flight of the plane. What do they make you see and feel? What words describe clouds, wind, sky, and space? How would *you* describe the young pilot's feelings about his plane, flying, and space?

Make a list of several words which give the sound effects of each of the following:

1. laughter
2. shouting
3. footsteps on gravel
4. an object falling
5. water coming from a faucet
6. eating potato chips
7. writing on the chalkboard
8. a car rounding a curve too fast
9. unwrapping a candy bar

3 Imagery: Simile and Metaphor

READING AND THINKING

You have listened to the music of poetry, let its rhythms and sounds affect you through your sense of hearing. You have been on the alert for a certain kind of *imagery* in the poems you have read. *Imagery* is the word we will use to mean descriptive language which appeals to the senses—*sight* (visual sense), *hearing* (auditory sense), *taste* (gustatory sense), *smell* (olfactory sense), and *touch* (tactile sense).

Although imagery is more often found in poetry, it is present in prose as well. You are already familiar with two ways of creating imagery from Lesson 4 in Chapter 8. At the top of page 323 are examples of the ways that were used in that earlier lesson. Be prepared to identify each type of comparison.

1. "They [*the scars*] were as old as erosions in a fishless desert."
2. "Mr. Chillip laid his head a little more on one side, and looked at my aunt like an amiable bird."
3. "The moon was a ghostly galleon tossed upon cloudy seas."

The types of descriptive comparison quoted above are probably more useful and more used than any other single method of description. Knowledge and understanding of them can aid you in your reading and writing of both poetry and prose.

- What other similes or metaphors can you use to describe the moon?
- What other similes or metaphors can you use to describe a person?

WORKING TOGETHER

Listen as one of your classmates reads "The Eagle" and two stanzas of "Color in The Wheat." Be ready to point out the metaphors and similes in the poems and to explain what two things are compared in each metaphor and simile.

Remember that in order to discuss these comparisons, you will have to know the meanings of words in the poems. In "Color in the Wheat" find out the meaning of *russet, sheen, amber,* and *alchemy;* in "The Eagle" be able to define *crag* and *azure.*

THE EAGLE
He clasps the crag with crooked hands;
Close to the sun in lonely lands,
Ringed with the azure world, he stands.

The wrinkled sea beneath him crawls;
He watches from his mountain walls,
And like a thunderbolt he falls.

Alfred, Lord Tennyson

323

COLOR IN THE WHEAT

Like liquid gold the wheat field lies,
   A marvel of yellow and russet and green,
That ripples and runs, that floats and flies,
   With the subtle shadows, the change, the sheen,
      That play in the golden hair of a girl—
        A ripple of amber—a flare
      Of light sweeping after—a curl
      In the hollows like swirling feet
        Of fairy waltzers, the colors run
        To the western sun
      Through the deeps of the ripening wheat.

Broad as the fleckless, soaring sky,
   Mysterious, fair as the moon-led sea,
The vast plain flames on the dazzled eye
   Under the fierce sun's alchemy.
      The slow hawk stoops
        To his prey in the deeps;
      The sunflower droops
        To the lazy wave; the wind sleeps—
      Then swirling in dazzling links and loops,
        A riot of shadow and shine,
        A glory of olive and amber and wine,
      To the westering sun the colors run
      Through the deeps of the ripening wheat.

Hamlin Garland

324

A. If you were to paint the scenes and objects described by the poets in the poems on pages 323 and 324, you would have no trouble knowing what colors to choose. Like paintings, poems can glow with color. They can also vibrate with movement.

In your notebook, list the words that describe color and movement in the poems on pages 323 and 324. Add as many color and motion words of your own as you can. These will be a storehouse of good words to help *you* paint word pictures.

B. Use some good color or motion words to write a few lines of verse that paint a word picture of something familiar to you.

C. Read the following poems to yourself. Then answer the questions about them on a sheet of paper. Be prepared to discuss your answers with the class.

THE SKY

I saw a shadow on the ground
And heard a bluejay going by;
A shadow went across the ground,
And I looked up and saw the sky.

It hung up on the poplar tree,
But while I looked it did not stay;
It gave a tiny sort of jerk
And moved a little bit away.

And farther on, and farther on
It moved, and never seemed to stop.
I think it must be tied with chains,
And something pulls it from the top.

It never has come down again
And every time I look to see
The sky is always slipping back
And getting far away from me.

Elizabeth Madox Roberts

325

A train is a dragon that roars through the dark.
He wiggles his tail as he sends up a spark.
He pierces the night with his one yellow eye,
And all the earth trembles when he rushes by.

Rowena Bastin Bennett

The poets give you word pictures of a bluejay and a train in motion. What words show their movements? What picture-making tools does each poet use?

4 Personification

READING AND THINKING

When non-human things are described as acting like *persons*—given human actions—we call this *personification*. Personification is another picture-making tool many poets use. In the following three poems, note how the poets personify *skyscrapers*, *night*, and *grass*.

- What qualities of persons are given to skyscrapers in the poem by Rachel Field?

SKYSCRAPERS

Do skyscrapers ever grow tired
Of holding themselves up high?
Do they ever shiver on frosty nights
With their tops against the sky?
Do they feel lonely sometimes
Because they have grown so tall?
Do they ever wish they could lie right down
And never get up at all?

Rachel Field

● In what ways is *Night* like a person in the following poem by James Stephens?

CHECK

The Night was creeping on the ground!
She crept and did not make a sound,

Until she reached the tree; and then
She covered it, and stole again

Along the grass beside the wall!
I heard the rustling of her shawl

As she threw blackness everywhere,
Along the sky, the ground, the air,

And in the room where I was hid!
But, no matter what she did

To everything that was without,
She could not put my candle out!

So I stared at the Night! And she
Stared solemnly back at me!

James Stephens

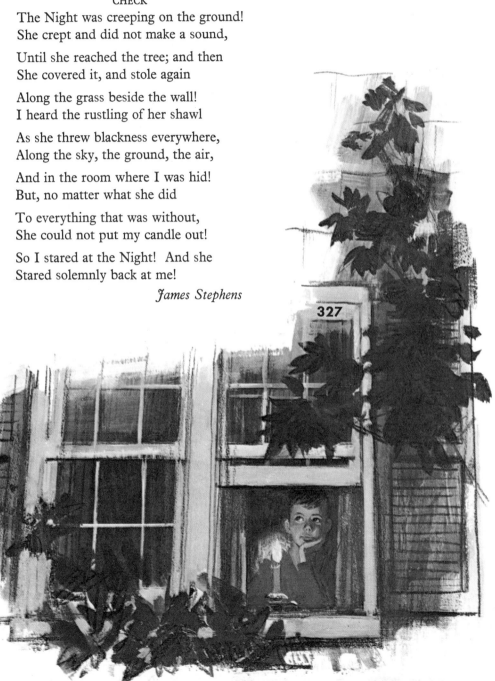

327

- What actions of the grass are like human actions in this poem by Emily Dickinson?

THE GRASS

The grass so little has to do,—
A sphere of simple green,
With only butterflies to brood,
And bees to entertain,

And stir all day to pretty tunes
The breezes fetch along,
And hold the sunshine in its lap
And bow to everything;

And thread the dews all night, like pearls,
And make itself so fine,—
A duchess were too common
For such a noticing.

And even when it dies, to pass
In odours so divine,
As lowly spices gone to sleep,
Or amulets of pine.

And then to dwell in sovereign barns,
And dream the days away,—
The grass so little has to do,
I wish I were the hay!

Emily Dickinson

WORKING TOGETHER

A. At home or in groups, practice reading the preceding three poems aloud, letting the mood and drama of each line—its sounds, its meaning—guide your reading. Follow punctuation signals in determining where you will pause, and for how long. Obviously, if your pace is too rapid, your listeners will hear a garble of words. Give each word proper recognition, without exaggerating your speech. (Remember to open your mouth wider to form such sounds as the *ou* in *ground*, the *a* in *grass*, and the *ow* in *grown*.)

B. Consider which words you would emphasize in reading each poem orally. Make a list of these important words on the chalkboard. What pattern or order, if any, can you see among these emphasized words?

C. Explain how punctuation in a poem affects your oral reading of it. Which marks indicate pauses? Which indicate longer pauses than others? Which guide the tone and pitch of your voice?

D. Read the following poems and decide which of them contain *personification*. Give reasons for your choices.

I SAW THE WIND TODAY

I saw the wind to-day:
I saw it in the pane
Of glass upon the wall:
A moving thing,—'twas like
No bird with widening wing,
No mouse that runs along
The meal bag under the beam.

I think it like a horse,
All black, with frightening mane,
That springs out of the earth,
And tramples on his way.
I saw it in the glass,
The shaking of a mane:
A horse that no one rides!

Padraic Colum

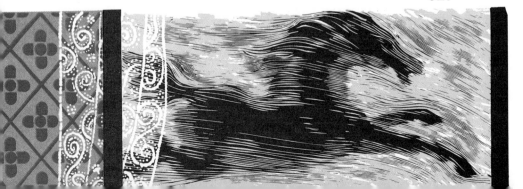

THE PUZZLED CENTIPEDE

A centipede was happy quite,
Until a frog in fun
Said, "Pray, which leg comes after which?"
This raised her mind to such a pitch,
She lay distracted in the ditch
Considering how to run.

Anonymous

PRIMER LESSON

Look out how you use proud words.
When you let proud words go, it is
   not easy to call them back.
They wear long boots, hard boots; they
   walk off proud; they can't hear you
   calling—
Look out how you use proud words.

Carl Sandburg

CITY

In the morning the city
Spreads its wings
Making a song
In stone that sings.

In the evening the city
Goes to bed
Hanging lights
About its head.

Langston Hughes

330

Write a personification of each of the following non-living things: (1) a flame, (2) a shoe, (3) a book, (4) a rock, (5) a bus.

5 Vivid Words: Nouns, Verbs, Adjectives

READING AND THINKING

The creative, vivid use of language that you aimed for in writing your own stories is perhaps nowhere more striking than in poetry. You probably noticed in the poems you have already read that nouns, verbs, and adjectives in poetry are used to produce vivid, specific images. Look for vivid language in the following poems.

THE BUCK IN THE SNOW

White sky, over the hemlocks bowed with snow,
Saw you not at the beginning of evening the antlered buck and his doe
Standing in the apple-orchard? I saw them. I saw them suddenly go,
Tails up, with long leaps lovely and slow,
Over the stone-wall into the wood of hemlocks bowed with snow.

Now lies he here, his wild blood scalding the snow.

How strange a thing is death, bringing to his knees, bringing to his antlers
The buck in the snow.
How strange a thing,—a mile away by now, it may be,
Under the heavy hemlocks that as the moments pass
Shift their loads a little, letting fall a feather of snow—
Life, looking out attentive from the eyes of the doe.

Edna St. Vincent Millay

331

SKATING

When I try to skate,
My feet are so wary
They grit and they grate:
And then I watch Mary
Easily gliding,
Like an ice-fairy;
Skimming and curving,
Out and in,
With a turn of her head,
And a lift of her chin,
And a gleam of her eye,
And a twirl and a spin;
Sailing under
The breathless hush
Of the willows, and back
To the frozen rush;

Out to the island
And round the edge,
Skirting the rim
Of the crackling sedge,
Swerving close
To the poplar root,
And round the lake
On a single foot,
With a three, and an eight,
And a loop and a ring;
Where Mary glides,
The lake will sing!
Out in the mist
I hear her now
Under the frost
Of the willow-bough
Easily sailing,
Light and fleet,
With the song of the lake
Beneath her feet.

Herbert Asquith

332

SMELLS

Why is it that the poets tell
So little of the sense of smell?
These are the odors I love well:

The smell of coffee freshly ground;
Of rich plum pudding, holly-crowned;
Of onions fried and deeply browned.

The fragrance of a fumy pipe;
The smell of apples, newly ripe;
And printer's ink on leaden type.

Woods by moonlight in September
Breathe most sweet; and I remember
Many a smoky campfire ember.

Camphor, turpentine, and tea,
The balsam of a Christmas tree,
These are whiffs of gramarye . . .
A ship smells best of all to me!
                    Christopher Morley

SILVER

Slowly, silently, now the moon
Walks the night in her silver shoon;
This way, and that, she peers, and sees
Silver fruit upon silver trees;
One by one the casements catch
Her beams beneath the silvery thatch;
Couched in his kennel, like a log,
With paws of silver sleeps the dog;
From their shadowy cote the white breasts peep
Of doves in a silver-feathered sleep;
A harvest mouse goes scampering by,
With silver claws, and silver eye;
And moveless fish in the water gleam,
By silver reeds in a silver stream.
                    Walter de la Mare

333

WORKING TOGETHER

A. Examining each of the preceding poems separately, mention the nouns, verbs, and adjectives that you think are especially effective in creating imagery in each.

B. Compile a list of verbs that clearly describe the *movements* of each of the following:

1. babies	3. ships
2. cats	4. skiers

C. List verbs that clearly describe the *sounds* made by each of the following:

1. hoofs	3. water
2. horns	4. wind

D. Make a list of adjectives that vividly describe the *taste, feel,* or *smell* of each of the following:

1. blossoms	3. feathers	5. gingerbread	7. lemonade
2. cotton	4. fur	6. ice cream	8. spinach

E. What adjectives vividly describe the *color* of each of the following?

1. leaves	3. sunlight
2. sky	4. water

WORKING BY YOURSELF

Choose an object in the classroom or one you can see from the window—one that has an interesting shape, color, or texture. Carefully select vivid descriptive words to create in three or four sentences a word picture of this object. Arrange your sentences and study them carefully. Can you polish or sharpen any words? Can you add or subtract any words? Try to develop a poem pattern in the arrangement of your sentences.

6 Using Few Words

READING AND THINKING

If you attempted to summarize the statement of each poem you have read in the preceding lessons, you would find it necessary to use many more words than the poems themselves use. Much of the power of poetry lies in its ability to say much in a very few words. Here are two short poems that have a great deal to say:

FRAGMENT FROM NOTHING
And Hate,
Fear's ugliest child,
Held to her skirts
And while she curtseyed,
Glared up like a toad.

Elizabeth Coatsworth

- Why is hate *fear's* child?
- Why does she curtsey?
- What does the curtsey tell you about her?
- How does the simile "like a toad" affect your impression of Hate?

OUTWITTED
He drew a circle that shut me out—
Heretic, rebel, a thing to *flout*,
But Love and I had the *wit* to win;
We drew a circle that took him in!

Edwin Markham

- What does the circle represent?
- Who was outwitted? How?
- Can you think of a personal experience that illustrates the point of "Outwitted"?

Read "We Never Know How High We Are" and "The Wayfarer." Then cooperate on a summary of the ideas you find in each poem, and the mood each poem creates.

WE NEVER KNOW HOW HIGH WE ARE

We never know how high we are
Till we are called to rise;
And then, if we are true to plan,
Our statures touch the skies.

The heroism we recite
Would be a daily thing,
Did not ourselves the cubits warp
For fear to be a king.

Emily Dickinson

THE WAYFARER

The wayfarer,
Perceiving the pathway to truth,
Was struck with astonishment.
It was thickly grown with weeds.
"Ha," he said,
"I see that none has passed here
In a long time."
Later he saw that each weed
Was a singular knife.
"Well," he mumbled at last,
"Doubtless there are other roads."

Stephen Crane

Ask yourselves the meaning of such words as *high, rise, true to plan,* and *warp* in the first poem; *wayfarer, weeds,* and *a singular knife,* in the second.

Be aware of the double use a word may have in a poem. That is, a word may be used according to its dictionary definition, and it may represent something else as well in the context of the poem. The words *pathway*, *weeds*, *knife*, and *roads* illustrate this double meaning. Try to see both meanings before you write your summary of the poem.

WORKING BY YOURSELF

Select a poem—from your reader, or from a library book—that you understand well enough to explain fully in your own words in a paragraph or two. Comment on the feelings created in the poem, the rhythms, and any language that strikes you as especially vivid. The poem should be at least ten lines long and one that you have not discussed before.

7 A Review

A. Does it surprise you to know that you use many similes and metaphors in your everyday speech? Haven't you often said something like this: "Jane's new kitten is a little ball of fur" or "My fingers are like icicles"? What poet's tool did you use in the first sentence? In the second?

Not all similes and metaphors are good ones; some, like the following ones, have become so overused that they are dull. Improve on each by writing a more original comparison.

1. Teeth like pearls
2. Hungry as a bear
3. Red as a beet
4. Slow as molasses
5. Quick as a flash
6. Strong as a lion
7. Quick as a wink
8. Eyes like stars
9. Heavy as lead
10. Soft as silk
11. Sly as a fox
12. Hard as nails

B. Read the following poems by Vachel Lindsay and on a sheet of paper write each metaphor you discover. Then change each metaphor into a simile. Write as many metaphors of your own as you can that describe the moon, the sun, and the wind. Write about each personification you find in the poems.

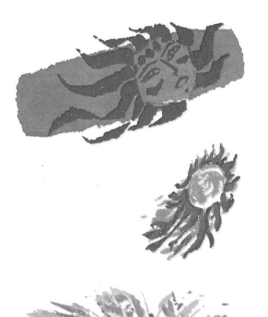

AN INDIAN SUMMER DAY ON THE PRAIRIE

IN THE BEGINNING

The sun is a huntress young,
The sun is a red, red joy,
The sun is an Indian girl,
Of the tribe of the Illinois.

MID-MORNING

The sun is a smoldering fire,
That creeps through the high gray plain,
And leaves not a bush of cloud
To blossom with flowers of rain.

NOON

The sun is a wounded deer,
That treads pale grass in the skies,
Shaking his golden horns,
Flashing his baleful eyes.

SUNSET

The sun is an eagle old,
There in the windless west.
Atop of the spirit-cliffs
He builds him a crimson nest.

Vachel Lindsay

THE MOON'S THE NORTH WIND'S COOKY
The Moon's the North Wind's cooky.
He bites it, day by day,
Until there's but a rim of scraps
That crumble all away.
The South Wind is a baker.
He kneads clouds in his den,
And bakes a crisp new moon *that . . . greedy*
North . . . Wind . . . eats . . . again!
Vachel Lindsay

C. It may surprise you to learn that not all poets are grown-ups, that boys and girls your age and younger write poetry.

The poems below are modeled on a form of Japanese poetry called *haiku*, and follow the typical pattern of five syllables in the first line, seven in the second, and five again in the last line. Usually haiku take a brief moment or a fleeting impression, often something in nature, and describe it in an unusual way. After you have read the two haiku below, try your hand at writing some, perhaps with your teacher's help at first, then on your own.

Clouds like gray warships
Are stealing silently by
Into the dark night.
Sam Wilder, Age 12

Sparks from the candles
On the high altar of night
Glow in the dark sky.
Leslie H. Walter, Age 14

You may have noticed a simile in the first haiku and a metaphor in the second. These images help you see how the clouds and the stars made the writers *feel*.

You too can paint word pictures. It takes only sharp eyes and ears that observe color, movement, form, and sound.

339

D. Use your powers of careful reading, observation, and imagination on the following poem by Robert Frost. Then go on to answer the questions at the end of the poem, either in writing or in a class discussion. As you read, listen to the *sound* of the poem. Robert Frost had a good ear for the sounds of ordinary speech, sounds which you should hear in "Mending Wall."

MENDING WALL

Something there is that doesn't love a wall,	1
That sends the frozen-ground-swell under it,	2
And spills the upper boulders in the sun;	3
And makes gaps even two can pass abreast.	4
The work of hunters is another thing:	5
I have come after them and made repair	6
Where they have left not one stone on a stone,	7
But they would have the rabbit out of hiding,	8
To please the yelping dogs. The gaps I mean,	9
No one has seen them made or heard them made,	10

But at spring mending-time we find them there.   11
I let my neighbor know beyond the hill;   12
And on a day we meet to walk the line   13
And set the wall between us once again.   14
We keep the wall between us as we go.   15
To each the boulders that have fallen to each.   16
And some are loaves and some so nearly balls   17
We have to use a spell to make them balance: 18
"Stay where you are until our backs are turned!"   19
We wear our fingers rough with handling them.   20
Oh, just another kind of outdoor game,   21
One on a side. It comes to little more: 22
There where it is we do not need the wall: 23
He is all pine and I am apple orchard.   24
My apple trees will never get across   25
And eat the cones under his pines, I tell him.   26
He only says, "Good fences make good neighbors."   27
Spring is the mischief in me, and I wonder   28
If I could put a notion in his head: 29
"*Why* do they make good neighbors? Isn't it   30
Where there are cows? But here there are no cows.   31
Before I built a wall I'd ask to know   32
What I was walling in or walling out,   33
And to whom I was like to give offense.   34
Something there is that doesn't love a wall,   35
That wants it down!" I could say "elves" to him,   36
But it's not elves exactly, and I'd rather   37
He said it for himself. I see him there   38
Bringing a stone grasped firmly by the top   39
In each hand, like an old-stone savage armed.   40
He moves in darkness as it seems to me,   41
Not of woods only and the shade of trees.   42
He will not go behind his father's saying,   43
And he likes having thought of it so well   44
He says again, "Good fences make good neighbors."   45

Robert Frost

1. What does the *wall* symbolize or represent in this poem?

2. Define a "frozen-ground-swell."

3. What do you think is the *Something* ". . . that doesn't love a wall"?

4. Why do hunters destroy the wall? What is the difference between their reason and nature's?

5. What do the lines, "No one has seen them made or heard them made, / But at spring mending-time we find them there" suggest about the importance of the wall?

6. What is there about the picture of the two neighbors repairing the wall in lines 13 to 20 that makes their action seem to the narrator like ". . . just another kind of outdoor game?"

7. Why does mending the wall seem senseless to the narrator? (See lines 23–31.)

8. Lines 32–34 point out the danger of building walls. Summarize this danger in your own words.

9. What would the narrator prefer his neighbor to say for himself? Why?

10. Why does the neighbor appear to the narrator to be ". . . an old-stone savage armed"?

11. What kind of darkness is meant by the lines, "He moves in *darkness*, as it seems to me, / Not of woods only and the shade of trees"?

12. Explain the meaning of line 43. Note that *behind* can also mean *beyond*.

13. Explain in your own words what the neighbor means by "Good fences make good neighbors." Do you agree with him?

14. How would you describe the characters of the two men?

15. Summarize what you think is the main point Robert Frost wished to make in "Mending Wall."

You have concentrated mainly on digging out the rich meaning of the poem "Mending Wall." Now use your knowledge of poetic language to point out examples of simile, metaphor, personification, and picture-making language in the poem.

E. Read "Theme in Yellow," and go on to the activities which follow the poem.

THEME IN YELLOW
I spot the hills
With yellow balls in autumn.
I light the prairie cornfields
Orange and tawny gold clusters
And I am called pumpkins.
On the last of October
When dusk is fallen
Children join hands
And circle round me
Singing ghost songs
And love to the harvest moon;
I am a jack-o'-lantern
With terrible teeth
And the children know
I am fooling.

Carl Sandburg

If you were to paint the scene and objects described in "Theme in Yellow," you would know just what colors to use. List all the color words you can find in Carl Sandburg's poem above. Add your own color words to the list. These will be a storehouse of words to help you paint your own word pictures.

343

Handbook

Your Handbook is a ready helper in answering many of the questions you may have about the English language. The items in the Handbook are arranged in alphabetical order so that you can easily find the information you need.

Sometimes when you are looking for a topic, for example *Auxiliary*, you will discover that the Handbook tells you to look for information under another topic, such as *Verb*.

Abbreviation. An *abbreviation* is a short way of writing a word. In most cases, a period follows an abbreviation.

Dr. Richard Cohen	Richard Cohen, *M.D.*
Mrs. R. W. Wilson	*Mr.* Corelli
Ross Thompson, *Jr.*	*St.* Joan
Ross Thompson, *Sr.*	*Rev.* Daniel Jackson

1066 *A.D.*   332 *B.C.*   9:45 *A.M.*   8:30 *P.M.*

A few abbreviations do not require periods.

+ Some government agencies: *FBI, NATO*
+ Television and radio stations: *KDKA, WTAE-TV*
+ Certain technical terms: *TNT, SOS, mph*
+ Most abbreviations should not be used in stories and reports. Ones which may be used are *Mr., Mrs., A.M.,* and *P.M.* (also written *a.m.* and *p.m.*).

Adjective. An *adjective* is a word which modifies a noun; that is, it describes the thing which a noun stands for, or names. Sometimes phrases are used as adjectives. A single-word adjective usually appears before the noun it modifies or after a linking verb. Adjectives are characterized by certain common endings.

344

+ Some common adjective endings are listed below:

-able	-ate	-ic	-ish	-ly
-al	-en	-ical	-ive	-ous
-ant	-ent	-ing	-less	-some
-ary	-ful	-ious	-like	-y

Adjectives show degrees of comparison in the following ways:

+ Use the *positive degree* to describe a single situation, idea, person, or thing.

The ocean water was *cold*.   The climb is *dangerous*.

Joseph was *angry*.   That is a *comfortable* chair.

+ Use the *comparative degree* to describe two situations, ideas, persons, or things. To form the comparative degree of one-syllable and some two-syllable adjectives, add *-er*. Many adjectives of two syllables and nearly all of more than two syllables form the comparative degree with *more* and *less*.

The ocean water was *colder* than the lake water.

Joseph was *angrier* than I had ever seen him before.

The climb is *less dangerous* in dry weather.

That is a *more comfortable* chair than this one.

(Note the spelling change which occurs in forming the comparative degree of adjectives ending in *-y*: *angry, angrier*.)

+ Use the *superlative degree* to compare more than two situations, ideas, persons, or things. To form the *superlative degree* of one-syllable and some two-syllable adjectives, add *-est*. Many adjectives of two syllables and nearly all of more than two syllables form the superlative degree with *most* and *least*.

The ocean water was the *coldest* I had swum in.

Joseph was the *angriest* of all.

The climb is *least dangerous* on the western slope.

That is the *most comfortable* chair in the house.

+ Some words when used as adjectives have irregular comparative and superlative forms.

Positive	Comparative	Superlative
bad	worse	worst
good	better	best
little	less (*or* littler)	least (*or* littlest)
many, much	more	most

+ Some adjectives are usually not compared because they are said to possess a quality completely, or absolutely, for example, *perfect, unique, round, square, eternal.*

Adverb. An adverb is a single word or a group of words which usually tells *how* (manner), *when* (time), or *where* (place). Adverbs can occupy various positions and can often be moved from place to place in a sentence for variety. This movable quality is one identifying characteristic of an adverb.

Carefully Terry attached the propeller to the model plane.
Terry *carefully* attached the propeller to the model plane.
Terry attached the propeller to the model plane *carefully*.

Many, but not all, adverbs are characterized by certain common endings.

+ The most common adverb ending is *-ly*: *quickly, lazily, quietly, happily.*

Adverbs show degrees of comparison in the following ways:

+ Form the comparative degree of most adverbs (especially those formed from adjectives by adding *-ly*, such as *quickly, angrily, carefully*) by placing *more* or *less* before the positive degree. We express the comparative degree of a few adverbs by adding *-er* to the positive degree form.

346

Positive	Comparative
quickly	more quickly *or* less quickly
early	earlier
fast	faster

✦ Form the superlative degree of most adverbs by placing *most* or *least* before the positive degree. A few require -*est*.

Positive	Superlative
quickly	most quickly *or* least quickly
early	earliest
fast	fastest

✦ Some adverbs have irregular comparative and superlative forms.

Positive	Comparative	Superlative
badly	worse	worst
far	farther	farthest
well	better	best

✦ Some adverbs cannot be compared: *always, here, never, now.*

Antonym. An *antonym* is a word which means the opposite or nearly the opposite of another word: *hot, cold; young, old.*

Apostrophe ('). Use an *apostrophe* in the following ways:
✦ To take the place of the missing letter or letters in a contraction (*See* **Contraction.**)

> We *have not* found the answer.
> We *haven't* found the answer.

✦ To show ownership or possession (*See* **Possessive.**) Do not use an apostrophe with a possessive pronoun.

> The senator shook the *president's* hand.
> The senator shook *his* hand.

347

+ To form the plural of figures, letters, and words being discussed as words

> Steven got three *B*'s and two *C*'s on his report card.
> His 3's look like 8's.
> I used too many *and*'s in my story.

Auxiliary. (*See* **Verb.**)

Bibliography. A *bibliography* is a list of the books, magazines, articles, and other printed sources of information which a writer used in preparing a report. Giving credit to those whose ideas a writer has used is more important than the form of the bibliography, but it is desirable to have the whole bibliography arranged in the same way. The examples below will show one way of listing the *author*, the *title*, the *place of publication*, the *name of the publisher*, and the *copyright date* of references.

1) Book

> Vail, Esther C., *Snow King Lookout*. Boston, Ginn and Company, 1964.

2) Magazine Article

> Corbin, Richard, "Poetry and Hard Fact." *Elementary English*, Vol. XLIII, No. 3 (March, 1966), pp. 203–208.

3) Encyclopedia Article

> "Language and Forms of Literature," *Compton's Pictured Encyclopedia* (Volume 8). Chicago, F. E. Compton Company, 1965.

Capital Letters. Use *capital letters* for the following purposes:
+ To begin all proper names, including:

1) *Persons, titles, and initials*

Peter Bryan, Jr.	Rev. James **R.** Stewart
Lt. **T. S.** Johnson	Professor Friedman

2) *Streets, avenues, and highways*
Valley View Drive   Pennsylvania Turnpike
Tremont Street   Seventh Avenue

3) *Days, months, and holidays*
Monday   December   Halloween

4) *Races and nationalities*
British   Indian   Spanish

5) *Geographical names*
New England   Allegheny Mountains
Great Lakes   Germany

6) *Businesses and organizations*
National Educational Association
American Legion
Girl Scouts
Carter's Bakery

7) *The Deity, religions, and sacred writings*
God   Christianity   Bible
Buddha   Buddhism   Koran

8) *Particular buildings and places*
Washington Monument   Zion National Park
Elmhurst School   Harvard University

9) *Departments of government*
State Department   Senate   Parliament

10) *Historical events and documents*
Declaration of Independence

11) *Brand names of products*
Ford   Wheaties   Lux

12) *Abbreviations of proper names*
Y.M.C.A.   N.Y.   Geo.   Calif.

13) *Proper names used as adjectives*
Roman mythology   French perfume

+ To write the pronoun **I**

+ To begin the first word of a sentence, a quotation, and of most lines of poetry

> **R**oger said, "**L**et's race to the corner."

> *   *   *

> **G**odfrey Gordon Gustavus Gore—
> **N**o doubt you have heard the name before—
> **W**as a boy who never would shut a door!

+ To begin the first word, the last word, and every important word in a title (Capitalize everything except articles, prepositions, and conjunctions: "**T**he **C**harge of the **L**ight **B**rigade.")

+ To begin the first word in the greeting and the first word in the closing of a letter

> **D**ear Janet,   **D**ear Sir: **S**incerely yours,

+ To begin the first word of each topic or each sentence in an outline

> I. **M**eans of transportation
> A. **C**overed wagons
> B. **M**ule trains

+ Do *not* capitalize:

> 1. Seasons (fall, winter, autumn, spring)
> 2. Directions (north, south, east, west) unless they name a region (the **S**outhwest, the **E**ast)
> 3. Subjects of study (history, algebra, science) unless they name a language (**E**nglish, **S**panish)

Colon (:). Use a *colon* in the following ways:

+ After the salutation of a business letter

> Dear Sir: Dear Mr. Rankin: Gentlemen:

+ To separate hours from minutes in showing time

> 8:30 P.M.   10:45 A.M.

✦ To introduce a list, except when the list directly follows a verb or a preposition

> Five students were invited to the contest: Paul, Rob, Jennifer, Marsha, and Fred.

> The five students invited to the contest *were* Paul, Rob, Jennifer, Marsha, and Fred.

> We were given money for the purchase *of* a net, six shuttlecocks, and four badminton rackets.

Comma (,). Use a *comma* in the following places:

✦ Between the name of a city and the name of a state

> Santa Fe, New Mexico   Denver, Colorado

✦ Between the day and the year in a date

> July 26, 1939

✦ After the name of the state or the year if other words follow in the sentence

> They moved to 5053 Hampton Street, Rockhill, Utah.
> On June 27, 1966, they bought the old house.

✦ After the greeting of a friendly letter and after the closing of all letters: Dear Peter,   Sincerely,

✦ To separate a direct quotation from the rest of the sentence when the tag is at the beginning of the sentence or when the quotation is a statement and comes first

> Peter said, "Let's start skating now."
> "Let's start skating now," Peter said.

✦ To separate words or groups of words in a series

> Chip plays football, baseball, and tennis.

✦ To separate the name of the person who is spoken to from the rest of the sentence

> Sally, please close the window.

✦ To separate words like *Yes, No,* and *Oh* at the beginning of a sentence from the rest of the sentence

> Yes, I heard you.

✦ To separate the two parts of a compound sentence

> We hoped to go on a picnic, but the rain spoiled our plans.

✦ To separate a dependent clause which comes at the beginning of a sentence from the rest of the sentence

> After the game was over, we stopped for ice cream.

✦ To separate a phrase at the beginning of a sentence if it makes the meaning clearer

> Instead of thirty, nine arrived for practice.

✦ To set off appositives and word groups which interrupt the sentence

> Bob, my cousin, is captain of the football team.
>
> This school, as you know, was built in 1950.
>
> It's a good game, isn't it?

✦ To separate from the rest of the sentence modifiers which add information to the sentence but are not absolutely necessary (nonrestrictive modifiers)

> Jeff, who lives next door to me, is my best friend.

Conjunction. A *conjunction* is a word which shows a connection between sets of words, phrases, or clauses.

> Penny *and* Dave looked for the lost paper.
>
> It wasn't in the wastebasket *or* on the desk.
>
> They hunted for an hour, *but* they could not find it.

✦ A *coordinating conjunction* joins two independent clauses in a compound sentence. *And, but, or,* and *nor* are coordinating conjunctions.

✦ A *subordinating conjunction* is often used to introduce the part of a complex sentence which functions as a modifier of

352

the main idea. A list of words often used as subordinating conjunctions follows:

after	because	so that	whenever
although	before	though	where
as	if	unless	wherever
as if	in order that	until	whether
as though	since	when	while

Contraction. A *contraction* is a single word made from two other words. An apostrophe takes the place of the missing letter, or letters. Below is a list of some common contractions.

aren't	are not	*it's*	it is, it has
couldn't	could not	*let's*	let us
doesn't	does not	*o'clock*	of the clock
don't	do not	*they're*	they are
haven't	have not	*weren't*	were not
I'll	I shall, I will	*won't*	will not
isn't	is not	*you've*	you have

Determiner. A *determiner* is a word which appears before a noun and signals that a noun is coming. An adjective may be placed between a determiner and the noun it modifies. The words *a*, *an*, and *the* are always determiners. (Sometimes they are called *articles*.) Other words often used as determiners are *this*, *that*, *these*, *those*, *some*, *few*, *most*, *many*, *all*, *both*, *each*, *every*, *any*, *his*, *her*, *its*, *our*, *my*, and numbers (*one*, *two*, *three*, *ninety-nine*).

> *An* elephant at *the* zoo ate *a* peanut.
> *That* elephant at *our* zoo ate *one* peanut.

Discussion. Some class discussions are organized more formally than others. Your class may participate in several of the kinds of discussions listed on page 354.

+ An *informal discussion* is the most common way of exchanging ideas among all the members of the class. Usually the only rules for such a discussion are to keep to the topic and to take turns speaking. The leader, usually the teacher, will guide the discussion. The order of the speakers is not planned ahead of time.

+ In a *round-table discussion* four to eight members discuss a topic informally around a table. At the end of their discussion the audience may add ideas or ask questions of the speakers.

+ In a *panel discussion* three or more speakers face the audience and give prepared speeches. Each speaker represents a different viewpoint or subtopic of the main topic. A chairman opens the discussion, calls upon the speakers, and ties together the ideas discussed at the conclusion of all the speeches. Then the speakers may question one another or express different opinions. Later the audience may take part in the discussion.

+ Below are some suggestions to help each person do his part well in a discussion.

Leader or chairman

1. Introduces the topic clearly and in an interesting way
2. Introduces each speaker with a brief explanation
3. Does not let any speaker take more than his share of time
4. If possible, summarizes points
5. In a general discussion, sees that one person speaks at a time, keeps the discussion moving, and keeps it from becoming a heated argument

The speakers

1. Make notes of the important points they plan to discuss
2. Know their ideas well enough so that they can discuss them easily
3. Speak clearly, using acceptable English
4. Do not interrupt
5. Disagree courteously if there is a difference of opinion

Each member of the audience
1. Listens courteously and attentively
2. Makes notes of questions to bring up later
3. Speaks only when called upon
4. Adds only information which is related to the topic and which has not yet been brought up
5. Asks questions or disagrees politely; has a good reason for disagreeing

Exclamation Mark (!). An *exclamation mark* is used to show strong feelings. Exclamation marks are most forceful if they are used only occasionally.

Ouch! Stop it!

Homonym. A *homonym* is a word which sounds the same as another word but has a different meaning and often is spelled differently.

There was a *pause* in the kitten's purring while he licked his *paws*.

Hyphen (-). A *hyphen* is used for the following purposes:
+ To divide words between syllables at the end of a line of writing (If you are not sure of the right place to divide a word, look in your dictionary.)

con-sid-er	com-mand	base-ball
be-have	re-port	de-pend

(*Note:* Words of one syllable should never be broken at the end of a line. Never write *scho-ol*, for example.)
+ To separate the parts of compound numbers from *twenty-one* to *ninety-nine* and to separate the parts of fractions (except one half) when written as words

thirty-two days   two-thirds of the class

355

Letter Writing. The parts of the forms for a friendly letter and a business letter are illustrated in the examples which follow.

✦ A *friendly letter* has five parts: (1) *Heading*, (2) *Greeting*, (3) *Body*, (4) *Closing*, and (5) *Signature*. A friendly letter is less formal than a business letter and should reflect your own personality. The best friendly letters are conversational.

Heading	1212 North Utah Street Arlington, Virginia 22201 May 7, 19————
Greeting	Dear Aunt Carol and Uncle Chuck,

Body	Thank you very much for writing. I love to get letters.
	    It doesn't feel too different, being thirteen, but when a mother asks me how old I am before asking me to babysit, and I say I am thirteen, I'm sure that sounds more impressive than twelve.
	    I haven't had much time to try out being thirteen yet. Ever since my birthday, I've had a nasty old cold. The robe my mother gave me has come in handy.

Closing	Love,
Signature	Becky

+ A *business letter* is usually sent to a stranger. To make a good impression, the appearance of the letter should be neat and the content should be clear, correct, and gracious. A business letter has six parts: (1) *Heading*, (2) *Inside address*, (3) *Greeting*, (4) *Body*, (5) *Closing*, and (6) *Signature*.

Heading	152 Clifton Drive Ames, Texas 18206 January 10, 19_____
Inside address	Hoyt Publishing Company 4571 Bristol Avenue Baywood, New York 10261
Greeting	Gentlemen:
Body	Please send *Hobbies for Young People* magazine to me, beginning with the February issue. I am enclosing a money order for $2.50 for a one-year subscription.
Closing	Sincerely yours,
Signature	Michael Chavez

+ An envelope should be addressed with care so that it will be delivered properly. Avoid confusing abbreviations and use a ZIP Code number. The sample envelope on page 358 shows the proper form for the address and the return address.

```
┌─────────────────────────────────────────────────────────┐
│                                                         ┌──────┐│
│  Return      Michael Chavez                             │Place ││
│  address     152 Clifton Dr.                            │stamp ││
│              Ames, Texas 18206                          │here. ││
│                                                         └──────┘│
│                                                                 │
│                        Hoyt Publishing Company                  │
│  Address               4571 Bristol Avenue                      │
│                        Baywood, New York 10261                  │
│                                                                 │
└─────────────────────────────────────────────────────────────────┘
```

Negatives. A statement can be changed, or transformed, to a negative statement by adding the word *not*. Other negative words are *no, none, never, no one, nothing,* and *hardly*. The use of two negative words in a single statement should be avoided in standard English.

AFFIRMATIVE	I have seen him before.
NEGATIVE	I have *not* seen him before.
NON-STANDARD	I have*n't never* seen him before.

Note-taking. Perhaps the most important point to remember about taking notes is to write them in your own words. It will be easier to write an original report if you have not copied someone else's words in your notes.

There are many ways to take notes, depending on the purpose for which you intend to use them. If the notes are for a report, you may find it helpful to write them on small cards or slips of paper, which you can later arrange in the best order for an outline. Notes should be brief, related to the topic, and accurate.

+ On page 359 is a sample note for a report on lemmings.

Subject of note	Color and size
Note	Scandinavian lemmings are yellowish-brown, spotted, and about 5 inches long.
Source	*World Book Encyclopedia,* volume 12, p. 167.

Noun. A *noun* is a word which usually has the following characteristics:

✦ A noun can be made plural: *cat, cats; beach, beaches.* Many nouns add *-s* or *-es* to form the plural. A few add other endings or change form inside the word: *child, children; man, men.*

✦ A noun often has a determiner such as *a, an,* or *the* before it. An adjective may appear between the determiner and the noun.

A huge *rock* fell over *the cliff.*

✦ A noun usually fits the test sentence:

(The) _____ seemed good.

✦ A noun may be made possessive by adding *'s* or just an apostrophe.

✦ A *proper noun* is the name of a particular person, place, or thing. It begins with a capital letter. Most proper nouns do not have determiners, but in a few cases the word *the* is almost a part of the name: *the Connecticut River, the Baseball Hall of Fame.* In most cases, proper nouns are not made plural.

Sue   Mt. Everest

✦ A *pronoun* is a word which may be used in place of a noun and its modifiers: John lives here. *He* is my friend.

Outline. An *outline* of a story or a report is a brief listing of the main ideas in the order in which the ideas are to be presented. Ideas can be organized in a *sentence outline*, which provides the key sentences in the report, or a *topic outline*, which lists the main points in single words or brief phrases. (*See* page 286.)

Paragraph. A *paragraph* is a number of sentences grouped together to tell about one topic. Usually a paragraph contains a topic sentence which tells the main idea. The other sentences explain or prove the main idea. Even if a paragraph does not have a topic sentence, it should have a unifying idea. In some paragraphs there is a concluding sentence which restates the main idea, brings the thoughts presented to a climax, or serves as a transition leading to a following paragraph.

In writing conversation, start a new paragraph each time the speaker changes.

Paragraphs may be organized in many ways:

+ Events may be told in the *time order* (chronological order) in which they happened. This order is often used for narrative paragraphs and sometimes for paragraphs of explanation.

+ Items may be told in *space order*, such as *left to right, top to bottom,* or *near to far*. This kind of organization is used in paragraphs of description.

+ An idea may be developed by giving *reasons* or *examples*. This type of organization is used in paragraphs which tell ideas, facts, or opinions.

Parentheses ( ). Use *parentheses* for the following purposes:

+ To show that doubt exists about a possible fact

    Aesop was born in Phrygia in 600 B.C. (?)

+ To confirm figures, especially in letters

    I am sending five dollars and sixty cents ($5.60).

+ To enclose information added to a sentence which does not change the basic meaning or structure of the sentence

> Istanbul (formerly Constantinople) is a city in Turkey.

> William Shakespeare (1564–1616) was born in Stratford-on-Avon.

Parliamentary Rules. To be successful any class or club meeting must be an orderly one. Some reminders for conducting such a meeting follow.

A. *Order of business*
1. The meeting is "called to order" by the president or chairman.
2. The *minutes* of the preceding meeting are read by the secretary. (The *minutes* are a report of what happened at the meeting.)
   a. They may be approved as read.
   b. They may be added to or corrected, and then approved.
3. The treasurer's report is given and accepted.
4. Reports from committees are called for by the chairman or president.
5. Unfinished business is taken up.
6. New business is taken up.
7. The program is presented, if one is scheduled.
8. The meeting is *adjourned* (ended).

B. *Motions*
1. The member who wishes to speak stands.
2. He speaks when the chairman *recognizes* (calls upon) him.
3. When a member speaks, he "addresses the chair," by saying, "Mr. President," or perhaps "Madam Chairman."

4. If the member has an idea that he wants the group to vote upon, he makes a motion. He says, "I move that . . ."
5. The motion must be seconded to be voted upon. Another member who agrees with the idea says, "I second the motion." This member does not need to stand.
6. The chairman repeats the motion. He calls for discussion. Then he calls for a vote on the motion. "All those in favor raise their right hands." The chairman counts the hands raised. "All those opposed raise their right hands." Again he counts.
7. The chairman announces the result. The motion is "carried" or lost. A *majority* vote (one half plus one of the total number of members) carries the motion.

C. *Duties of the chairman*
  1. Before the meeting:
    a. He learns the order of business and plans the agenda (plan of things to be done).
    b. He collects any information that may be needed.
  2. During the meeting:
    a. He presides (takes charge) in a businesslike way.
    b. He talks no more than necessary.
    c. He makes sure that everyone is courteous.
    d. He sees to it that the order of business is followed and motions are properly made.

D. *Duties of the secretary*
  1. He may be responsible for notices of meetings.
  2. He keeps the records, such as the following:
    a. Lists of committee members
    b. Club constitution
    c. Notes about unfinished business

3. He keeps the minutes (the records of what is done at meetings) which should include items such as the following:
   a. Date, place, time, and kind of meeting
   b. The name of the person presiding
   c. All motions, whether carried or not

Period (.). Use a *period* for the following purposes:

+ At the end of most statements and commands (In most cases the period is a signal that the voice will fall slightly and then pause after the sentence is spoken.)

> The ice on the sidewalk makes it slippery.

> Watch your step.

+ After most abbreviations and initials

> Oct.   Mr.   P.M.   Ave.

Phrase. A *phrase* is a group of words which does not contain a subject and predicate working together.

+ A *prepositional phrase* contains a preposition and the noun or pronoun which is its object. Sometimes a determiner or an adjective will appear before the noun.

> Put the apples *in a bowl.*

+ A *verb phrase* contains a verb and any auxiliaries working with it.

> Rick *should have known* the way.

+ Many grammarians refer to a noun with its determiner and any adjectives working with it as a *noun phrase.*

> *The fresh, ripe berries* were served with cream.

+ A *participial phrase* modifies a noun. The participial phrase consists of a verb form (a participle), its modifiers, and its object, if it has one. The phrase functions as an adjective.

> *Lifting the lid of the box,* Penelope peered inside.

363

Possessive. A *possessive* is a word which is used to show ownership. There are two ways to form *possessive nouns*.

✦ When a noun does not end in *s*, you add *'s*: Joe's arm.

✦ When a noun does end in *s*, you add only an apostrophe:

The players' jerseys were all muddy.

Possessive pronouns do not have apostrophes.

Predicate. (*See* **Sentence.**)

Preparation of a Paper. Your teacher may have a form for you to follow in preparing your stories and reports or may tell you to follow the form given below.

Name ———————— Room ————

Date ————————

Title

    The arrangement of your paper may be simple, but it should be neat and give all the necessary information. Start the heading of the paper far enough to the left to leave room for a margin. Indent the first line of each paragraph about one and one half inches from the left edge. Leave a margin of about an inch on the left side of the paper and almost that much on the right. Keep the margins as straight as you can.

Preposition. A *preposition* is the first word of a prepositional phrase. The last word of the phrase is a noun or pronoun which is called the *object of the preposition.* A determiner and adjectives may appear between a preposition and its object. Each prepositional phrase works as an adjective or as an adverb.

The prepositional phrase indicated by brackets in the first example below works as an adjective; the phrase in the second example works as an adverb.

Prep N(pro)

The girl behind me / had a cold.

Prep Det N

The car / stopped at the corner.

✦ Prepositions do not change their forms. Only about fifty words are commonly used as prepositions in English. Research studies show these to be the most common: *of, in, to, for, at, on, from, with,* and *by.* Other words often used as prepositions are listed below.

about	around	due to	off	till
above	below	during	onto	toward
across	beneath	except	opposite	under
after	beside	except for	out	underneath
against	between	inside of	out of	until
along	beyond	instead of	over	unto
alongside	despite	into	over to	up
among	down	like	through	upon
apart from	down from	near	throughout	without

Pronoun. A *pronoun* is a word which may be used to take the place of a noun or a noun and its modifiers.

A wild animal escaped.

It escaped.

✦ Pronouns may change their forms. They may show that they are subjects, objects, or possessives. Some possessive pronouns are used as determiners.

1) Pronouns which are used only in subject positions:

I	*he*	*she*	*we*	*they*

2) Pronouns which are used only in object positions:

me	*him*	*her*	*·us*	*them*

3) Pronouns which may be used as subjects or objects:

it   *you*

4) Possessive pronouns:

my, mine	*our, ours*
your, yours	*your, yours*
his, her, its, hers	*their, theirs*

✦ Apostrophes are not used with possessive pronouns.

Proofreading. (*See* **Revision.**)

Punctuation. When you *speak* words you can use gestures and the tone, volume, and pace of your voice to help make your meaning clear. In *writing* words, you cannot use these aids to communicate your meaning. Therefore, users of written English have developed a system of signals you can use to let your reader know when he should pause and when he should come to a complete stop in his reading. These signals act like traffic lights and signs; they steer readers and help them get the intended meaning from what they read. These signs we call *punctuation marks*.

Punctuation marks not only act as traffic signals to guide readers, but they also act as sign posts to show just how words and word groups are being used. Notice how they help you know what meaning you should get from the following expressions:

1) "My dog," said Tom, "is very smart."
2) My dog said, "Tom is very smart."
3) This is your hat.   (statement of fact)
4) This is your hat?   (a question)
5) $6.25   (six dollars and twenty-five cents)
6) 6:25   (twenty-five minutes past six o'clock)
7) "Beth, Ann and Scott are coming." (Two are coming.)
8) "Beth, Ann, and Scott are coming." (Three are coming.)

(*See* **Apostrophe, Colon, Comma, Hyphen, Period, Question Mark, Quotation Marks, Semicolon.**)

Question Mark (?). A *question mark* is used at the end of a sentence which asks a direct question. It signals that a response is expected. This mark is often called an *interrogation point.*

Why was Shirley absent today?
Did Nancy call Shirley last night?

Quotation Marks (" "). *Quotation marks* are used to show the exact words of a speaker. Note the way the sample statement, question, and exclamation below are punctuated.

John said, "The score is tied."
"Who is pitching?" I asked.
"Play ball!" cried the umpire.

+ *Do not* use quotation marks to enclose an *indirect quotation.*

Direct quotation: Mrs. Tolan said, "Tulips will be blooming soon."

Indirect quotation: Mrs. Tolan said that tulips would be blooming soon.

367

+ Quotation marks are used around the titles of stories, poems, songs, and magazine articles. Titles of books, magazines, plays, movies, and newspapers are underlined.

> I read a story called "New Puppy" in <u>The World of Dogs</u> magazine.

Revision. The process of revision includes all the steps you take to improve and correct your stories and reports. As you work on your papers, ask yourself the questions given below.

+ *Survey, Revise*

1) Does the topic sentence of each paragraph state my topic and the main point I want to make about it?

2) Do all my details relate to the topic? Do they help to prove the point I am trying to make?

3) Have I arranged the details according to a plan? Are my descriptive details arranged according to a space order or a time order? Are my reasons arranged in a special order, such as most important to least important, which makes them easy for a reader to understand?

4) Does my concluding sentence bring my ideas to a satisfying conclusion?

5) Do the words I have chosen say exactly what I want them to say?

+ *Proofread, Correct*

1) Have I used capital letters correctly?

2) Do I have all the necessary marks of punctuation?

3) Are all the words spelled correctly?

4) Is my handwriting neat and clear?

5) Have I followed directions about spacing, title, and page numbering?

6) Does my paper look as though I wrote with care and cared about what I wrote?

368

Semicolon (;). Use a *semicolon* in the following ways:

+ In place of a conjunction between two closely related independent clauses

> The gray skies darkened menacingly; thunder rumbled loudly in the distance.

> Nancy wanted to leave the party early; Benjamin did not.

+ Before connecting words like *besides, however, moreover, nevertheless, then,* and *therefore* when they join independent clauses

> A large crowd filled the theater; *nevertheless,* many seats remained unoccupied.

> We spent two hours watching the parade; *then* we drove to the stadium for the game.

+ Between items in a series if the series contains commas

> Their tour will take them to four state capitals: Harrisburg, Pennsylvania; Albany, New York; Providence, Rhode Island; and Boston, Massachusetts.

Sentence. Almost every *sentence* has two parts: a subject and a predicate. The subject tells what the sentence is about. The predicate tells what the subject *is, was, does, did,* or *will do.* It may tell what *is, was,* or *will be done* to the subject.

When spoken, the sentence has a pause before it and after it. A statement will usually end with falling pitch. A question which does not begin with a question word will end with a rising pitch. In written form, a sentence is indicated with a capital letter at the beginning and a mark of punctuation (period, question mark, or exclamation mark) at the end.

1) A *declarative sentence* tells, or declares, something.

2) An *interrogative sentence* asks a question.

3) An *imperative sentence* gives a command.

Often, no subject appears in an imperative sentence, for example, *Stop*. It is sometimes said that the subject of an imperative sentence is understood to be *you*. If an imperative is transformed to a question, *will* must be supplied. (*Will you stop?*)

4) An *exclamatory sentence* shows surprise, anger, or excitement.

PATTERNS OF SENTENCES

Each major sentence pattern in English has a subject and a predicate. The main word in the subject is a noun or a pronoun. The main word in the predicate is the verb. In studying a sentence, look first for the main words of the pattern. The basic sentence patterns studied in this book are illustrated by the following examples:

1) **N V** pattern

N   V

Ducks /swim.

N   V

The shoppers in the plaza /ducked hurriedly under awnings.

2) **N V N** pattern

N   V   N

Cats /climb trees.

N   V   N

The agile cat /climbed the elm tree outside my window.

3) **N LV Adj** pattern

N   LV   Adj

The campers /were weary.

$$\overset{\textbf{N}}{\text{The six hungry campers}}\,/\overset{\textbf{LV}}{\text{were}}\,\text{too }\overset{\textbf{Adj}}{\text{weary}}\text{ to build}$$
a fire.

4) **N LV N** pattern

$$\overset{\textbf{N}}{\text{A senior}}\,/\overset{\textbf{LV}}{\text{is}}\,\overset{\textbf{N}}{\text{captain.}}$$

$$\overset{\textbf{N(pro)}}{\text{I}}\,/\overset{\textbf{LV}}{\text{am}}\,\text{.the }\overset{\textbf{N}}{\text{sister}}\text{ of the tallest boy in eighth grade.}$$

5) **N V N N** pattern

$$\overset{\textbf{N}}{\underset{\textit{subject}}{\text{Mother}}}\,/\overset{\textbf{V}}{\underset{\textit{verb}}{\text{gave}}}\quad\overset{\textbf{N(pro)}}{\underset{\textit{indirect object}}{\text{me}}}\quad\text{a }\overset{\textbf{N}}{\underset{\textit{direct object}}{\text{cookie.}}}$$

$$\overset{\textbf{N(pro)}}{\underset{\textit{subject}}{\text{We}}}\,/\overset{\textbf{V}}{\underset{\textit{verb}}{\text{chose}}}\quad\overset{\textbf{N}}{\underset{\textit{direct object}}{\text{Larry}}}\quad\overset{\textbf{N}}{\underset{\textit{object complement}}{\text{president.}}}$$

6) **N V N Adj** pattern

$$\text{The }\overset{\textbf{N}}{\underset{\textit{subject}}{\text{class}}}\;\overset{\textbf{V}}{\underset{\textit{verb}}{\text{found}}}\quad\overset{\textbf{N}}{\underset{\textit{direct object}}{\text{Larry}}}\quad\overset{\textbf{Adj}}{\underset{\textit{object complement}}{\text{capable.}}}$$

KINDS OF SENTENCES ACCORDING TO STRUCTURE

1) A *simple sentence* contains a subject and a predicate.

Carl /*swam* to shore.

2) A *compound sentence* combines two or more simple sentences (independent clauses) by joining them with words such as *and, but, or,* and *nor.*

The *sun* /*was* warm, and the *wind* /*blew* softly.

3) A *complex sentence* consists of one or more independent clauses to which is attached a dependent clause that acts as a modifier and begins with a connective such as *if, when,* and *since.*

When *Allen* /*arrives,* the *game* /*can begin.*

Speaking. Perhaps the following suggestions will help you speak more effectively:

+ Take a deep breath before you speak. This will relax you.

+ Hold your body and head erect. This will strengthen your voice as well as improve your appearance and make what you have to say more convincing.

+ Speak loudly enough to be heard.

+ Speak with enthusiasm and sincerity, and your feelings are likely to be contagious.

+ Speak more slowly than you do in ordinary conversation.

+ If you use note cards as reminders of facts and figures, look at them only when necessary.

+ Keep yourself reasonably still. Fidgeting may distract your audience. Move when it is natural to do so.

Subject. (*See* **Sentence.**)

Synonym. A *synonym* is a word which means the same thing or about the same thing as another word: *awkward, clumsy; big, large.*

Topics for Writing. "Know thyself," wrote a wise man centuries ago. That's good advice. Sometimes when boys and girls say, "I'm supposed to write a theme for Monday, and I don't know what to write about," it is because they do not know themselves. How do you get to know yourself? You get to know yourself when you begin to discover how many interests— hobbies, sports, collections, handcrafts, books, art, music—you have developed, how many places—zoos, museums, fairs, parks, historical centers, government buildings—you have visited, and how many people—parents, relatives, friends—have played important parts in your life. These experiences—exciting,

372

interesting, frightening, pleasant, unpleasant—provide material to think about, talk about, and write about. "I am the sum total of all I have experienced," wrote another wise man. When you wonder what to write about, look into your life. As you sort out your experiences, think about them, and write about them, you will find that you get to know and understand yourself better. Some of the following subjects may remind you of something in your life to write about.

1. The day you would most like to relive
2. The place you know best
3. An organization to which you belong or a hobby you enjoy
4. A quality you admire (dislike) in others
5. A place you would like to visit or revisit
6. Your favorite summer (winter) activities
7. The experience each of these adjectives best describes: most embarrassing, most surprising, most rewarding, most disappointing, most exhausting, most pleasant
8. Important people in your life

+ Remember to make your titles interesting. Here are some titles other students have used:

1. Never Take a Girl (Boy) Shopping
2. How to Be Unpopular
3. Lawns Shaved—One Dollar
4. Fasten Seat Belts!
5. The Life of a Safety Pin
6. If I Knew the World Would End Tomorrow
7. Chaos in the Kitchen
8. Bringing Up Parents
9. "But Mom, It Followed Me Home"
10. The Perils of a Paper Route

Verb. A *verb* is the main word in the predicate of a sentence. In the most common word order, the verb follows the subject of a sentence.

✦ *Regular verbs* show past time by adding *-d* or *-ed* in the past tense. *Irregular verbs* show past tense by changing form.

✦ Verbs may use *auxiliaries* (helping verbs) to help show the time of action.

He *is walking*.   He *has walked*.

✦ The verb in a sentence should agree with the subject in number. In the present tense the verb adds *-s* with *he*, *she*, *it* or a person's name: He *plays*. When a verb has an auxiliary, the auxiliary changes form to agree with the subject.

He *is* playing.   They *are* playing.

✦ Some verbs express the action of the subject.

Gretchen *combed* her hair.
The kite *sailed* over our heads.

✦ Some verbs link a subject and a complement. These verbs are called *linking verbs*. Some commonly used linking verbs are: *appear, become, feel, grow, look, remain, seem, smell, sound, taste,* and all the forms of *to be* (*am, are, is, was, were, being,* and verb phrases ending in *be* or *been*, such as *has been, will be, should have been, might have been,* and *can be*).

The air *feels* colder in this room.
My feet *are becoming* tired.

✦ Some verbs can function either as action or as linking verbs.

N   V   N
Mrs. Olivetti *tasted* the sauce.

N   LV   Adj
The sauce *tasted* too salty.

Index

74, 75, 91, 148–149, 151, 158, 159, 179; N V N Adj, 154–155, 168; N V N N, 74, 78, 149–155, 160
in subject, 91, 107, 132, 142, 152, 157, 168, 196–197
N V agreement, 84, 105–107
plural forms of, 41, 81–83, 84, 87, 106, 108
positions in sentences, 73–74, 76, 148–151, 168, 197
possessive forms of, 85–89
signals to identify: change in form, 81–83, 109; determiners, 75, 76, 77, 80, 109, 125; endings, 81–83, 109; position in sentence, 74, 75, 109; substituting pronouns for, 77, 108
substitution for, 75, 76, 80, 115–116, 188–191, 192–194
test frame for, 74, 80
using more specific, 115, 116, 260, 261, 331–334

Object complement, 152–155

Object of preposition
noun clause as, 193–194
nouns as, 74, 128, 129, 150, 195, 197, 198
pronouns as, 128, 129, 131, 150–151, 168

Oral language activities
giving explanations, 53–63, 64, 298
giving reports, 47, 298, 301, 303, 304, 305–306, 307
making announcements, 54–55
reading aloud, 58, 104, 107, 113, 120, 198, 233, 248, 252, 263, 279, 296
reading poetry, 49, 52, 315, 316, 317, 319, 320, 321, 328–329

standards for speaking, 47, 294–295
using voice effectively, 43–48, 49, 52, 102, 263, 294, 295, 320, 328–329
See also Conversation, Discussion, Speaking

Outlines
for paragraphs: developed by descriptive details, 215–216, 220; developed by example, 62–63, 211, 220, 221, 222–225; developed by space order, 235, 307; developed by time order, 226, 307
form of, 60, 211, 214, 215, 220, 221, 222, 223, 282, 286, 288, 290–293, 296, 300, 303, 307
organization in, 221, 222–224, 306–307
practice in making, 211, 215–216, 220, 221, 225, 282, 287, 288, 289, 307
topic outline-sentence outline, 286–288

Paragraphs
beginning, 208, 249–251
chart of, 211
concluding, 217–221, 235, 243, 292
concrete words in, 238–241, 253–254
developing by descriptive details, 116, 123, 254, 258, 261
developing by reasons, 59–60, 62–63, 64, 135, 215–217, 220, 221, 222–225
developing by space order, 231–235, 243
developing by time order (chronological order), 225–230, 241–242
importance of structure in, 207–211
linking words in, 229–230, 243, 248, 275, 292, 294
order in (coherence), 228, 241–243, 248

organizing and writing, 221, 235, 243, 337

outlining, 211, 215–216, 220, 222–223, 235

proofreading, 236–237, 293, 294

revising, 115–116, 120, 167

sentence variety in, 237

topic sentences in, 208, 210, 211, 212–214, 220

worksheets for, 214, 215, 220, 221

Period. *See* Handbook

Phrases
defined, 128

moving for sentence variety, 173, 174, 202, 203, 204

participial, 162–163, 169, 180–181, 204

prepositional, 128–129, 131, 132, 133, 150, 172–175, 176, 201, 202, 203

Poems
"The Blitzen Oasis After Rain," 51

"The Buck in the Snow," 331

"Check," 327 ("Night Was Creeping")

"City," 330

"Color in the Wheat," 324

"The Cowboy's Life," 50

"Crossing," 318–319

"The Eagle," 323

"The Flag Goes By," 314–315

"Fragment from Nothing," 335

"The Grass," 328

"High Flight," 321

"I Saw the Wind Today," 329

"An Indian Summer Day on the Prairie," 338

"Mending Wall," 340–341

"A Modern Dragon," 326

"The Moon's the North Wind's Cooky," 339

"Outwitted," 335

"Paul Revere's Ride," 49

"Primer Lesson," 330

"The Puzzled Centipede," 330

"Silver," 333

"Skating," 332

"The Sky," 325

"Skyscrapers," 326

"Smells," 333

"The Sounds in the Morning," 52

"Splinter," 320

"Theme in Yellow," 343

"Under a Telephone Pole," 320

"A Vagabond Song," 316

"The Wayfarer," 336

"We Never Know How High We Are," 336

Poetry
haiku, 339

imagery in, 322–326, 331–334, 338–339, 340–342, 343

interpretation of, 315, 317, 320, 326–328, 329, 335–337, 340–342

language of, 313–343

pattern poems, 334

personification in, 326–331, 338–339, 340–342

reading orally, 49, 52, 315, 316, 317, 319, 320, 321, 328–329

rhythm, 313–317, 337

sensory impressions in, 321, 322–326, 331–334, 337

sounds in, 49, 52, 318–322, 340

writing, 325, 334

Possessives, 85–88

EFGHIJK   765432
PRINTED IN THE UNITED STATES OF AMERICA